T0193120

The Alchemy of Becoming

(all that you are meant to be)

DIANE FULFORD
KAREN DIGUER

BALBOA.PRESS
A DIVISION OF HAY HOUSE

Balboa Press books may be ordered through booksellers or by contacting:

Balboa Press
A Division of Hay House
1663 Liberty Drive
Bloomington, IN 47403
www.balboapress.com
844-682-1282

Because of the dynamic nature of the Internet, any web addresses or links contained in this book may have changed since publication and may no longer be valid. The views expressed in this work are solely those of the author and do not necessarily reflect the views of the publisher, and the publisher hereby disclaims any responsibility for them.

The author of this book does not dispense medical advice or prescribe the use of any technique as a form of treatment for physical, emotional, or medical problems without the advice of a physician, either directly or indirectly. The intent of the author is only to offer information of a general nature to help you in your quest for emotional and spiritual well-being. In the event you use any of the information in this book for yourself, which is your constitutional right, the author and the publisher assume no responsibility for your actions.

Any people depicted in stock imagery provided by Getty Images are models, and such images are being used for illustrative purposes only. Certain stock imagery © Getty Images.

Cover design by Sarah B. Uncommon Artscape
Illustrations by Valerie Fulford

Print information available on the last page.

ISBN: 978-1-9822-6014-9 (sc)
ISBN: 978-1-9822-6016-3 (hc)
ISBN: 978-1-9822-6015-6 (e)

Library of Congress Control Number: 2020924322

Balboa Press rev. date: 02/10/2021

To all of you who have found your way to this book, know that it is the path that awaits your awakening. And while there are many paths, the only true path is the one that lies within, as uniquely experienced. The path lit as you walk it, is the premise and promise of this book. This book is dedicated to all who journey and to the luminaries throughout time and of our time answering the universe's call to the knowing of ourselves and the world in higher consciousness.

CONTENTS

EPILOGUE AS PROLOGUE

It is only when looking back that they understood with absolute clarity, what had to be. The hindsight of 2020.

The world pressed the pause button. "I can't breathe" became the universal cry of the oppressed, of those left behind and kept out; the cry of fauna and flora, of Gaia herself. The crack, that had long been there, became an abyss. Unbridgeable. The chasm too vast, too deep. The views too polarized, no common ground upon which to heal, upon which to move forward. The world in fragments—institutions and economies gasping for air. And through it all there were those bent on covering up the crack, getting things back to normal as if normal had never been the problem. But there were those who chose to follow the light. "There is a crack in everything, that's how the light gets in."

And the light reminded them that all change must first come from within. That the path forward is the one less travelled, the one unknown yet coming from a deep knowing. That what is broken can never be healed from the same level of consciousness from which it was created. That through the *in-sight* of higher consciousness, the breakthrough, the lit path, makes itself known. That alchemy of realizing all that is, as new, is made whole and indivisible, through consciousness. Alchemy replaces fear with truth, love, and light. The alchemy of transformation.

And so looking back, they were thankful for the many who chose to journey, following their own spiritual paths (for there are many such paths). That they had transformed not only themselves but through their presence, the world around them. They were thankful for the emergence of communities spanning the globe so that no one had to travel alone. And they were thankful for the luminaries of their time, bridging science and spirituality, daring to be unconventional and exposed, forging the way for others to follow.

And what they witnessed was a new world order made in the conscious evolution of choice. The world anew, breathing. The natural world respected, nurtured. Systems reimagined, dependencies and interconnections understood, separation an illusion. Equanimity amongst humans, divinity in every soul. Force redundant, individuals empowered. Senses expanded beyond the known. Inspired by love, fear relegated to where it serves. Living in truth, gratefully and mindfully. Becoming, who you were always meant to be. Individuated divinity.

FOREWORD

One of the most indelible memories while biking through Southern France with my husband, is of staying in a small hotel that was once the residence of a well-known alchemist. The giveaway was the wall-sized fireplace in an otherwise modest stone room. That image has stayed with me and it is only now that I understand why—that alchemy would play a rather profound role in my life. While the alchemists never did succeed in transforming a base metal into gold, or of finding the secret to eternal life (or did they??), what was magic was the process they followed. A process replicated throughout nature that not just changes but forever transforms: from a tadpole to a frog, from a caterpillar to a butterfly, from a delicious meal to sustenance and energy for a body, from life happening to you, to life happening from within you.

This process, that we have not been able to call anything but a journey, is one that for me at least, is an ongoing voyage of discovery. Unlike other travels, however, it is not about witnessing the breathtaking wonders of our planet, but of travelling through my own inner landscape. A place until recently rarely visited, yet even more amazing in its complexity and beauty ... and so very accessible! No crowded airports, cramped plane rides or annoying jet lag. It was always there, anxiously awaiting my visit.

My awakening was far from dramatic. I had that perfect life—a steadfast partner, two wonderful children, grandchildren who literally highjacked my heart, a varied and interesting career and early retirement with enough resources to live, travel and play out my remaining days in comfort. But ... (yes you knew this was coming) something was missing. There was a feeling deep inside that I needed more, something more than a shiny new car or a trip to Italy could satisfy. My health was also declining, catching every cold and flu virus that went around, low energy, and an alarming bout of alopecia which was a sign that something indeed was up with my immune system.

Then I got the tap on my shoulder—from my close friend who also happens to be my sister-in-law, Diane. "Karen," she said, "I need to talk to you about something." And she told me of her unusual and rather lonely path—of being called to explore her own inner landscape, the constant messages from her spirit guides and of the mandate with which she had been tasked. It's no wonder she took so long to share this with me—as I was the poster child for a left-brain skeptic. Surprisingly, perhaps to both of us, I immediately embraced this path. The crack had opened, and I was so ready to explore the light that was peeking through. I will remain eternally grateful that she took that risk. The process allowed me to peel back the layers of the persona created to conform and succeed as defined by our societal standards and find my true self. I am now enlightened by higher guidance and my own compass. My immune system is strong, energy levels restored, and can boast of a biological age decades below that of my chronological count. Even better, I am happy, fulfilled and dedicated to raising my level of consciousness to explore further, and credibly share this process with others.

It has been my privilege to be a part of this unfolding, and of documenting this unique experience and methodology. There are sections of this guide that may be difficult to grasp at first, but as you progress in your journey, I encourage you to go back periodically and reread them as their meaning and vibration will take hold.

If you are reading this, you have already taken a leap of faith. Take the next one and the one after until they are replaced with conviction, knowing and a sovereign, empowered you. There is no going back, only forward, always expanding.

Karen Diguer

INTRODUCTION

"A journey of a thousand miles starts—with a single step." Lao Tzu

I was gifted this work, as channelled through me. It is a methodology for spiritual transformation. There is a need, I was told, to complement the many spiritual works with a simple methodology. It is a step-by-step process, a how-to guide for those inspired and seeking answers to; "How do I get there, wherever there is?" and "What exactly should I do?"

The architecture of the methodology is based on the 7 stages of alchemy. Alchemy is a medieval forerunner of chemistry thought capable of transforming base metals into precious ones (especially gold and silver), often referred to as "the Philosopher's Stone." The more mystical application was the search for an elixir that grants eternal youth and immortality through the purification of the soul. While such quests were abandoned, alchemy nonetheless captured the concept of taking something ordinary and producing something extraordinary through a process of breakdown, separation of elements, purification, fermentation, and distillation. Think grapes to wine.

In this methodology, the word alchemy is not used loosely to suggest transformation. Rather, it is the spiritual code to transformation and each of the 7 alchemic states are to be followed in a precise and prescribed sequence.

While this may appear rigid and impersonal, nothing could be further from the truth. It is deeply personal and individualized. Indeed, no two people will have the same self-work to do, share the same experience nor journey at the same pace. However, all will have the same 7 steps and sequence to go through. It's like eating, I was told. Everyone goes through the same steps to ingest the food they eat through a mechanical and chemical breakdown of food into fragments for absorption into the bloodstream or elimination from the body. But what is needed for optimal health is very individualized from the caloric need to the variety and balance of foods to food combinations, taste preferences and sensitivities—all depending on one's body chemistry. No two people will have the same needs, but they will go through the same steps for ingestion.

But while alchemy forms the architecture, each step is informed by great spiritual minds and their works. One-by-one, I was led to each author and their work. In some cases, I was to pull out certain key concepts (only from pages x to y), in other cases, asked to modify or add to their concepts. Sometimes I had to read and reread until I finally understood their insights and how they fit into the methodology.

While many of the works were spiritual in nature, many were surprisingly deeply scientific in basis. Not having a science background, I found myself often stretched to the limit to grasp the brilliance of works from Newtonian to Quantum physics. The more spiritual works stretched me in other ways, often having to believe and trust before I could see. Both were invaluable.

So, this methodology is a compendium, if you will, of insights, beliefs, and experiences held by those I have been introduced to, be they physicists, biologists, medical practitioners, channelers, mediums, neuroscientists, psychologists and spiritual guides—with one thing in common—their understanding and connection to consciousness. I have the privilege of synthesizing their works, as pieces of a puzzle, put together in a particular sequence. There are many more inspiring minds, but these are the ones I was guided to for completion of this level 1 book.

I have been through this journey, through each step of the methodology and as I did so, it became clear that I had to await the elevation of my own consciousness before I was guided to particular authors. It was as if each author held the key to unlock the next stage of the transformation process. In that way, each was indispensable to the journey.

This is a methodology for transformation of self, but to what end? The words I was repeatedly and consistently given is that this is a journey to discover who you are meant to become. It is a journey of becoming. It is a journey of deconstructing and reconstruction of self at the vibrational level. It is a journey of becoming conscious of the evolution of your consciousness. It is a journey of empowerment, of healing, of mastery, of understanding who you are meant to forever be—coming as *individuated divinity*.

This is a lot to take in. But these phrases took on more meaning as I underwent the journey, and such will be the case for all those who journey.

But here is a brief primer. Becoming is *a being in motion*. We are meant to be evolving as a species not just biologically but as consciousness. And this is BIG. We are the first humans in significant numbers to be aware of our consciousness; the first in history to be aware that we are part of a universal consciousness that is evolving in tandem with itself as an expanding universe. This awareness means we have choice in how consciousness is evolving; we are co-creating the universe through consciousness. We are, today, the sum total of the history of evolution of our species as humans. But our evolution up to this point has been unconscious. Now and forever more, our evolution as humans will unfold as the conscious exercise of evolutionary choice. There is so much responsibility in that shift.

The exercise of that responsibility is inherent in this journey. It is the responsibility of becoming; we become the quality of choices we make— the quality of what and how we choose to manifest—how we show up in life. And how we show up in life, each thought, each belief, each action is reflected in the unfolding of universal consciousness. There is quality in elevated consciousness, shifting from density to lightness, from contraction to expansion. The journey is about the quality of our becoming through higher consciousness. The path to higher consciousness can only be achieved at a vibrational level of change—the knowing of ourselves as divinity.

I was told that the journey as a methodology follows the laws of the creation of the universe. Jude Currivan wrote that "the universe is ordered, patterned, rational, meaningful, and intelligent, in-formation, exquisitely balanced, incredibly co-creative, staggeringly powerful and yet fundamentally simple." Such is this methodology; the intelligence and eloquence of creation imprinted in the vibratory field of its alchemy.

The methodology is intended to serve as a bridge to expanding consciousness. Indeed, the metaphor of *bridging* ran throughout this work; from bridging the thinking mind to the state of knowingness, from Cartesian thinking to intuitiveness, from navigating an outer landscape to the landscape that lies within, from the physical to the metaphysical, from Newtonian to Quantum physics, from spirituality to science, from a world of fear to one of love, and from the known to the unknown. There is no judgment here. The aim is not to forego one for the other. Our growth lies in the understanding and embodiment of all that is, as oneness or as a unified theory.

There are levels to this understanding. This book is the first of four, intended to take one through to progressively higher and deeper levels of learning. It is a journey of continuous refinement, of mastery, of seeking what lies beyond the known. As such, the benefits of this journey accrue incrementally throughout each stage of this first level and throughout subsequent levels. The choice to journey and how far to travel is yours to decide, and know that you will be guided in that choice.

Above all it is your journey. It is not held or taken by anyone other than you. Each of us is personally unique; there has never been, is, or will be another such person. The messages were clear and unequivocal that this methodology is willingly given to empower any and all who choose to discover their unique selves and their purpose. Everyone without exception has the ability to ignite the power within themselves and to be spiritually connected and guided every step of the way.

What follows in this book is co-authored by Karen. This work would not have been realized without her wisdom, advice, encouragement, and insistence that this book must come to be. Higher guidance was ever-present for both her and me, in all aspects of this work from the structure, content, choice of wording and tone. Each page is a transmission of not only information but of an imbedded energetic vibration of consciousness. You are not just informed but transformed through this alchemic process. The book is designed in 7 parts.

Part One, is an overview of the 7 alchemic stages that form the architecture of the methodology. It is intended to give the journeyer a feel for each stage as it relates to the whole of the alchemic process. The theme that runs through this first book is authenticity and sovereignty. Living your truth from a place of sovereignty. This is foundational. All that follows is predicated on the integrity of an unshakeable, unbreakable you. This first part encapsulates the why of the journey; why these steps in this order and to what end. It provides but a tantalizing glimpse into the journey where neither your complete buy-in nor understanding is expected.

Part Two, breaks each of the seven stages into discrete sets of instructions. The quest for higher consciousness demands work. But the work here is all done through the transmission of energy and until you do it, it is almost impossible to conceive. It requires you to be open to new beliefs, understandings, and skills beyond what you have likely experienced. But it is a self-guided approach, clearly laid out and at a pace you determine. You are from the outset connected to your higher guidance ensuring that the experience is personalized to the needs of your body, mind, and soul. Through higher guidance you will never be given more than you are prepared for and more will not be accessible until you have successfully completed the work at each step. The pace with which you journey is unique to you and in part, predicated on the time you choose to devote to this work. You honour the journey required for body, mind, and soul transformation and *becoming* lies in each step as you walk it.

Part Three, is about applying your new-found guidance and higher consciousness to the everyday challenges of living in our three-dimensional reality. Instead of life happening to you, life happens from within you, for you. You find yourself in the flow of life with higher guidance at your disposal promoting your health and well-being. You understand this guidance is there 24/7, and that *matter does not matter.* You can ask for help on anything from the mundane to the important. But the law of non-interference means that you must ask. You may not always like the answer, but you learn to trust that what you receive is exactly what your soul needs at that moment. There is no obligation or judgment on whether you heed or act on this advice. It is freely given. There is magic in this and you find yourself grateful for this wondrous gift. Part 3 is designed to get you started with some ideas on how to make good use of this gift.

Part Four, is a list of the *invariant laws* which anchor the integrity of this work. The prime directive of this methodology as gifted, is to raise consciousness. In so doing, there are a number of invariant laws that underpin the alchemic process in raising consciousness. *Invariant* as these laws apply universally—to all, regardless of age, gender, level of consciousness, geographic location, circumstances, animate or inanimate, seen or unseen. These laws had to be applied throughout the methodology without exception. They apply to this first level of transformation as well as to subsequent levels.

Part Five, is a brief description of the other levels of transformation. These are each to be the subject of discrete books expanding on spiritual foundations supporting the progressively higher alignment of body, mind, and soul as indivisible and individuated divinity. This overview is intended to provide a glimpse into the continuing journey for those willing to go further. *As above, so below* is the governing law. The higher the consciousness, the more truth, love, and light allow for a greater depth of understanding and healing. You journey deeper to reveal the power vested in you to heal and uplift the world around you. There is an urgency and responsibility to raise collective consciousness.

Part Six, is a primer on the fundamental concepts underpinning the level 1 journey. This is where science and spirituality are thankfully coming together, albeit with a way to go! Neither one is complete without the other. This part attempts to capture but a sound bite of the science with an explanation of how it informs the spiritual nature of the journey and methodology. It covers such topics as consciousness, energy, the basic differences between Newtonian and Quantum physics, the new biology of epigenetics and the body's energy systems including the chakras. This really amounts to a launching pad for further exploration with suggested books and videos.

Part Seven, is a fairly comprehensive section to acknowledge the luminaries who are forging the way forward for us all. This is a tribute to the great minds and their works, and we acknowledge how their insights have informed this methodology. Their works are all without exception worth reading and reading again. You might find some hard to fully comprehend but as your own consciousness is raised, you will find yourself going back to their works with greater understanding and appreciation. We are grateful to every one of them. More such luminaries and their works will be highlighted in subsequent levels of transformation.

In closing, you are already on your way to becoming all that you are meant to be... The universe thanks you...

Diane Fulford

☙❧

PART ONE

OVERVIEW OF THE SEVEN
STAGES OF ALCHEMY

Transformative Level 1
THE ALCHEMIC ARCHITECTURE OF THE JOURNEY

The following chart summarizes the overall architecture of the journey. As you proceed through the seven alchemic stages, each category will be discussed in detail to enable you to understand where you are in the process, the purpose of each stage, what work is required, and the key learnings and accomplishments. Each stage must be completed before the next one is undertaken as it is a methodical build of your understanding and vibrational frequency. It has been constructed to allow for independent progress.

	Calcination	Dissolution	Separation	Conjunction	Fermentation	Distillation	Coagulation
Alchemic State	Reducing (to ashes)	Suspension (in water)	Isolating (purifying)	Amalgamation (coming back together)	Interaction (of purified elements)	Condensing (reduction)	Transformation (progressive)
Journey Stage	Questioning	Resolve	Purifying	Surrendering	Practicing	Mastering	Becoming
What Happens	Acknowledgement of Breakdown or Yearning	Suspending Disbelief	Deprogramming + Reprogramming of Self	Reordering of Self	Reordering of Life	Moving from Practice to Mastery	Be-ing
The Work	Pushing the Pause Button	Connecting to Inner Guidance — Connecting to Higher Guidance	Releasing Misspent Energies — Balancing Positive Energies	Forgiveness and Acceptance of New Self	Attuning Life Structures to New Self	Manifesting from Higher Self	Body Mind Soul Oneness
Foundational Competencies	Introspection	Empowerment	Healing	Reframing	Meditation	Self Transcendence	Embodiment
Aspects of Consciousness	Seeking	Awakening	Awareness	Knowing	Self-Realization	Insightful	Enlightened
Revelation	"there is a crack in everything – that's how the light gets in"	"you are a soul with a body not a body with a soul"	"healing is the process of releasing and correcting dis-harmonic energy"	"when I let go of what I am, I become what I might be"	"mindful living is the choice to harmonize life and self"	"from seeing is believing to believing is seeing"	"be the change you want to see in the world"

CALCINATION

"There is a crack in everything. That's how the light gets in."

Leonard Cohen

There comes a moment...

when your world shifts, sometimes ever so subtly, but you feel the wobble. You pause momentarily to question whether life is all you thought it should be; whether you could call yourself "happy"; whether you feel fulfilled. The moment is fleeting and then life simply takes over and you carry on.

But a shift is a shift. And the shift produces the tiniest of cracks in your world. Just a filament really, but it is persistent. You think it can be papered over, covered up with a course correction; a little more sleep, a better eating choice, some exercise, a shopping spree, a mini getaway—something—and then you can resume, and all is under control. Under control. That is the illusion. And it works until it doesn't. Such is the nature of illusions.

Sometimes abrupt and traumatic, sometimes gradual and subtle, it is the cycle of breakdown to breakthrough. The breaking down of you and your life. Like a crack, it can start out small but over time becomes more pronounced, and harder to dismiss. *"What is the meaning and purpose of my life? Why am I working harder only to achieve less happiness and fulfillment? Why do I oscillate between feverish resolve to tackle everything on the (endless) to-do list and numbing myself from feeling too much of anything? Why is my body breaking down and betraying me? Who and what can fix me?"*

The insights come not from the crack but the light that comes through. Focus not on the crack but rather on what is illuminated. Push the pause button. Pause long enough to reflect, to be introspective even if it is painful or uncomfortable or unfamiliar. Take off the *everything is fine mask*. Allow yourself to feel vulnerable and honest. Lean into that moment and give it a voice.

This is the essence of the first stage of the journey. The questioning. The breaking down. The wondering whether life has more to offer or whether you have more to offer life. The emerging understanding that, whatever your circumstances, be they dire or quite exceptional, you are meant to evolve at a deeper level to enable a more meaningful connection to yourself and the world around you. In alchemy, it is the reduction to ashes that begins the transformation of the ordinary to something extraordinary.

The light is a beacon for that yearning, for those who become "seekers" of themselves.

DISSOLUTION 2

"You are a soul with a body, not a body with a soul"
– Ankush Modawal"

There comes a moment...

when you are prepared to suspend disbelief; when you are prepared to suspend what you hold as beliefs. The known world making room for the unknown. That is a big leap of faith. You make that bargain with yourself. OK, maybe just for a few days. You don't have to announce it to the world. Keeping it under wraps is part of the bargain. There's always a way back.

Whatever the bargain, you separate yourself just enough from life as you know it to venture beyond the conventional. It is about choosing to expand by opening up to new possibilities; to imagine that there just might be something beyond what our senses confirm as our only reality. A soul with a body? Really? Well, just maybe.

In alchemic terms this is the Dissolution stage; the suspension of elements in liquid to render them malleable. You have to park your skepticism to become less rigid, to become more malleable. This is *awakening*. And awakening is the beginning of everything you are meant to discover. A grand portal leading not OUT into the world but INTO a world that lies within—your inner landscape. A landscape filled with an inner power you are about to ignite. Energy is that power.

This stage brings forth understanding that you are vibrating energy in a universe where everything is vibrating at a unique vibrational speed. What appears to be solid is only energy whose vibration has been so lowered as to appear solid and stationary to our senses. Everything is energy. There is no separation; we are all connected by energy to everything and everyone. Separation is not only an illusion, but an impossibility.

Why is this so foundational to the journey? Well, we tend to try to change ourselves by controlling what we say and how we act. For example, we know that we should not anger so quickly so we either tell ourselves we will not get angry and we hide our anger, or we decide to avoid situations or persons that make us feel angry. But this type of change is about control, not transformation. Transformation can only happen at the level of vibration. Real and permanent transformation means recalibrating ourselves vibrationally, clearing our dissonant, negative energies and resetting or shifting our vibration into a higher frequency of energy. There is a reason why we anger. We have trapped many negative emotions within our bodies, based on fear and unworthiness, that leave us prone to defensive behaviours. These emotions are trapped through previous experiences and they trap as negative energy.

So, one must accept that thoughts, emotions and feelings are energy just like sound and light waves are energy. We are like a container holding a mix of low, dense energies and higher, lighter energies. Everyone has a unique blend of this energy mix which forms our *vibrational signature*. You are your thoughts, emotions and beliefs and they manifest in the body, mind, and soul. You are your unique vibrational signature.

It is at this stage that we become awakened to the energies beyond what we can detect with our 5 senses. We learn to connect with inner guidance and with higher guidance; a spiritual guidance that is your indispensable Sherpa on this journey.

**As we hone the skill to connect to higher
guidance, we become limitless.**

SEPARATION

"Healing is the process of releasing and correcting disharmonic energy"

There comes a moment...

when the connection to higher guidance takes you to the next stage of the journey—that of recalibrating yourself through the purification of body, mind, and soul. This is a process of separating out and getting rid of lower frequency energies, followed by a process to bring in elevated energies, all to attain a higher vibrational self. To be everything we are meant to become, we need to be beings of light, whole and healthy.

The work starts here—on healing the body, mind, and soul through raising consciousness. You cannot heal physically, emotionally, or spiritually at the same level of consciousness that created or led to the *dis-ease* or *dis-order* in the first place. You can manage the symptoms and distortions, but true healing can only be achieved through higher consciousness.

This is the alchemic stage of separating and isolating base elements from their combined state to purify each of them in turn. And so, it is with our body, mind, and soul. We *decode* through a guided process of isolating and then releasing trapped and blocked energies in a unique and personalized sequence. We are deconstructing our vibrational signature to remove the lower frequencies in favour of higher frequencies. It is a purification process.

As vibrational vessels we each hold emotions, experiences, and beliefs within us. We are a unique mosaic of these emotions, experiences, and beliefs, held as memories and habits which form our personality and identity. At any moment, we are the sum of our past which is a great predictor of our future as we tend to repeat the same patterns of behaviour. For most of us, we hold a number of fear-based experiences which reinforce fear-based beliefs and behaviours. We are hardwired to survive, and our evolution has been (ironically) guaranteed based on fear as our greatest source of protection. We have learned to conform to the collective and our sense of self tends to be a reflection of how we think others see and judge us. Our validation is at best conditional on fulfilling expectations as set by others, and adopted by us. We risk being more image than authentic. The mask we wear for others, we wear equally for ourselves. And while fear may have guaranteed our evolution to date, it will not in the future.

This process of purification is designed to shed that which over time and through control and fear has masked our authentic self. We peel off the mask layer by layer to uncover our authentic selves. Remember that this journey is about discovering who you are meant to *become.* The starting point to becoming is who and what you are NOW, unmasked. We are meant to be authentic and living our truth as sovereign individuals. Sovereign in our own right as in a refusal to conform for the sake of those societal dictates not in our highest interest or for our greatest good. So, the transformation of *life happening TO you to life happening FROM within you* is really life happening through your authentic and sovereign self. This is shifting from *awakening* to a state of *awareness*, awareness of your authentic self.

This journey is an invitation to travel deeper within to reset; to systematically release misspent energies. Through this guided process, we gain powerful insights into what specific events and experiences have burrowed deep within our psyche and physical body making us act and react in repeated behavioural patterns. It is why certain people, words, feelings, or situations push our buttons or leave us feeling edgy, on the defensive or simply deflated and defeated.

These underlying triggers are negative emotions that become trapped at a specific age in conjunction with a particular event or situation. These trapped energies attach themselves to organs and other parts of the body causing distortions to their functioning. With higher guidance, they release in a sequence unique to you, as if the release of one trapped energy holds the key to releasing the next. The process is as mysterious as it is powerful. It is through the energetic release of these underlying emotional triggers that the healing begins. We repair.

The need for releasing lower frequency energies applies ever more at the subconscious level. It is at this level that our automatic programming becomes the focus. Certain of our behaviours are patterns deeply entrenched to the point where we act, feel, or respond without thought or even awareness. As Joe Dispensa says, this is about *breaking the habit of being yourself.* This takes work and resolve. There is comfort in the familiar, in the known no matter how dysfunctional. Becoming is choosing not to settle for who and what you are now. It is choosing not to be limited by the confines of the known.

After we decode, we encode. The release of negative, dense frequencies creates *space* to encode positive attributes. We bring in what serves us. Here again, higher guidance isolates and identifies positive attributes in a very specific and ordered fashion to create harmonic balance. We invite these elevated energies through a process of intention and affirmations. We learn the power of setting intentions and of creating meaningful affirmations that work their alchemic magic at the vibrational level.

And after all of this separation, isolating and purifying we are ready for the next stage of putting it all back together...

"Know thyself" is a prerequisite to "Becoming."

CONJUNCTION

"When I let go of what I am, I become what I might be." — Lao Tzu

There comes a moment...

when the new vibrational signature takes shape. You have deconstructed and deprogrammed, purified and have begun healing towards a new self. You have kept what always was good, shed what did not serve and brought balance to your strengths. You are now a different mix of energy frequencies having shed the densest in favour of bringing in more lightness. Now is the period of adjustment, a period of transition towards a new *reordered self*.

In alchemic terms, this is when the separated and purified elements are put back together in a combined state albeit a reconfigured state. This represents a reordering of the altered elements as they mesh and forge. It is in fact the chemistry of creating something unknown from combining the altered parts. The emergence of the extraordinary from the ordinary is preparing itself.

This stage is often compared to the cocoon or chrysalis stage transforming caterpillar to butterfly. There is a breaking down of the caterpillar to a malleable liquid within the cocoon. This liquid state is the body reduced to imaginal cells which are undifferentiated, like stem cells. The imaginal cells reorder to form an entirely new body. It is a period of transition.

So too is this an important transition phase within the journey. Transition, but far from a resting phase. There are many shifts taking place, a reordering of self at the vibrational level. You are healing at an impressive rate. Your biological age is considerably reduced and consequently you may experience periods of being very tired. Going through a transition takes considerable energy; coming out of a transition brings higher forms of welcome energy.

What this stage requires of you is everything and nothing. Everything that it requires and nothing you can think of. To *think* is not to *know* and this stage is the transition, the preparation from a life experienced through thinking to a life realized through *knowing*. And you may only know in the moment you stand in, not before or after. The Conjunction stage is that pause, to experience your reordered self in the moment. In the surrender to the moment, you acquaint yourself with the knowing that is *heart centred*. It is the transition to head and heart coherence.

Within the journey this is the *surrendering* stage. And here, surrendering does not mean giving up but denotes a state of graceful acceptance. Breathing through the changes; embracing the new self as it is going through a reordering; letting go of resistance and fear. Really experiencing a new-found authenticity and assurance rooted in sovereignty. Understanding that validation and self-worth come from within. All change comes from within.

This is discovering the power to *reframe* yourself in the context of your life. Reframing is a choice for self-determination, the hardwiring if you will, of a new belief system. Choose to live in trust rather than fear; choose to live your truth rather than someone else's; choose peace over drama;

choose to be authentic rather than perfect. These are not just empty phrases; they are life changing. You now have the vibrational capacity and elevation to do so. This is not easy. There are moments of insight, but so too will you slide back. But this time, when you slide back to your old self, you will know it; you will feel the vibrational discord. Like an inner compass, it will let you know when you are not aligned to your true north.

It is a metamorphous of self that, as you go forward, will not go unnoticed by others. Prepare yourself for this. Expect that many will be inspired by your new self while others will not welcome the changes. They may fear abandonment, or it may hold up an unwanted mirror. But this is when your reordered self deepens into a state of *knowingness*; you believe in the authentic self that is emerging. It is a relief to give up falseness and pretence. You feel liberated and at peace with yourself. You stand your ground with understanding and compassion for others but stand your ground, you will. It is conviction not permission that allows you to move forward.

And this is the moment when you have one last grace note to extend to your old self and your old life: that of forgiveness. Einstein is often paraphrased as advocating that you cannot solve a problem with the same level of consciousness that created it. So too this goes for transgressions. You had to await this higher vibration and consciousness to forgive what wrongs occurred at the lower and denser vibrational plane of your past. Forgiveness is not an intellectual exercise; rather it is the ultimate form of surrender. It is freedom. Freedom from guilt, from regret, from hurt, from anger, from fear. Every transgression was a lesson; every person who wronged you, a teacher.

It is conviction not permission that allows you to move forward.

FERMENTATION 5

"Mindful living is the choice to harmonize life and self in authenticity"

There comes a moment...

when you, as a newly ordered self, are ready for the road test. The road test is life; the transition from a former life that was happening TO you to life happening FROM within you, for your highest good. You now have the vibrational capacity to live from a place of inner power, knowing and mindfulness.

The shift from a life happening to you to one happening from within you is life altering. While you have the vibrational capacity, it is your will, your intention, that sets this profound shift in motion. The Fermentation stage is about making life choices, not predicated on past habits and behaviours but on the highest choice available to you. Making a *mindful* choice, a choice of the highest good, will support the highest ramifications for your soul's requirements for its growth. You come to appreciate that all life choices, even the smallest ones have ramifications not only on you but upon the world. You are the only one accountable for your choices.

You no longer see yourself as a victim, survivor, conformist, pleaser or unworthy. This is now life as manifested by you. You are reframing what you send out to the universe and attracting that which you desire from a place of trust, openness, and goodness. You cannot help but notice the synchronicities that spontaneously and magically manifest—from the mundane (the perfect parking spot) to the sublime (how did I happen to be at the right place at just the right time?)

With this understanding, the challenge now is to *attune* your higher self to an elevated life and lifestyle. Your former self set up behaviours and patterns in every aspect of your life from what you ate, how you slept, worked, played, and interacted with those in your life. Each of these life structures requires adjustments to match or attune to your elevated vibration. They need an upgrade to match your upgrade. This is the attunement so necessary to maintain an elevated or higher vibrational resonance. At any point in time, you and your life are in a dance of resonant harmony or disharmony. There is no separation; you and life are enmeshed as vibrations impacting each other. It is only through life experiences that your potential as becoming, as emerging, is self-realized.

Bruce Lipton, in his book "Biology of Belief" described how a healthy cell introduced into an unhealthy Petri dish would become unhealthy over time but the inverse was likewise true; put an unhealthy cell in a healthy Petri dish and the cell will turn healthy over time. Your life is like your Petri dish. Your vibrational well-being is dependent on its interaction with its environment. The good news is that denser vibrations naturally want to entrain to higher vibrations. This means that the tendency will be for life to adjust to your new level of vibration over time. And in turn, you will find yourself attracted to people, places and situations that expand you, and inspire you. Some changes will be subtle, others more obvious but these shifts serve to be in better resonant accord (as in tune and a-c-c-h-o-r-d) with your elevated vibrational signature.

In alchemic terms, this is the Fermentation stage. The organic process of elements adjusting and interacting with each other and their environment. You and life are this organic process. It is a back and forth, an ebb and flow of refinements to create a compatible harmonic resonance between you and life, as one inseparable dynamic. And as with fermentation, a change agent is added to the mix, such as yeast to transform grapes to wine. Your yeast, your agent of transformation is *authenticity.* Approach all aspects of your life with the goal of attuning your authenticity to an authentic life.

In Brené Brown's book, "The Gifts of Imperfection" she contends that authenticity is not something we either have or don't have. It is a mindful practice—a conscious choice of how we want to live. It is about the choice to show up and to be real. Being authentic in a culture that dictates everything from how much we should weigh to what our homes should look like, to what jobs we hold, is a daunting task. Authenticity demands wholehearted living and loving (particularly of ourselves). It demands the practice and discipline of *mindful living.* Living with intention, audacity, and authenticity.

When we choose to be elevated, to be true to ourselves, people around us may struggle to make sense of how and why we are making changes. Some will find it worrisome; some will ridicule, some may withdraw. Still others will find you a source of strength and inspiration.

This is not a question of seeking permission or approaching change with trepidation; this is a resolve to adjust with understanding, compassion, and inclusion. Validation comes from within. This is not easy and there will be times when you want to slide back to what is familiar, accepted, and comfortable no matter how dysfunctional it may be. When this happens (and it will surely) meditate. Go deeper still. Find that inner compass, power and resolve to remain true to yourself and live life in your truth.

Live life with mindfulness.

DISTILLATION 6

"From seeing is believing, to believing is seeing"

There comes a moment...

when practice becomes mastery. Mindful living at the master level is the belief in your power to create. What takes you there is the all-important shift from seeing to observing. What you see, you react to; when you observe, you create what comes next.

Seeing is with the eyes; observing comes from the elevated perspective of the third eye. There is only one third eye as it reconciles what both eyes see. Observing is the *space* you hold between moments. It is the space that is just before what happens next. It is the briefest of pauses but oh so powerful. There are infinite possibilities that exist within that space. It is a pause that expands and fills the moment with choices. With mindful observing you *create* what comes next as a choice among infinite possibilities.

The choice is *realized* in that moment—in the words chosen, the feelings expressed, the actions taken that set in motion what comes next. The power of creating rather than reacting. And you understand that all subsequent moments are predicated on the one before. When you choose to turn left rather than right, life unfolds along a different path; when you choose to be the voice of openness and inclusion rather than feeding drama—you shift the energy.

As observer you are not caught up in the fray of the moment but hover just above, inviting perspective, *insight,* and intention into the unfolding of the moment. You appreciate that you are co-creating the expanding universe with the exercise of each mindful choice. The mastery of mindful living is in accepting responsibility to raise consciousness with each breath and each moment. You bring a soul whispered wisdom to the moment you stand in.

In alchemic terms, distillation is the process of reducing something to its essence. Distillation creates potency, purity, and resilience. It helps preserve and stabilize all that has not been discarded. Your true self as your higher self is your essence, your divinity. The essence of who you are with the power to elevate everything and everyone as a mindful choice. So here the journey takes an important leap. It is no longer just about you. It is not just about accepting responsibility for yourself or about raising your own consciousness. No. Your journey of healing, of sovereignty, of wholeness, of authenticity, of higher consciousness has led you here. To go beyond yourself.

This is *self-transcendence.* It is mindfulness for the collective good. To create or manifest not just what is in your interest but to go wider and broader with your reach. In each moment you have that choice; after all, there is no separation. What you throw out to the universe reverberates right back. The challenge we face on a planetary scale can only be addressed through a collective focus on higher consciousness.

**Pay it forward—know that the choice for higher
consciousness reverberates and multiplies endlessly.**

COAGULATION 7

"*Be the change you want to see in the world*"

There comes a moment...

when what you have mastered integrates and completes the transformation of self at this level. You have arrived to find yourself. The journey is many things but above all, it is a journey of discovery—the discovery of whom you are meant to become. It is a journey of becoming—come to be. Be. Be-ing. Be in motion—Being.

Be the body, mind, and soul embodiment of your authentic self. All else evolves from that state of being. *Be* elevated and be the one who elevates consciousness. *Be* sovereign in the power vested in you—in your knowing. *Be* mindful in your words, emotions, and actions as the gift to create. *Be* a beacon of light and inspiration. *Be* the change the world so desperately needs.

All is possible because you have chosen to evolve; to shift; to awaken. You have had the resolve to deconstruct and reconstruct, shedding density to welcome light into a new reordered self and reordered life. You have found your inner compass, rejecting a life dictated to you and embraced a life defined by you. You have shifted from conforming out of fear, to authenticity powered by trust. You have shifted from discord and dis-ease to a vibration of health, harmony, and coherence. Such is the power of transformation.

Yet, challenges remain. There are many demands and responsibilities in mindful living at such an elevated level. You are forging the way. The path can be lonely. And you will see more cracks. You will feel the struggles of others; you are ever more conscious of the challenges inherent in being good stewards of the planet. But as always, the cracks let in the light. It is the gift of imperfection. Earth is not in perfect rotation; it wobbles, ever so slightly. It is the wobble that ensures just enough variation to allow for continuous evolution. So too must you welcome the wobbles as the way through to elevated consciousness for all. Be-ing is always in motion.

Live your truth in peace, love, and gratitude.

AND FINALLY...

There comes a time...

As above, so below

when you understand that the end is just the beginning. This is a continuous journey of "becoming." It is the evolution of consciousness as you ascend to higher vibrational planes—a refinement of self in a continuous cycle of breakdowns to breakthroughs. That is how all of nature regenerates. You go deeper within to attain higher levels of consciousness and enlightenment. *As above, so below.*

And so, you start anew. You go through the 7 alchemic steps to achieve the next level of transformation. Yes, there are levels (see Part Five—Levels of Transformation—Overview). You begin at the beginning with a beginner's mind. However, your starting point is from your higher self with a more open mind, accepting that learning and transformation come with claiming your future as one worthy of being a wayshower for a life and *presence* in higher consciousness. Consciousness wants to keep expanding and elevating. The state of be-ing is always moving; always becoming.

There are deeper truths to be uncovered; there is greater healing to be had; there are greater powers to master; there is greater service to others that awaits; there is understanding of who and what you are as *individuated divinity* to be revealed.

The never-ending journey of the awakened awaits...

෴

PART TWO

INSTRUCTIONS

CALCINATION

*"There is a crack in everything—that's how
the light gets in"* — Leonard Cohen

	Calcination	Dissolution	Separation	Conjunction	Fermentation	Distillation	Coagulation
Alchemic State	Reducing (to ashes)	Suspension (in water)	Isolating (purifying)	Amalgamation (coming back together)	Interaction (of purified elements)	Condensing (reduction)	Transformation (progressive)
Journey Stage	Questioning	Resolve	Purifying	Surrendering	Practicing	Mastering	Becoming
What Happens	Acknowledgement of Breakdown or Yearning	Suspending Disbelief	Deprogramming + Reprogramming of Self	Reordering of Self	Reordering of Life	Moving from Practice to Mastery	Be-ing
The Work	Pushing the Pause Button	Connecting to Inner Guidance Connecting to Higher Guidance	Releasing Misspent Energies Balancing Positive Energies	Forgiveness and Acceptance of New Self	Attuning Life Structures to New Self	Manifesting from Higher Self	Body Mind Soul Oneness
Foundational Competencies	Introspection	Empowerment	Healing	Reframing	Meditation	Self Transcendence	Embodiment
Aspects of Consciousness	Seeking	Awakening	Awareness	Knowing	Self-Realization	Insightful	Enlightened
Revelation	"there is a crack in everything – that's how the light gets in"	"you are a soul with a body not a body with a soul"	"healing is the process of releasing and correcting dis-harmonic energy"	"when I let go of what I am, I become what I might be"	"mindful living is the choice to harmonize life and self"	"from seeing is believing to believing is seeing"	"be the change you want to see in the world"

Introduction

Calcination is the first step in the transformation process. There are many breakdowns throughout one's life but this one leads you down a different path. A crack opens; something tells you to take the path less travelled. Rather than patching up the crack and carrying on, you choose to see what is illuminated by the light that comes in. You follow the light.

In alchemic terms, this is reducing what needs to be transformed through rendering it to ashes. It is the breaking down or breakdown so necessary for breaking through. It is altering the state from ordinary to extraordinary, from a base metal to precious metal, from corrupted to pure.

The crack, such as it is, is acknowledged. There is a crack. It can take the form of a significant crisis in your life—a health issue, a loss of a loved one, the end of a relationship, the unexpected termination of a job, a personal failure, a tragic accident—whatever the nature, it happened to you. You had little to no control and it caused suffering, or you were the cause of suffering. It can be life altering. There is a before and after, whatever the crack.

The crack can be more subtle. It can be a slow build of hopes and expectations dashed. You find yourself at a certain age and point in life not where you expected to be. Wasn't there supposed to be something better given all that invested effort, given all the planning, given all the expectations everyone had of me and that I had for myself?

The crack can take the form of opportunity foregone. Why didn't I follow my gut rather than follow the herd? Why didn't I stand up for my convictions and values at that critical juncture? Why do I always retreat when I have an opportunity to shine? These are the cracks of regrets and they play out as endless loops of negative self-worth until you believe you are no better than those failed moments.

The crack can take the form of yearning, yearning for more meaning in life. What is it all about anyways? What will be my legacy? How really am I spending my time? What is my purpose? Why do I fill every waking moment tackling an endless list of things to do? Why is it so hard to live in the moment? Why, despite all measures of success do I feel unfulfilled? Why is there always a shiny new thing that I absolutely need to make my life meaningful? Why is bigger and better always better?

For every one of these cracks, there is an opening of introspection that reveals itself; the moment that you know the real answers come from within. Make no mistake, this is profound. The path most often taken is not to go within. That is uncomfortable—just more suffering. We avoid suffering at all costs. And we fail to see what suffering offers. So instead, we simply patch things up, get it behind us as quickly as possible and carry on. We do so by seeking validation from the outside. We seek remedies and people to fix things from the outside. We rationalize our actions.

To some degree we are both victims and survivors of a life largely happening to us. We define ourselves through the collective barometers of what constitutes normal behaviour and determinants of success. We wear a mask to hide what we do not want others to see, and what we choose to ignore within ourselves. We seek the comfort and familiarity of others like us. We are good at camouflaging.

What we send out to the universe we get back in kind. This is the law of attraction. If we think ourselves unworthy, we will be confirmed as unworthy. We adopt certain behaviours and habits that invite repeated sets of circumstances and experiences into our lives even as we would wish for something else.

So, transformation starts with the most important pause you will ever take. The pause to turns inwards. Inwards is where transformation takes place. You become a *seeker* of who you really are; the stripped-down, unmasked version of your authentic and sovereign self. You have an inner landscape far different than the outer landscape you are tied to. All change must first come from within. This is the journey of transformation that lies ahead.

The Work
Pressing the "Pause Button"

Acknowledgement of the crack and the desire to pay attention to this interruption leads to a metaphorical pushing of the pause button. Pressing the pause button takes a certain amount of courage as it disturbs the predictable flow of life that you have established through years of practice—inviting disruption within you and around you. The time for looking inward and exploring different paths is now.

Preparing for your journey

As with any journey, the experience will be enriched through some advance information. In many respects, this journey guides you into unfamiliar territory. While exciting, it will at times be outside of your comfort zone. It is meant to be by design; it cannot be otherwise. It is having the courage and resolve to move past the known and familiar to accept an evolution of self not otherwise possible. This journey is deeply personal and is fundamentally a choice for expansion of mind, body and soul through the connection to consciousness. It is by far the most wondrous journey of all, for those who choose to travel.

Carving out time

As with any commitment or practice, the challenge is fitting this into an already busy life. We all have demanding lives and contend with personal challenges. What makes things even more difficult is that most of us put ourselves last on the list of things that must get done to get through the day. Only after the needs of everyone else are met can we turn our attention to the investment and nourishment of ourselves. And then we are usually exhausted. Trust that investing in yourself will pay dividends.

Your presence is required

You must be willing to show up and be present, meaning your presence in the NOW: in the moment because that is the only time and space when change can occur. This is really challenging at the start but in time you will be seized with the wonder and importance of the changes taking place; indeed, you will crave this time as you become one with the experience. Rather than another add-on to your day, everything you do, every interaction, every demand will be fuelled by an inner power gifted through this transformation. It is an investment in self with unlimited dividends.

Carve out time with intention and whatever time you devote to this, make it count. There is no right amount of time; it can be an hour to three hours a week and that can vary from week to week. It can be any time of the day when you make alone time.

Pace of journey

The pace with which one goes through the steps of this journey is unique and in part predicated on the amount of time you can devote to this. Again, there is no right or wrong but in general this is something you do not want to race through having checked appropriate boxes. In fact, that may be an indication that you are not *getting it*. This is about the process; about enjoying and understanding that the journey is the destination.

Length of journey

This is not like a six-week course in which you are declared transformed, certificate in hand. No, this is who you are becoming, what you are becoming and your purpose in becoming. It comes in layers and stages and levels of evolving. It is like school, where the learnings are a build and bridge to the next grade. Patience is required. When you do not fully understand, you will be stopped; forced to pause and ponder until the answers come; until your body, mind and soul are aligned and ready to move on. But it is also your choice, your will to pause, take a prolonged break or quit at any point in the journey. Wherever that may be, is better than your starting point.

You are not alone

The resolve to journey and invest in yourself must come from within. Few are in a position where they are encouraged to do so by those around them. Indeed, the level of skepticism for spiritual development of this nature remains high, for now. This is changing rapidly. There are many and many more every day, who are seeking their own journey; they just have not expressed it. But communities of like-minded seekers are forming globally. There are new media platforms devoted to spiritual development that are credible sources of information. This manual is intended to connect you to the communities and platforms and practitioners that occupy this space. Once considered the realm of the "woo-woo," you will be amazed at the number of physicists, medical practitioners, scientists, psychologists and the like who are forging the way. You will be amazed at the calibre and authenticity of mediums and channelers and those with extraordinary gifts, all sharing their insights with the world. The ones referenced in this manual are credible and brilliant sources of learning.

But you travel alone

It is your personal journey and those around you may not be supportive. They may be fearful of the changes you will undergo or may think that they too must journey lest they be abandoned. Some will ridicule; some will be inspired and find a welcome outlet to their own yearning. Others will applaud and support you with encouragement and help to find the time you need to invest in yourself. Whatever the case, the journey is yours to travel alone. No one but you can provide the introspection needed to know where and how changes must be made; no one but you can find the self-worth and validation required to persevere through periods of self-doubt or skepticism by others. All change, all validation comes from the travel within.

Conviction not permission

You are not seeking permission. Seeking permission is tentative and confusing for all those around you. It is a choice you have made to invest in your own spiritual development. Period. Unapologetic. It must be so. For those skeptical or fearful, the least amount said the better; let the change speak for itself; let your growing conviction speak for itself. Those who feared abandonment are likely to find relationships deepening when they serve. You will find yourself more centred, less judgmental, more understanding and compassionate and more sovereign in your presence. As your conviction and belief grow, you will know just when to open up.

Expressing the journey

When you do open up, it will be important to find a comfortable way to express the journey to others. Finding the right words and feelings to express the experience with authenticity will serve you well in your connection with others. It is not a question of convincing others of the merits of the journey; rather it is being able to express it as simply and heartfelt as possible. There will come a time when your conviction is unshakeable and unbreakable, and you will want to share this experience with those close to you. There will be a time when your enthusiasm and belief in the journey is so strong that you will want everyone close to you joining in this experience. Be discerning, and trust there is a right time and place to engage others.

Empowerment

When we are broken, our belief is that we should seek someone from the outside to fix us. This journey is about fixing ourselves from within. So instead of giving power away, we own it. It is a journey of empowerment; of igniting the power that lies within to heal the body, mind and soul through energy and the connection to higher guidance and consciousness. We all, without exception, have been gifted with this power which lies latent within most of us, awaiting some sort of awakening. Once unleashed, this power is understood, honed, and eventually mastered throughout the course of this journey.

This is not to say that medical help of any nature (physical or mental) is unwanted or unnecessary. That is simply not the case. It does suggest, however, that there is much we can do to help heal mentally and physically by understanding the impact of negative fear-based structures, beliefs, emotions, experiences and behaviours we hold, as accumulated and reinforced throughout life.

Physical and emotional experience

You will feel it all. The wonder, the doubt, resistance, surrender, discouragement, excitement, impatience, vitality, exhaustion—yes all of it. You will feel times of great progress and times you feel discouraged. The journey is directional but not linear; meaning you are evolving but more like spirals or a vortex where upwards and downwards are in a dance but all the while you are being propelled upwards.

DIRECTIONAL BUT NOT LINEAR

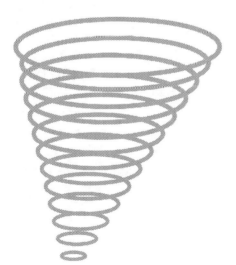

- Coagulation
- Distillation
- Fermentation
- Conjunction
- Separation
- Dissolution
- Calcination

Living life to the fullest

This journey is not about *renunciation,* meaning having to give up material pleasures. The journey over time will serve to accentuate and appreciate more fully all that you experience through your senses. You will come to see with new eyes, create with greater inspiration, forge deeper more meaningful relationships, nourish yourself with food, music, and sensation. We are meant to learn through the experience of all that is to be human. And we are to do so with higher emotions of gratitude and love.

Paying attention

In many respects, the journey is about awareness. Waking up and paying attention. Living with intention and passion for this experience of life. It is about learning how to manifest what you desire and deserve through conscious intention and higher emotions. Pay attention to the synchronicities that fall at your feet; do not dismiss them as random acts or coincidences, for such things do not exist. The promise and responsibility are that you get to create a life by you, from within.

Notes

Keeping your own notes throughout the journey is especially important. We all learn in different ways and it is helpful to translate information, insights and experiences into your own internal language or shorthand. This is a personal record of the journey and you will find yourself referring to events and dates to verify or track specific steps of the journey. Furthermore, you will want to personalize or contextualize the steps through your own reflections and life experiences. Not everything seems meaningful at the time it occurs; insights tend to come as you connect the dots backwards or in hindsight.

Journals

Journaling is different than note keeping and you may want a dedicated journal for this work. Not everyone is comfortable or at ease in expressing themselves through writing. This type of journaling is not about recording daily events; rather it is about capturing your musings, your deepest thoughts and literary and writing skills are not important. Sometimes images or symbols may come to mind. Whatever form this takes, we would encourage you to capture it. Your higher guidance may send you messages through your journaling. You begin to write and inspirations will come *out of nowhere* and you will be amazed at the insights gained in this way. You can ask questions of your higher guidance or spirit guides and they know how best to furnish the answers you need.

Getting started

This is a journey of self-discovery and learning. A highly recommended starting point is the following:

- **A subscription to Gaia:** This is a powerful and highly credible platform for spiritual and consciousness awakening. There are thousands of videos covering wide-ranging topics and includes all forms of yoga and numerous meditation series for the beginner to advanced levels. Throughout the 7 stages of this methodology, you will be referred to numerous interviews with authors to gain more insight on their works.
- **Explore and read:** First book recommendation is "Soul Shifts" by Barbara De Angelis. See Part Seven—The Luminaries, for more information on this and many other authors whose works have inspired this methodology.
- **Alchemy:** Understand the power of Alchemy through the Mystery School teachings of Theresa Bullard. Regina Meredith interviews Theresa on Gaia's Open Minds in an episode entitled "Teaching the Mysteries" (season 11, episode 12). Also, Theresa has her own Gaia series called "Mystery Teachings" where she explores alchemy (season 1, episode 4).
- **Refer to Part Six—Stepping Stones to Greater Understanding:** For further understanding on a variety of topics from consciousness to quantum physics.

Summary

All change comes from the courage to travel within. The discipline and ability to reflect inwardly to honestly examine one's own thoughts and feelings is a fundamental competency that will serve you well throughout your spiritual wakening. Know thyself is a prerequisite to "The Alchemy of Becoming."

Transformative Level 1
DISSOLUTION

"You are a soul with a body not a body with a soul" — Ankush Modawal

	Calcination	Dissolution	Separation	Conjunction	Fermentation	Distillation	Coagulation
Alchemic State	Reducing (to ashes)	Suspension (in water)	Isolating (purifying)	Amalgamation (coming back together)	Interaction (of purified elements)	Condensing (reduction)	Transformation (progressive)
Journey Stage	Questioning	Resolve	Purifying	Surrendering	Practicing	Mastering	Becoming
What Happens	Acknowledgement of Breakdown or Yearning	Suspending Disbelief	Deprogramming + Reprogramming of Self	Reordering of Self	Reordering of Life	Moving from Practice to Mastery	Be-ing
The Work	Pushing the Pause Button	Connecting to Inner Guidance / Connecting to Higher Guidance	Releasing Misspent Energies / Balancing Positive Energies	Forgiveness and Acceptance of New Self	Attuning Life Structures to New Self	Manifesting from Higher Self	Body Mind Soul Oneness
Foundational Competencies	Introspection	Empowerment	Healing	Reframing	Meditation	Self Transcendence	Embodiment
Aspects of Consciousness	Seeking	Awakening	Awareness	Knowing	Self-Realization	Insightful	Enlightened
Revelation	"there is a crack in everything – that's how the light gets in"	"you are a soul with a body not a body with a soul"	"healing is the process of releasing and correcting dis-harmonic energy"	"when I let go of what I am, I become what I might be"	"mindful living is the choice to harmonize life and self"	"from seeing is believing to believing is seeing"	"be the change you want to see in the world"

Introduction

"The Alchemy of Becoming" starts with the resolve to be that seeker of your inner landscape, a seeker of yourself. So instead of dismissing the crack, you resolve to follow the path of light coming through. The resolve might be more tentative at this point; it is more of a bargain with yourself to explore without grand announcements or big life changing commitments. For the most part, it is a quiet resolve with an exit strategy, a way back, if and when needed. But that's really all it takes. A journey of a thousand miles does indeed start with a single step, even if tentative.

You separate yourself from life as you know it, just enough to find that quiet inner space, that in time you will find wondrous. But for now, it is just exploratory, and you may view it as no more productive than daydreaming given how much it seems to intrude on one's busy life. But this space is not about the *doing*; it is about *being*. You get to know yourself not just through what you do in life but through the "be-ing" that you are. Through the unique life force that you are.

This methodology is the exploratory map to yourself, to the unbelievable untapped potential that lies within you. The uniqueness of this journey is that it transforms through working with energy fields. There is truly little physicality associated with it. It does not take will power, or exertion, dietary supplements, or force of any kind. Not force, just power. You hold a life force power, supernatural in fact, that awaits your awakening to it.

You *awaken* to its existence and life is never quite the same (in a good way). But in addition to resolve, awakening requires that you suspend what you believe in. You suspend what you think you know and what you think you are certain of. This awakening is not of the 3rd dimensional world with Newtonian laws that govern the physical nature and predictability of life as we know it. Although not of this dimension it is nonetheless, very real. And you will discover that science and spirituality are finding common ground; that this whole thing is not so woo-woo after all. You will find that the new physics of Quantum mechanics and Astro physics and even epigenetics all point to unseen forces of energy rewriting the textbooks of what we thought we knew as certain.

It starts with understanding that absolutely everything is vibrating energy—you, animals, trees and even seemingly inanimate substances such as rocks or furniture. And even the space in between is just another form of energy. Boundaries of objects or of our physical bodies do not really exist. There is no separation; everything is connected by energy. Separation is a persistent illusion given our sensory limitations.

This concept also extends to thoughts, emotions, words, numbers, and geometric symbols. These are all forms of energy. Your thoughts are every bit as real as the chair you sit on. And all energy encodes information. Energy is encoded with instructions, memory, information, and consciousness.

Every person (and in fact everything) has a *vibrational signature* meaning that you are a unique composite of different frequencies of energy and that the energy you hold also holds consciousness. Your vibrational signature reflects your level of consciousness. We all hold lower, denser frequencies and higher-level frequencies. How much we hold of each, determines where our vibrational signature sits. Those who hold traumas and negative experiences, and thoughts will have a lower vibrational signature than those whose life experiences have been generally more positive.

The transformation through "The Alchemy of Becoming," is all about empowering yourself to raise your level of consciousness through changing the composite of frequencies that make up your vibrational signature. You learn what produces discord and dis-ease within your energy systems and how to function with coherence of energy.

All of this does not have to be understood or in fact believed before embarking on this journey. You will not only understand in time; you will embrace the concepts. For now, it is simply about keeping an open mind to these possibilities.

In alchemic terms, dissolution is the process of suspending elements in water to make them more malleable. The same holds true for your mind. Suspend the hardness of your perceptions and beliefs in favour of a beginner's mind, malleable to go beyond what is known.

The Luminaries
The notion of a vibrational signature is beautifully captured in Barbara De Angelis' book "Soul Shifts". See Part Seven—The Luminaries, for more information.

The Work
Guidance 1: Seeing energy at work

When contemplating these new ideas and concepts, there is nothing that matches seeing and experiencing it for yourself. Simple metal wands made from everyday wire coat hangers and drinking straws *(see Figure 1)* can illustrate that you and your thoughts are indeed energy. Having your first experience seeing and manipulating

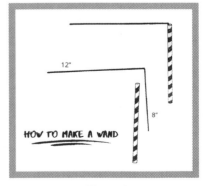

Figure 1

your energy demonstrates that everyone has this innate ability. Processing and understanding the implications of your personal power grows as you progress in this journey.

Consider the wands your personal *truth tellers*.

1. Holding the wands loosely and without moving them, witness how they respond to your body and the energetic field that encompasses it. This illustrates that you are energy.

2. Now explore how the wands respond to statements that are true and untrue. Try simple statements such as "my name is (your true name)" versus "my name is (someone else's name"). The wands will open away from you with a true statement and fold inwards for a false statement. Experiment with different statements and watch them respond accordingly. A true statement generates positive energy, a false one negative energy, thus the expansion and contraction. Just as truths and untruths carry different energies, so do your emotions.

> **Need More Proof?**
>
> Pam Grout's two books "E-Squared" and "E-Cubed" offer lab experiments proving that reality is malleable, consciousness trumps matter and you can shape your life with your thoughts. All the experiments are fun, light-hearted, easy to do but contain serious messages and lots of wisdom. They are designed to prove the principles that there is an invisible energy force or field of infinite possibilities and that you impact this field according to your beliefs and expectations. Furthermore, the experiments are designed to demonstrate and confirm that you are connected to accurate and unlimited guidance and that the universe is limitless, abundant, and accommodating.

3. Again, holding the wands loosely and without moving them, think about an upsetting personal experience. Note how the wands contract inwards in response to this negative energy. Then switch to a positive experience—thinking of someone you love deeply, or a walk along a beach on a perfect day and you will see the wands expand and move outwards in response to this positive energy *(see Figure 2).*

4. Your thoughts are powerful energy forces as well. As you hold the wands, they will likely be swirling in response to your body, so command them to be still (it does not matter if you say the command out loud or to yourself). Once they have settled, command them to move to the left, to the right, point to a window, a compass direction, etc. Experiment at will and enjoy the powerful body/mind connection that this clearly demonstrates.

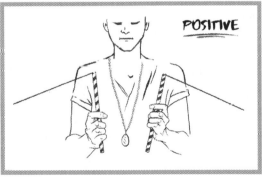

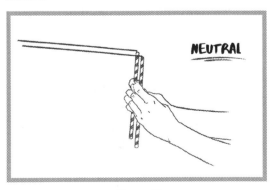

Figure 2

Guidance 2: Connecting to inner/higher guidance

Once you have seen, witnessed and experienced your own ability to move energy with your thoughts and emotions, the foundation has been set for your next metaphysical experience—the ability to connect to inner/higher guidance.

The prime directive of this methodology is attaining higher levels of consciousness. Your guide for this journey comes from the connection with your spirit guides. All questions are directed to them and the guidance comes from them. You learn to connect with them in many ways and over time the connection grows stronger and effortless as your vibrational frequency rises. We all begin this journey with a denser, lower frequency and the first steps of the journey are all designed to release lower densities and attract more elevated vibrational frequencies. All of this is done in a unique, personalized manner with the help and direction of your spirit guides. The relationship you develop with spirit guides will be yours to determine. They can take on many forms from guardian angels, to archangels, to a committee of higher guidance with multiple personalities or areas of specialty, to religious figures, to God, Source or the Divine. It literally is immaterial. The important thing here is to connect to something greater than you, something spiritual that connects with your soul. Your soul, as life essence is the bridge between the body/mind and spirit.

> If you have difficulty standing for a period of time due to injury, or if the sway does not feel right for you, there are other ways to connect using your hands. Dr. Hesu Whitten has a short video on YouTube "Muscle Testing Yourself" that explains several proxies.

Learning the sway

1. Stand with your weight equally distributed between your right and left legs *(see Figure 3)*.
2. Relax your shoulders, close your eyes and go inward. If you practice meditation, go into this state to ready yourself.

3. Set an intention to be open to communicating with your inner/ higher guidance.

4. Ask yourself the same kinds of yes/no questions you did when practicing with the wands. A positive response will cause an involuntary sway forward. A negative response will cause you to sway backwards.

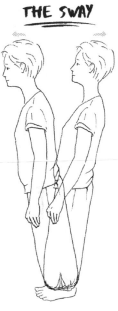

THE SWAY

5. The same reactions hold true for positive/ loving thoughts and negative/hateful thoughts. Experiment with questions that have obvious answers—this will help you gain confidence with this technique and trust in its perfect wisdom.

6. Observe the strength of the response. One of the wonderful characteristics of this technique is that it conveys nuance. A powerful sway forward means a strong yes, while a slight sway may mean "It's OK."

Figure 3

Developing a relationship

They have been waiting your awakening. They know you and the guidance they provide is always in your highest interest. They will never lead you astray nor will they give you a task for which you are not ready. They will never override your will. You are always in the driver's seat. You will develop an intimate relationship with them founded in trust and love. They are always present, day and night. They are remarkably enthusiastic and will keep sending you encouraging messages. There is no limit to the advice they will provide nor limitations to the frequency or importance of what is being asked; from the mundane to the urgent, matter does not matter. There comes a time when you find yourself in silent almost continuous conversation as background in your day. That negative chatter is replaced with higher frequency messaging keeping you centred, self-assured and peaceful. You go from not really believing they exist to not imagining life without them! A curious and wondrous phenomenon indeed.

ARE GUIDES ACCOUNTABLE FOR THEIR ANSWERS?

Answer from the guides...

"We provide what your soul needs at that moment. All power lies in the present moment. What your soul needs for its growth is never a decision but advice and insight into what is needed for the soul's trajectory to know itself in higher consciousness. Will and responsibility are always yours. Like asking the wisest and truest friend you have, the decision to have asked the question is yours, the responsibility to receive an answer is yours and the decision to act on the answer is yours and yours alone. Just like the truest friend, the gift of an answer is freely given with no expectations or judgment attached. This is aligned to your sovereign selves.

Please understand this, there is no abnegation of your power here, of your divinity. We are here to help you help yourselves—we are not here to fix you. All the requirements for your soul already lie within you. We remind you through your knowingness what you already know."

Am I really connecting?

We encourage everyone to connect through the sway (using the body as a pendulum) or if needed, with a hand proxy. At first you will feel unsure that you are connecting. You will wonder if it is your imagination or if your thinking mind is cleverly getting in the way. The curious thing is that the more you just go with it, the more the trust will come. The exercises you will be led to in this methodology will not "harm" you even if you are convinced you got it wrong. We are in no way suggesting

Rules for Connecting using the Sway

- All questions need to be phrased to be answered with a yes/no
- Matter doesn't matter. In other words, you are free to ask questions that range from the mundane to the extraordinary.
- You must not be attached to the outcome/answer you are seeking. You can subconsciously force the sway one way or another, so keeping a neutral mind is extremely important.
- You cannot ask a question about the future, only the past or present. The future has not been predetermined and will be dependent on your thoughts and actions.

that you start asking critical life and death questions. You must be discerning in your learning. Connecting is based on first learning to be in a neutral mind. This is a particularly important skill.

A neutral mind is one where you learn to not be attached to a particular answer or outcome or based on what you think you know. This takes practice. If you ask a question of your guides, you must be open to whatever the answer is. Unbiased and unattached to wanting a particular answer. You are not bound in any way to the answer. Whether you heed the advice or answer given, is entirely within your prerogative. Free will has been granted to us all and your will here must be first applied in posing the question and in choosing to respond or act to the answer provided. There are no consequences to ignoring the answers or advice and going another way. The answer to all questions is freely given with no conditions or expectations. Take it or leave it, at will.

Note that the answers from your guides are geared to what your soul needs at that moment for your growth and well-being. So, answers can come in increments or progression rather than end state answers. Sometimes you fail to get an answer (no forward or backward movement) and that is a signal that the question is phrased in such a way that a question is not aligned to what you need. Figure out another way of asking the question or accept that this is not the time to ask that particular question.

The Luminaries
Regina Meredith Interviews Jean Slatter on Gaia's Open Minds. Author Jean Slatter explains how to use your body as a divination device (i.e., sway) or using just your fingers.

The use of charts to connect with your guides

A type of *coding* is used to by-pass the thinking mind. This coding is in the form of charts which provide a number of possible answers to a series of questions you will be asking. The charts are designed to create boxes of answers which are identified through an intersection of a particular column and row. There are many such charts in the next alchemic stage you are about to embark on (Separation). Each box contains a set number of words which your guides will lead you to. You are asked to familiarize yourself with the set-up or architecture of the chart (number of columns, rows, and words). Once familiar with the design, you are asked to put it aside and do the exercise blind, meaning you do not look at the particular words. You simply are asking your higher guidance to direct you to the right column, row, and word through a set sequencing of questions (is the trapped emotion in column A? In an even-numbered row? Is it the first word in the box?) Viewing the words invites the thinking mind to leap in as it attaches meaning or value to the words. Doing it blind allows no possibility of attachment and practices the feel of a neutral mind. Having no idea what word you are being directed to, leaves you in an open state to receive the guidance. Once the position of the word is determined, you refer to its coordinates in the chart to reveal the word (emotion) your guides have led you to. It is now up to you to accept the word as uncovered and trust that it is the right word for you to be working with.

Know that even if you are unsure you have interpreted your guide's instructions correctly, there is a higher GPS system at work which will energetically course correct your work. Just go with it. You will soon be convinced through the uncanny ability of this process, that your higher guidance is truly at play here.

The use of a logarithmic scale to connect with your guides

In other exercises, you will be asked to assess the effectiveness of what you are doing. You do so by asking your guides for a mark out of ten, using a logarithmic scale. A logarithmic scale is different than a linear scale. In a linear scale, the difference between numbers is of the same value. In a logarithmic scale, the differences are exponential and determined by the power of the base axis, usually a factor of 10. Thus, the difference between 7.1 and 7.2 is tenfold. This type of measurement is used in describing the strength of an earthquake. Apparently, our guides love to communicate through the power of numbers as well as geometric designs and words! Suffice it to say that what may appear to be a small incremental change in a mark assigned to your efforts is likely to indicate exponential levels of improvement.

Guidance 3: Metrics

Level of consciousness

Measuring progress is both important in its own right and a source of encouragement. You will feel many changes but there are several measurements which can be taken periodically throughout the journey, providing numerical confirmation of progress. At the onset of the journey, you will want to create an assessment of your starting point.

For example, it is helpful to know the level consciousness you are starting out with on your journey of becoming. Your vibrational signature correlates to your level of consciousness. This is determined using a scale of consciousness developed by David Hawkins in his seminal work, "Power vs. Force" with a numerical range between 0 and 1000 *(see Figure 4)*. This scale serves to stratify the expressions of consciousness from the lowest (shame, guilt) to higher forms of love to enlightenment. In the early 1990s, he measured the world consciousness level at 209 and believed that those born at a particular level would live out their lives at that same level. He believed the knowledge did not exist to transcend your 'consciousness lot in life.' We now know that not to be true and to do just that, is the prime directive of this methodology. (For more information on consciousness in general, refer to Part Six—Stepping Stones to Greater Understanding of this book.)

Using this logarithmic scale, ask your guides for your level of consciousness. To do so, and without looking at the chart, simply ask if your level of consciousness is over 200. If you get a YES, ask if it is over 210 and then 220, etc. in increments of 10. Once you reach a number where the answer is NO, you can refine the number by asking if it is below or above intervening numbers. Once you have the number or approximately the number, record your level of consciousness and the date on which it was measured *(see Appendix 1)*.

Using the sway, if you get neither a yes or no (movement forwards or backward) you know you are very close to the precise number. If you are unable to do this now, at the onset of this journey do not worry. You will be able to do it in time. Furthermore, you can ask for the information retroactively (what was my level of consciousness at such and such date?)

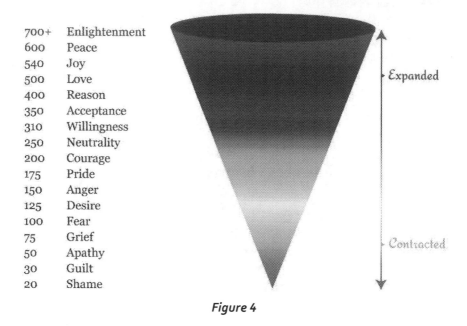

700+	Enlightenment
600	Peace
540	Joy
500	Love
400	Reason
350	Acceptance
310	Willingness
250	Neutrality
200	Courage
175	Pride
150	Anger
125	Desire
100	Fear
75	Grief
50	Apathy
30	Guilt
20	Shame

Figure 4

Other measurements

As beings of energy, we each vibrate at a unique level which we call your vibrational signature. Your vibrational signature acts like an antenna allowing you to tune into the wave frequency you are emitting. It is like we are all radio stations emitting a unique signal, invisible to the eye. By turning the dial, you tune into your particular "station" or vibrational wave which contains information about you.

All information and measurements are optional. For example, you have the choice to measure your biological age, as different from your chronological age. Here you simply ask whether your biological age is less than x as you go down in small increments from your chronological age. Note that some people start their journey with a biological age greater than their chronological age. Whatever the case, you will find that your biological age usually decreases during the course of the journey as the body's source of *dis-ease* and energy blocks are cleared from the physical body.

You are also able to determine an overall assessment of your physical and emotional health. **This is not a medical assessment nor is it designed to replace any medical consultation, advice, diagnosis, or care provided to you.** This state of your energy health and well-being with your guides should be considered complementary or preventative. Here you can simply ask your guides for a numerical reading (using the logarithmic scale) of the health of any particular organ or other system of your body (e.g., nervous or lymphatic system) and record that number. The record of these measurements is kept by you for your purposes only. Know that you are doing this, not out of fear, but with the trust of many improvements to come.

Many other practical applications and benefits with communicating with your guides will come in time. You will want to reference Part Three— Applying Higher Guidance to Everyday Life. However, the advice from our guides is to crawl before we walk. Learn the feel of the neutral mind to do this correctly. This is a great power you are learning to harness and there are many dividends in learning it well and applying it judiciously in your life.

Remember that the lower your vibrational level or signature, the denser the energetic field is around you. A denser field means more veils between you and your guides, making the clarity of communication more challenging. As your vibrational signature and level of consciousness elevate, there will be less density to navigate. So, focus primarily on the steps that follow to raise your level of vibration. The Separation stage which follows is dedicated to doing just that.

Summary

The change you experience in the Dissolution stage is perhaps one of the most significant ones you will encounter on this journey. That you have proven abilities beyond those associated with your five senses are a revelation and opens you to many more possibilities. The ability to connect with higher guidance is your lifelong compass that is always with you. The shift in how you view yourself and the untapped power that you carry within, is a potent awakening of self.

<u>Important Information</u>

What follows in the Separation stage is a self-guided process to uncover, release and clear all lower frequencies that limit you, followed by a process to bring in and harmonize higher held frequencies. You are effectively creating a new vibrational signature. The steps are presented in a particular sequence and each must be followed in the order given. Furthermore, each step must be fully completed before moving on. Higher guidance will not permit you to move forward in the event you have inadvertently missed a step or failed to fully complete it. Nor will higher guidance allow you to proceed faster than what is in your highest good and readiness.

As such, you may experience a pause either within a step or between steps where you are to let the vibrational changes settle within you. These pauses are generally not lengthy (a day or two, or perhaps a week). However, at any point in the following Separation stage, should you find yourself stuck, unable to move forward, simply stop and reset. Ask your higher guidance if there is something you have missed or done incorrectly and, if so, go back and reread and redo that step.

The alchemy imbedded in the methodology is unique to your requirements and no two people will have the same experience. Take the time you need and journey well.

Transformative Level 1
SEPARATION

"Raising consciousness is the process of
releasing and correcting disharmonic
energies that distort our original energetic blueprint."

	Calcination	Dissolution	Separation	Conjunction	Fermentation	Distillation	Coagulation
Alchemic State	Reducing (to ashes)	Suspension (in water)	Isolating (purifying)	Amalgamation (coming back together)	Interaction (of purified elements)	Condensing (reduction)	Transformation (progressive)
Journey Stage	Questioning	Resolve	Purifying	Surrendering	Practicing	Mastering	Becoming
What Happens	Acknowledgement of Breakdown or Yearning	Suspending Disbelief	Deprogramming + Reprogramming of Self	Reordering of Self	Reordering of Life	Moving from Practice to Mastery	Be-ing
The Work	Pushing the Pause Button	Connecting to Inner Guidance Connecting to Higher Guidance	Releasing Misspent Energies Balancing Positive Energies	Forgiveness and Acceptance of New Self	Attuning Life Structures to New Self	Manifesting from Higher Self	Body Mind Soul Oneness
Foundational Competencies	Introspection	Empowerment	Healing	Reframing	Meditation	Self Transcendence	Embodiment
Aspects of Consciousness	Seeking	Awakening	Awareness	Knowing	Self-Realization	Insightful	Enlightened
Revelation	"there is a crack in everything – that's how the light gets in"	"you are a soul with a body not a body with a soul"	"healing is the process of releasing and correcting disharmonic energy"	"when I let go of what I am, I become what I might be"	"mindful living is the choice to harmonize life and self"	"from seeing is believing to believing is seeing"	"be the change you want to see in the world"

Introduction
Deprogramming and reprogramming of self

"The Alchemy of Becoming" is the transformation to higher consciousness. As previously mentioned, you have a unique vibrational signature that reflects your level of consciousness. The vibrational signature is a composite of dense and higher frequencies—healthy and unhealthy frequencies that animate your physical body and govern your behavioural patterns subconsciously and consciously.

Raising your vibrational signature requires you to do work. The work here is a series of steps all designed to discover who you are. This is a journey of self-reflection and self-discovery like none other. The work goes deep, very deep and you are guided every step of the way. This is a process of delayering, of uncovering your authentic self; that sovereign self, free from any pretence or persona. *Know thyself* is foundational to evolving, to becoming.

This stage requires that you bring forward everything you have learned and processed in the preceding Dissolution stage. You must accept that absolutely everything, no matter how solid it appears, is nothing more than vibrating energy. You must accept that everything manifests as energy and therefore can be changed with energy. You must, above all, accept the benevolence of higher guidance and be willing to develop a relationship of trust with that guidance. With this openness you are ready for the real transformative process in this Separation stage.

The most efficient way to raise your level of consciousness is to rid yourself of lower held frequencies as they are simply not aligned to your authentic self. These lower frequencies are like baggage you picked up along life's way; some inherited, some you simply absorbed as a child and some were of your own making through the choices you made. Traumas, fears, lies, greed, envy, shame, anger, intolerance, heartbreak, and all forms of suffering are part of life's lessons and our opportunity to grow and know ourselves through these experiences. But instead of growing, we often fail to see them for what they are and to process them accordingly. When that happens, they literally become a distortion within us, changing our nature, our personality and ultimately whom we become. They can erode our sense of worth, our self-esteem and in that way, we become victims to these unseen energetic forces.

Our thoughts and emotions are forms of energy. Love is a high frequency emotion while shame and guilt are low frequency emotions. When we are faced with an unpleasant or traumatic experience, the associated energy can become physically trapped within us. These trapped experiences manifest as distortions in the fabric and functioning of our organs and systems.

In **step one** in the Separation stage, we identify, separate, and release lower frequencies from the body. It is a purification process. In alchemic terms, the corrupted elements are separated and purified in turn to remove all undesirable and base elements. In a similar fashion, we are guided to isolate the lower frequency emotions from the higher held ones to release them. We come to understand the nature of the negative emotions we have held onto and when and how they occurred. There is no judgment with this process, only knowledge. As we release these lower frequencies from our bodies, a wonderful healing of body, mind and soul takes place. We feel the release in a form of lightness.

Step two of the Separation stage involves clearing blockages from our energy systems. The body has at least nine energy systems that circulate through and around the body providing a life force current to the functioning of our bodies. This current is a field of information analyzing, adjusting, optimizing, protecting, coordinating, and sequencing interdependencies in the highly complex organism that is our body. Energy systems running through the body pick up information from both trapped lower frequencies and higher frequencies held throughout various organs to relay a composite energetic picture of ourselves. This composite can signal a well adjusted, healthy, happy person with positive behaviours and personality traits; alternately, the composite can signal an individual struggling to offset too many negative emotions and experiences, precluding any hope of health and well-being.

Step three in the Separation stage is about isolating and releasing limiting programming—meaning programming that limits our potential for the higher expression of ourselves. Trapped emotions and blockages are like lines of code that together form our subconscious programming of limiting or negative behaviours. This is how it works; thoughts and emotions become our beliefs (as in what we come to believe in and the opinions we hold). Beliefs are powerful and they run much of our programming at the subconscious level. These beliefs influence our personality and behavioural tendencies. We identify ourselves with our belief system. We gravitate to certain behaviours and certain people that align to our beliefs. Those behaviours in turn produce or favour certain experiences. The experience reinforces the behaviour, and the behaviour reinforces the belief. This loop from belief to behaviour to experience (and reverse engineered from experience to behaviour and belief) is repeated and in so doing, becomes a habit. We are our beliefs and habits, as programming. Once we deprogram our negative beliefs, we have the opportunity to reprogram with those that are of a higher vibrational frequency.

This step helps us to identify areas of limiting programming expressed through lower frequency personality traits, whose origins are lower held views of ourselves and replace those traits with higher frequency programming.

The **fourth and final step** of the Separation stage is to refine your higher held frequencies. This is a process of isolating and balancing higher-level emotions. We need to hold a variety of positive emotions and traits that reinforce the expression of our authentic selves with conviction and a strong sense of sovereignty. Here sovereignty is meant to convey a powerful sense of self-worth and validation that comes from within. We no longer are defined by others. We no longer are defined by cultural norms, history, or fear of not fitting in, nor of not living up to expectations set by others. We are comfortable in our own skin, have a strong sense of our *presence* in this world and live our truth.

All the above steps build on one another to raise consciousness and your vibrational signature. As you rid your body of these lower frequencies to discover a more purified, authentic version of yourself, you transform body, mind, and soul through a healing process. Physical, emotional, and soul level healing is the promise and by-product of higher consciousness. You simply cannot heal anything at the same level of consciousness that caused the *dis-ease* to occur.

The Work

Trapped Emotions are held as lower frequencies—emotional experiences of a negative nature that you were unable to fully process and release. We all have them as part of life's experiences. We experience life through the contrasts of sadness and joy, fear, and hope, hate and love, etc. The negative experiences have a way of *sticking* to us. We are particularly sensitive to criticism or unpleasant and even nightmarish events that leave us shaken and a bit broken. They shape us whether we know it or not. They shape our behaviours, our perceptions, our relationships and all the choices we make. They can also register in our bodies, physically. They become trapped as they physically attach themselves to organs within the body.

The Luminaries
The identification and releasing of lower frequency emotions and energy blocks is inspired by the work of Dr. Bradly Nelson's "The Emotion Code." While Dr. Nelson's focus is primarily on healing rather than raising consciousness, the concept and idea of codification of emotions to facilitate identification, have been adopted. See Part Seven—The Luminaries, for more information.

Somehow it has long been known in Eastern traditions that we store anger in our liver, fear in our kidneys, grief in our lungs, upsets in our stomach, anxiety in our gut and that our heart can indeed break. Trapped emotions alter the perfect functioning of our organs. Even as they renew themselves many times over our lifetime, they replicate with the same distortion caused by the attachment of a negative trapped emotion. When enough of the negative experiences take up residence in an organ, it's very functioning can become compromised. The organ is in a state of *dis-ease* and in time, that state will manifest as inflammation or a chronic illness.

Through this Separation stage, your unique set of trapped emotions will be identified in a particular sequence and you will be able to energetically rid your body of their presence. You release them. And in so doing, your level of consciousness is raised. As you raise your consciousness, you are able to heal the *dis-ease* which occurred at a lower level of your consciousness. Healing is indeed a by-product of raising one's level of consciousness. This is a powerful experience. You will be amazed at the uncanny ability of your higher guidance to identify the exact time and event your body trapped the emotion.

Now let's discuss **Energy System Blockages** which are covered in Step 2. The body has a least nine energy systems. For centuries, and throughout numerous cultures, there has been an understanding and belief in energy systems that support and animate the physical body known as *Qi* or *chi* in China *prana* in the yogic tradition, *ruach* in Hebrew, *ki* in Japan, *baraka* by the Sufis, and *oreda* by the Iroquois. The body's energies are not just a force that causes your body to function but an intelligence that orchestrates all biological functions. The body's energy systems are fields of energy running through every part of your body and around your body, containing information for the functioning of literally every one of the trillions of cells and organisms of which you are made. They are your body's life force, the current of life and the body's innate intelligence and communication vehicles. When all the body's energy systems are brought into harmony, your body flourishes.

The Luminaries
Donna Eden was born with the ability to see energies around and within the body. Her book "Energy Medicine" is a wonderful source of knowledge about the body's nine energy systems, how they function and how to keep them flowing for peak performance. See Part Seven—The Luminaries, for more information.

Many things can influence the fluctuation of your energy systems from solar radiation flares, to moon phases, to barometric pressure changes, to the foods you ingest to exposure to viruses and bacteria. Your thoughts and experiences can also affect the flow of your energy systems and can even cause blockages that restrict the free flow of energy. A brief description of the nine energy systems is described in Part Six—Stepping Stones to Greater Understanding, and you may be familiar with the chakras, the auric field, and the meridian pathways that acupuncture is based on.

In the Separation stage, you will be able to identify in which of your nine energy systems you have blockages or imbalances and here too, you will be able to clear the blockages with the help of higher guidance. As with trapped emotions, there will be a specific order in which these blockages or imbalances are to be cleared. While trapped emotions impact the functioning of the organs, the energy system blockages appear to form or alter lifelong behaviours. For example, childhood traumas, limiting beliefs, cultural conditioning and even physical and emotional injuries can all cause blockages to the flow of the chakra currents. The manifestation of blocked energy is very often displayed in either excessive or deficient behaviours. For example, a bully who compensates for insecurity exhibits an excessive third chakra. On the other hand, a person who feels powerless and avoids conflict, exhibits a deficient third chakra.

Some of these trapped emotions and energy system blockages and imbalances manifest at birth. You inherit them. You come into this life with imprints both positive and negative, that govern physical characteristics, personality, and behavioural tendencies, intelligence, and creativity. While it is preferable, an in-depth understanding of the circumstances of a negative event is not a requirement to clear the blockages. An example of this is repressed memories. While you may be aware of a traumatic event, your subconscious mind may block details to protect you from deeper damage, but the damage that has been done can be healed through the release of that imprint.

As you go through the instructions of this section, you will note that there is even an order to whether you are to first release trapped emotions or clear blockages in your energy systems. These are, to some extent, intertwined and some individuals must start with one or the other. Some will be guided to flip between releasing a trapped emotion and clearing an energy blockage.

You will also note that you can clear blockages from all nine of your energy systems at once. However, some of you may choose to know what blockages or imbalances exist within a particular system and choose to clear that energy system as a discrete entity. Just as the heart holds prominence in the coherence of all other organs, the chakras appear to hold prominence in the coherence of other energy systems. A description of the nine energy systems is included in Part VI—Stepping Stones to Greater Understanding.

Whatever the order you are guided to, rest assured that you have the ability to remove all lower frequencies available to you at this first level of the methodology. Subsequent levels will go deeper within the body to release and clear deeper held negative frequencies. It is a layering effect and the higher your consciousness, the deeper you travel and heal within (see Part Five—Levels of Transformation—Overview).

Step 1: Identifying and releasing trapped emotions

Preparation

While you may initially be unsure of yourself when using *the sway* (or proxy) to identify and release your first trapped lower frequency emotions, do not worry! Your higher guidance will always be with you and automatically provide course correction if and when needed. Your adeptness and confidence will grow the more you use it.

If you are identifying and releasing a trapped emotion, your tools include:

- The Sway or proxy *(described in the Dissolution stage)*
- The Lower Frequency Emotions Chart *(see below)*
- The Lower Frequency Emotions Flow Diagram *(see below)*
- A small but powerful magnet *(purchased at any hardware store)*
- A log sheet to record details of each release *(see Appendix 2)*

Identifying Lower Frequency Trapped Emotions

Follow the Learning to Sway instructions in the Dissolution stage to ready yourself. A series of YES/NO questions are posed in a precise order to first identify a trapped emotion. You can also refer to the flow chart diagrams if you find that easier. Familiarize yourself with the Lower Frequency Emotions Chart. Note that the chart has 3 columns, 3 rows, and 6 words in each box. Resist looking at the chart as you go through the following steps:

1. Do I have any trapped emotions in my body?
   If you get NO, ask if you have energy blocks.
   If you get YES, proceed to Step 2 (Identifying and Clearing Energy Blocks) and then come back to trapped emotions afterwards.
   If you get NO to both releasing trapped emotions and clearing energy systems, check again to confirm as this would be a rare occurrence.
2. Am I ready to identify and release trapped emotions in my body?
   If YES, proceed to the 3 below.
   If NO, ask if you need to wait a few days to try again.

3. Identify the trapped emotion by asking:
   a) Is it in column A?
   b) Is in in column B?
   c) Is it in column C?
   d) Is it in row 1?
   e) Is it in row 2?
   f) Is it in row 3?
      Once you have identified the correct column and row, you can now proceed to identifying the exact emotion that lies within that box.
   g) Is it the first word? The second word? etc.
   h) Once you identify the word as being the first, second, third, etc., refer to the chart to identify the corresponding emotion.
   i) Confirm that you have the correct word? by asking: Is it (emotion named)? If YES, go to 4 below.
      If NO, repeat steps 2 and 3.
4. Is this trapped emotion of X inherited or acquired?

If inherited:
   a) Do I need to know more?
      If NO, proceed to releasing.
      If YES,

> **NOTES FOR IDENTIFYING TRAPPED EMOTIONS/ENERGY BLOCKS**
>
> Remember to approach all your questions with a neutral mind—with no predisposition to the answer.
>
> It is highly recommended that you do not look at the chart when you are going through the questions as it may trigger an unconscious bias towards a particular word.
>
> If you are having trouble understanding the meaning of your word, definitions can be found in **Appendix 4.**
>
> Inherited emotions are not uncommon and can be thought of in the same way as inherited family traits that are encoded in our DNA. Inherited emotions can go back generations and you may have no knowledge of that ancestor or what the particular circumstances may have been. Even though you may be told that you do not need to know more to release the emotion, feel free to probe as deeply as your curiosity takes you.
>
> Understanding fully the circumstances surrounding an acquired emotion, while preferable, is not essential to fully process and release it from your body. Remember that while recalling the event may cause uncomfortable memories to surface, it would not have been identified if you were not fully ready and capable of dealing with them.
>
> The number of negative emotions and energy blocks you uncover vary tremendously from one person to another. Accept that the ones uncovered are what's accurate for you and you alone.

Did this inherited emotion come from my mothers' side of the family?

Did this inherited emotion come from my fathers' side of the family?

Ask as many follow-up questions as needed (or wanted) to understand the incident and circumstances.

b) Am I ready to release the inherited trapped emotion of X?

If NO, go back and ask additional questions to understand the circumstances more fully or ask if you need to wait and process what you have learned.

If YES, proceed to releasing.

If acquired:

a) At what age did I attract this trapped emotion?

Was it between birth and 10 years?

Was it between the ages of 10–20?

Was it between the ages of 20–40? Etc.

Continue with isolating the exact age that the emotion became trapped. This may give you a clue as to what the situation was. If you intuitively know and can recall the exact circumstances, ask for confirmation that this is the source. If YES, proceed to releasing.

If you still need to dig deeper, use your intuition to identify the exact circumstance with these example questions.

- Did this situation relate to my relationship with my family member X, friend X? etc.
- Was this related to the time I spent at X?

Continue with these questions until you feel confident that you have isolated the incident. Understanding fully the source of the trapped emotion is preferable but not mandatory for processing and releasing it from your body.

b) Am I ready to release this trapped emotion of X from my body?
    If NO, go back and ask more questions to understand the incident more fully. A NO answer could also mean that you need more time to process what you have learned. You can ask if this is the case and then determine how long you will have to wait to release. If YES, proceed to releasing.

LOWER FREQUENCY EMOTIONS CHART

	COLUMN A	COLUMN B	COLUMN C
ROW 1	☐ Anger ☐ Ashamed ☐ Betrayal ☐ Regret ☐ Love Unreceived ☐ Vulnerability	☐ Confusion ☐ Defensive ☐ Discouragement ☐ Overwhelm ☐ Shame ☐ Unworthy	☐ Dread ☐ Effort Unreceived ☐ Fear ☐ Forlorn ☐ Self-abuse ☐ Horror
ROW 2	☐ Sorrow ☐ Frustration ☐ Grief ☐ Rejection ☐ Helplessness ☐ Worry	☐ Hopelessness ☐ Humiliated ☐ Indecisiveness ☐ Insecurity ☐ Jealousy ☐ Anxiety	☐ Lack of Control ☐ Lust ☐ Neglected ☐ Detachment ☐ Abandonment ☐ Depression
ROW 3	☐ Panic ☐ Peeved ☐ Resentment ☐ Bitterness ☐ Failure ☐ Hatred	☐ Sadness ☐ Shock ☐ Guilty ☐ Terror ☐ Disgust ☐ Lost	☐ Unnurtured ☐ Heartache ☐ Worthlessness ☐ Nervousness ☐ Despair ☐ Longing

Lower Frequency Emotions Flow Diagram

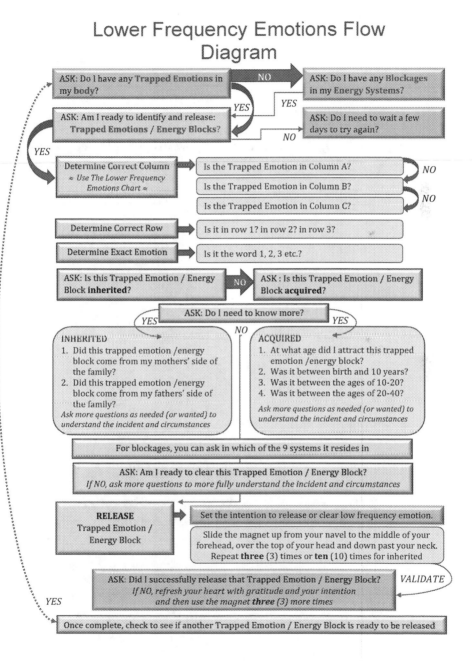

Releasing trapped emotions

A small but powerful magnet, available at any hardware store, is the only tool you need to release trapped emotions and energy blocks.

How does the magnet work?

The magnet is pure energy that disrupts the energy of your trapped emotion or energy block and literally magnifies your intention to release it from your body or clear it from your energy systems. The path of the magnet follows your Governing Meridian. Once released or cleared it is removed permanently.

Once you have received the OK to release, follow these steps:

1. Place the magnet at your navel.
2. Set your intention to release the trapped emotion of X.
3. While breathing deeply, slide the magnet up from your navel to the middle of your forehead, over the top of your head and down past your neck, as far as you can comfortably reach (see diagram).

USING THE MAGNET

4. If this is an acquired emotion repeat **three** times.
5. If this is an inherited emotion, repeat **ten** times.
6. Once you have completed this, set the magnet aside and ask if the trapped emotion has been released.
7. If NO, reset your intention and then use the magnet to release the trapped emotion.
8. If YES, start the identification process again to reveal your next trapped emotion. Note that you may have to wait several days before you can identify and release the next emotion. Some emotions may take longer to "process" than others.

9. Repeat the process until you confirm that you have no more trapped emotions in your body.

A confirmation that you have no more trapped emotions can signify either that:

a) The next emotion to be identified is an energy block (see Step 2) before returning to releasing another trapped emotion (Step 1) or,

b) You have released all trapped emotions and you are ready for Step 2.

Remember that trapped emotions and energy blockages are often intertwined and must be dealt with in a sequence unique to you. If you seem to get stuck at any point in this process (i.e., you are not allowed to go on, but cannot understand why) please see the *important reminder* at the end of Step 2.

Step 2: Identifying and clearing energy blocks

Preparation

Energy blockages are identified as lower frequency emotions which instead of being trapped in a physical location (organ) are instead held as a lower frequency field of information, flowing as current through your energy systems. These lower held frequencies can restrict, distort or block the energy frequencies of your body, causing dysfunctional or compromised states within the body, mind, or soul. As such, the Lower Frequency Emotions Chart is used for both. It can be confusing if you are led to start with your energy systems, but rest assured that the order in which they are revealed is the right one for you.

As a first step, please review the introductory section on Energy System Blockages. When you are identifying and clearing an energy block, your tools include:

*   The Sway or proxy (*described in the Dissolution stage*)

- The Lower Frequency Emotions Chart and Flow Diagram *(see above)*
- A small but powerful magnet *(purchased at any hardware store)*
- A log sheet to record details of each release *(see Appendix 3)*

Identifying Lower Frequency Energy Systems Blockages

Again, follow the "Learning to Sway" instructions in the Dissolution stage to ready yourself. Just as with identifying trapped emotions, a series of YES/NO questions are posed in a precise order to first identify an energy block and then to isolate the circumstances. You can also refer to the flow chart diagram if you find that easier. Familiarize yourself with the Lower Frequency Emotion Chart, remembering that the chart has 3 columns with 3 rows and 6 words in each box. Resist looking at the chart as you go through the following steps. Remember that you can clear energy blocks from your nine systems at once, though it might be interesting for you to ask what precise system the block was in, after each clearing (these are described in Part Six—Stepping Stones to Greater Understanding).

1. Do I have any blockages in my energy systems?
   If NO, check again as this would be a rare occurrence.
   If YES, proceed to the 2 below.
2. Am I ready to identify and clear blockages in my energy systems?
   If YES, proceed to 3 below.
   If NO, ask if you need to wait a few days to try again.
3. Identify the energy block by asking:
   a) Is it in column A?
   b) Is in in column B?
   c) Is it in column C?
   d) Is it in row 1?
   e) Is it in row 2?
   f) Is it in row 3?
      Once you have identified the correct column and row, you can now proceed to identifying the exact emotion that lies within that box.
   g) Is it the first word? The second word? etc.
   h) Once you identify the word as being the first, second, third, etc. refer to the chart to identify the corresponding emotion.

    i)   Confirm that you have the correct word? by asking: Is it (emotion x)? If YES, go to the 4 below. If NO, repeat steps 2 and 3.

4.   Is this energy block of X inherited or acquired?

If inherited:

a)   Do I need to know more?
If NO, proceed to clearing.
If YES,
Did this inherited energy block come from my mothers' side of the family?
Did this inherited energy block come from my fathers' side of the family?
Ask as many follow-up questions as needed (or wanted) to understand the incident and circumstances.

b)   Am I ready to clear the inherited energy block of X?
If NO, go back and ask additional questions to understand the circumstances more fully or ask if you need to wait and process what you have learned.
If YES, proceed to clearing.

If acquired:

a)   At what age did I attract this energy block?
Was it between birth and 10 years?
Was it between the ages of 10–20?
Was it between the ages of 20–40? Etc.

Continue with isolating the exact age that the blockage occurred. This may give you a clue as to what the situation was. If you intuitively know and can recall the exact circumstances, ask for confirmation that this is the source. If YES, proceed to clearing.

If you still need to dig deeper, use your intuition to identify the exact circumstance with these example questions.

- Did this situation relate to my relationship with my family member X, friend X? etc.

- Was this related to the time I spent at X?

Continue with these questions until you feel confident that you have isolated the incident. Understanding fully the source of the energy block is preferable but not mandatory for processing and clearing it from your energy systems.

b) Am I ready to clear this energy block of X from my energy system? If NO, go back and ask more questions to understand the incident more fully. A NO answer could also mean that you need more time to process what you have learned. You can ask if this is the case and then determine how long you will have to wait to clear the energy blockage. If YES, proceed to clearing.

The Luminaries
Want to know more about the chakras. Anodea Judith's "Eastern Body, Western Mind" is a comprehensive synthesis of the Chakra system. See Part Seven—The Luminaries, for more information.

Clearing energy blocks

Your magnet is the only tool you need to clear energy blocks. Once you have received the OK to clear, follow these steps:

1. Place the magnet at your navel.
2. Set your intention to clear the energy block of X.
3. While breathing deeply, slide the magnet up from your navel to the middle of your forehead, over the top of your head and down past your neck, as far as you can comfortably reach *(see diagram)*.
4. If this is an acquired block repeat **three** times.

USING THE
MAGNET

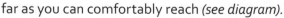

5. If this is an inherited block, repeat **ten** times.
6. Once you have completed this, set the magnet aside and ask if the energy block has been cleared.
7. If NO, reset your intention and then use the magnet to clear the energy blockage.
8. If YES, start the identification process again to reveal your next energy block.
9. Repeat the process until you confirm that you have no more blockages in your energy systems.

A confirmation that you have no more energy blockages can signify either that:

a) The next emotion to be identified is a trapped emotion to be released from the body (Step 1) or,
b) You have cleared all energy blocks and released all trapped emotions, and you are ready for Step 3.

Remember that energy blockages and trapped emotions are often intertwined and must be dealt with in a sequence unique to you.

Important Reminder

During this stage in the journey, you may find yourself stuck and unable or unsure how to proceed. Should you find yourself stuck the important things to keep in mind are as follows:

a) The above is a complex exercise given the possible intertwining of trapped emotions with energy blockages. These steps must be unravelled in a sequence unique to you. This may involve you switching back and forth between releasing trapped emotions and clearing energy blockages.
b) This is an exercise of self-discovery meaning that the incident and circumstances that led to the need to release or clear low frequency emotions should be uncovered as fully as possible. (While it is preferable to fully unpack the nature of the incident, there are limitations attached to uncovering

inherited and repressed events. In those situations, you will not be prevented from proceeding.)

c)   While releasing or clearing the emotion with the magnet, it is the intention to release or clear that particular emotion that is paramount. Remember to set the intention with each release or clearing command.

d)   It is also essential that your command is precise. You release trapped emotions and clear energy blocks. Words matter.

Ironically, uncovering the wrong emotion from the charts is less important than the above four considerations. Higher Guidance cannot recalibrate your intent or words, but they can recalibrate the emotion identified and enact an energetic GPS correction.

If you do find yourself stopped, determine (using the sway) if your issue lies in one of these four categories. If it is a), you may need to go back and repeat the whole process to ensure you have unlocked your sequence in the correct order. If it is b) go through your list of emotions and ask which one needs to be more fully explored. If it is c) ask which emotion you have not fully cleared or released. If it is d) isolate the emotion(s) where you have used the incorrect command.

Step 3: Breaking behavioural patterns

Our subconscious programming

The next step in releasing negative energies lies with your subconscious programming. Our personalities, behaviours and perspectives are formed largely by early life experiences. As negative experiences imbed much more than the positive, they play a critical role in the development of your world view, how you react to situations, others around you, and most importantly, how you truly feel about yourself. Too often, early life traumas and hurtful experiences create an overriding perspective of fear, unworthiness, and insecurity, that play out in your life.

Trapped emotions and energy system blockages set you up to form behavioural patterns at the subconscious level. This becomes your automatic programming. Automatic programming can also be a type of conditioning set up by things like cultural norms (*this is the way things are done here*), historical precedent (*it has always been done this way*) or societal rules of engagement (*this is what success looks like*). More subtle forms are imbedded in advertising and more troubling forms, in issues like gender, religious or racial biases. The need for control through fear underlies much of how we operate in the collective.

The Luminaries

For those who love the science in spirituality and the spirituality in science, Dr. Joe Dispenza is a must read or one to follow in his Gaia series Rewired. See Part Seven—The Luminaries, for more information.

You perceive and react to situations without conscious awareness. It is very much akin to driving to a destination and realizing that you do not remember how you got there. Somehow your body and the automatic program of driving a car took over. While thinking of other things, you managed to navigate the roads, traffic, and stop lights without conscious thought. Something out of the ordinary would have had to happen to jolt you back to conscious awareness of driving your car. This phenomenon would not happen to a new driver. It could only happen when you have enough experience to form a programming file within your memory bank. Your automatic programming is a bit like that. You are conditioned through repeated and confirming experiences to gravitate to and respond to situations in a familiar and habitual way. Even if the situation is unpleasant and at some level, you know it should or could be different, there is a gravitational pull to the familiar and expected. You actually confirm it every time. *That is exactly what I knew would happen* or *why would I have expected anything different?*, become confirming mantras.

At some level, automatic or subconscious programming allows for predictable outcomes in many daily functions of our lives. Like breathing, which most of us happily take for granted, automatic functions allow the freedom to focus our attention on other matters. It is estimated that up to 95% of what we do, think and feel is held at the subconscious level. So, our behavioural patterns, as imbedded programming, is potentially useful on one hand but limiting on the other. This step of the

Separation stage is designed to address areas of limiting programming by first creating awareness of the behavioural pattern and identifying the thought patterns that set up the habits. Behaviours and habits develop in response to deeper held beliefs. To deprogram subconscious habits and behaviours, we need to uncover the beliefs that underpin them. The process reveals just how much we become our habits and just how much our habits attract the same patterns of experience. Limiting programming is a subconscious feedback loop based on the limiting beliefs we hold, destined to repeat endlessly.

Undoing this automatic programming—our operating system, to borrow a computing term, is not easy. It is not easy as it operates with no awareness or conscious thought and sits squarely within your comfort zone. Dr. Joe Dispenza has written an entire book on this subject, aptly named "Breaking the Habit of Being Yourself".

Uncovering limiting beliefs and breaking habits, we often don't even know we have, requires a *whole brain state awareness*. To achieve this state, we consciously engage both the right and left hemispheres of the brain to bring the subconscious to the surface of our awareness. It is only in the knowing and acceptance of this limiting belief and its manifestation in behaviours and habits that we can release and replace it with positive programming.

The Luminaries
The whole brain state is described in Olympia LePoint's book "Answers Unleashed—the Science of Unleashing your Brain's Power." See Part Seven—The Luminaries, for more information.

Beliefs are complex. They tend to be an amalgam of what we have been told by authority figures, dictates of the culture in which we live, the interpretation of history and perhaps most vividly the direct experience of our lives. Beliefs are reinforced through the behaviours and habits that are the expression of the beliefs. At the subconscious level, beliefs are sensory, meaning that they are not so much what we *think* they are but how we have internally processed them or how we have *felt* them. In this way, beliefs are less evidentiary or necessarily rational (i.e., of the thinking mind) but sensed and interpreted by the subconscious mind.

These beliefs, deeply imbedded, manifest not only in behaviours and habits but as personality traits that we identify with. The *surface* display of limiting beliefs show up as limiting personality traits. Personality traits are themselves a complex amalgam of beliefs, emotions, behaviours, and habits.

The short cut to bringing awareness to the limiting beliefs is through the limiting personality traits. In other words, deprogramming is reverse engineered from identifying a personality trait, to understanding the personality trait as exhibiting a pattern of behaviour, leading to, and revealing the belief that underpins the whole dynamic. It is for this reason that the following deprogramming process starts with the identification of a limiting personality trait as depicted in a chart. We want to avoid *thinking* what limiting personality trait we have and trusting higher guidance to identify the trait or traits that lead to the awareness of the limiting belief that underpins it.

The process is to *displace* the limiting belief with a positive or desirable belief described in the reprogramming process that follows.

The deprogramming process

The process for this step again uses the sway, the Limiting Personality Traits Chart *(see below)* and a series of questions to identify the personality traits that have shaped your programming. While you may have more than one personality trait, it is important to do the work called for in **deprogramming and reprogramming**, one trait at a time. Familiarize yourself with the Limiting Personality Traits Chart. It has 3 columns, 4 rows and 5 words in each box. Resist looking at the chart as you go ask the following question:

- What is the first limiting personality trait that has shaped my subconscious programming? (isolate by identifying the column, row, and word)

	LIMITING PERSONALITY TRAITS CHART		
	COLUMN A	**COLUMN B**	**COLUMN C**
ROW 1	☐ Shattered ☐ Restless ☐ Angry ☐ Fearful ☐ Nervous	☐ Bitter ☐ Depressed ☐ Disrespectful ☐ Apprehensive ☐ Stressed	☐ Edgy ☐ Envious ☐ Arrogant ☐ Pessimistic ☐ Uneasy
ROW 2	☐ Heartbroken ☐ Inflexible ☐ Intolerant ☐ Judgemental ☐ Shameful	☐ Lost ☐ Low Self-Esteem ☐ Miserable ☐ Moody ☐ Apathetic	☐ Obsessive ☐ Passive ☐ Remorseful ☐ Fussy ☐ Domineering
ROW 3	☐ Resentful ☐ Secretive ☐ Abusive ☐ Distraught ☐ Melancholy	☐ Shutdown ☐ Tactless ☐ Aloof ☐ Condescending ☐ Defensive	☐ Uncaring ☐ Unloved ☐ Unsettled ☐ Weepy ☐ Wishy-Washy
ROW 4	☐ Helpless ☐ Needy ☐ Impulsive ☐ Thoughtless ☐ Hypocritical	☐ Perfectionist ☐ Indecisive ☐ Controlling ☐ Self-destructive ☐ Ungrateful	☐ Insecure ☐ Argumentative ☐ Cynical ☐ Aimless ☐ Stubborn

Once you have identified your first limiting trait, a new technique is used to work through this process which involves writing first with your dominant hand and then with your non-dominant one.

Note that while you have been encouraged to take and retain notes throughout this entire alchemic process, you may not want to retain the record of what you uncover writing with both your dominant and non-dominant hands. We store our deepest secrets and regrets in our subconscious and the fear of someone else reading them may inadvertently prevent you from letting them fully surface. Once completed, it may even be helpful to burn and bury them—performing a symbolic final shedding of these lower-density vibrations.

1. Using your dominant hand, write about the first personality trait identified. Write about the different facets that make up this trait and how you identify with it—*what age did this trait become*

imbedded in you; how it shaped your life; how it made you feel about others; about yourself and your overall outlook on life? How did it shape the experiences and events in your life? How might it have affected your relationships, your career, and even how you react in uncomfortable situations or meeting someone for the first time? Reflect on how you consciously try to hide this personality trait and how much energy that you had to expend to do so. Just allow the words to flow from your pen, unedited. Remember that no one else will see this other than you. It is important to fully experience any emotions and let the resulting feelings rise to the surface. You will not be given anything you are not ready to handle at any point in your journey. It is important to visualize this trait and sense its hold on you. Understand that this trait is the manifestation of an underlying belief system you hold. **What is that underlying belief?**

2. Wait at least one day to continue to the next step.
3. Using your non-dominant hand (yes this may be very arduous at first!) repeat the same process.
4. At this point, review what you have written with both your right hand and left hand and reflect on insights gained. Remember that your insights reveal what you hold subconsciously as beliefs. The personality trait is a manifestation of the beliefs you hold—it is the underlying belief that you are trying to isolate.
5. Ask if you have successfully understood the limiting personality trait and the belief that underpins it.
6. If NO, probe deeper using the dominant, non-dominant hand writing exercise. Ask again to get confirmation that you have been successful.
7. Once you have completed the deprogramming process for that trait, you are ready to displace that trait with a positive one.

WHY WRITING WITH EACH HAND?

Writing with your right hand activates the left hemisphere of your brain and the left hand your right hemisphere. While physically looking very much alike, there is a significant difference in how the right and left hemispheres process information.

The left brain is more verbal, logical, and analytical and *thinks* linearly. The right brain is more visual, creative, intuitive and *thinks* more holistically. They communicate and work with each other through bundles of nerve fibres creating a virtual information highway. You may clearly identify with one or the other hemisphere or have more balance between the two. Everyone is unique in their right brain/left brain composition.

Invoking one hemisphere at a time allows for a different perspective on the belief, held as programming, to reveal itself. You may be quite surprised at the differences that emerge. You are increasing "cross talk" between the two brain hemispheres to achieve a "whole brain state." When right and left hemispheres are in simultaneous communication, you are able to maximize a full response to overcome challenges.

If you ever wondered why labyrinths are constructed in such a distinct pattern—it is to allow for just this thinking process to take place. If you are mulling over a problem, the path you take forces the brain to switch from one side to the other encouraging a more balanced and fully thought-out analysis.

Spacing each session by a day helps ensure that you are starting fresh and are not being influenced by what you have already written.

The reprogramming process

Once you have successfully unpacked your limiting personality trait, it is time to displace the underlying belief from your programming and its manifestation in you as a limiting personality trait, with new programming that raises your vibrational level and serves you in positive ways. Note that displacing the limiting belief and corresponding personality trait you have identified is not accomplished through thinking of the opposite word (such as uncaring to caring); rather you will now be using the Positive Personality Traits Chart to identify and bring in a higher frequency trait that will effectively counteract the negative one and imprint it into your subconscious programming. The positive trait you uncover will act as a *vibrational antidote.* For example, if the word *restless* is uncovered, one might automatically think that the antidote word would be something akin to *peaceful.* However, the trait you uncover could be *creative,* which might be somewhat perplexing at first. In this case *creative* represents an outlet for restless—and the state of restlessness is resolved by redirecting that energy to a creative pursuit such as writing, painting, or designing a garden or new home.

Using the Positive Personality Traits Chart below, you now want to uncover the trait needed to vibrationally counter the limiting one. Be mindful of this vibrational correspondence. The chart has 3 Columns, 4 rows and 5 words in each box. Remember to avoid looking at the chart when you are identifying the words.

1. What is the personality trait that will displace xxxxxxxxx?
2. Using the sway (or proxy) isolate the column, row, and word.
3. Using the sway, confirm if you have identified the correct word.
4. If NO go back and redo steps 2 and 3.
5. If YES create a simple affirmation statement using the positive trait identified — "I AM xxxxxxx."
6. Proceed to the PYSCH K process

Note: You may feel the need to analyze or further explore the significance of the positive personality trait you have been given in order to displace the limiting belief. Know that this is actually counterproductive as the displacement is fully accomplished at the vibrational level. While the work to remove a negative frequency from your programming requires the *knowing* of it as a belief, bringing in a higher frequency trait only requires that you *claim* it through your affirmation and the PSYCH K process which follows.

	POSITIVE PERSONALITY TRAITS CHART		
	COLUMN A	**COLUMN B**	**COLUMN C**
ROW 1	☐ Compassionate ☐ Tolerant ☐ Forgiving ☐ Optimistic ☐ Thoughtful	☐ Serene ☐ Delightful ☐ Joyful ☐ Loving ☐ Grateful	☐ Kind ☐ Open ☐ Generous ☐ Humble ☐ Whole (Integrity)
ROW 2	☐ Patient ☐ Passionate ☐ Curious ☐ Resilient ☐ Trustworthy	☐ Gracious ☐ Liberated ☐ Caring ☐ Modest ☐ Empathetic	☐ Creative ☐ Determined ☐ Committed ☐ Self-accepting ☐ Independent
ROW 3	☐ Authentic ☐ Flexible ☐ Self-aware ☐ Supportive ☐ Moral	☐ Understanding ☐ Nurturing ☐ Honest ☐ Disciplined ☐ Sensitive	☐ Spiritual ☐ Quiet ☐ Inspirational ☐ Accepting ☐ Attentive
ROW 4	☐ Harmonious ☐ Self-assured ☐ Merciful ☐ Mindful ☐ Persistent	☐ Temperate ☐ Unselfish ☐ Ethical ☐ Altruistic ☐ Articulate	☐ Divine ☐ Intuitive ☐ Open minded ☐ Insightful ☐ Powerful

The PSYCH K process

The technique used to displace and imprint a new trait into your subconscious is known as "PSYCH K" (which stands for Psychological Kinesiology). PSYCH K uses specific body postures and movements that cause neurons to fire in both hemispheres of the brain, creating a state of "super learning." In effect you are using this positive personality trait to imprint a new belief system about who you are. It is important to note that the technique described below is not an intellectual exercise. For successful results it is important to experience the conflicting emotions between the limiting belief and your new desired one. Willpower and determination are not required and become a misdirected struggle. The feeling here is more of graceful surrender. Let the higher vibration of the positive trait displace the lower vibration held in the limiting trait.

Before you start, use the sway confirm that you are ready to start the PSYCH K process. If NO wait a few days and try again.

1. The PSYCH K process requires that you cross your ankles and hands in front of your body, but first you need to determine if it should be right over left or left over right. Using the sway determine:
   a) Should I cross my ankles right over left?
   b) Should I cross my wrists right over left?
2. Once you have the correct placement instructions, sit in a chair with your feet on the floor. Cross your ankles in the way you were directed.
3. Now cross your wrists in front of your body as you were directed and interlace your fingers. Lay them in your lap (see Figure 5).
4. Set the intention to bring in your new belief.
5. Keep repeating your "I am" statement as you allow any doubts to rise up and be displaced through your powerful and overriding affirmation. Remember that this is a vibrational exercise that requires no will or determination. Just feel it.
6. Continue this process until the negative thoughts have disappeared. This normally happens in as little as 2–5 minutes.

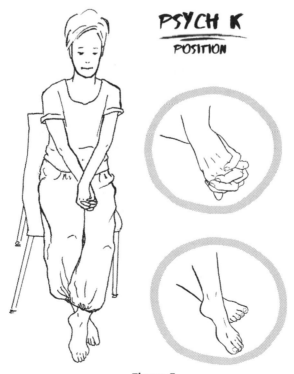

Figure 5

7. Using the sway and the 1–10 scale, now determine how closely your "I AM" statement aligns with your upgraded unconscious belief.
8. If you get a score higher than 9.0 proceed to step 10 below.
9. If your score is less than 9.0, repeat the above steps 1–8.
10. Ask if you have another negative trait that needs to be displaced from your subconscious programming.
11. If YES repeat the entire deprogramming and reprogramming process for that limiting personality trait and its corresponding positive one.
12. Continue this process, until all negative and positive personality traits have been identified and processed using PSYCH K.
13. Ask if you have completed the deprogramming and reprogramming steps.
14. If NO wait a few days and try again—sometime a period of time is required to fully absorb your upgraded programming.
15. If YES, proceed to "Balancing higher frequencies."

The Luminaries

PSYCH K is a tool developed by Robert M. Williams and has been used since 1988. This technique has been used successfully by thousands of people. You can see a full demonstration of this technique on YouTube (just search for Robert Williams). His companion book entitled, "PSYCH-K The Missing Piece/Peace of Your Life," also provides valuable information and instructions on this technique.

Step 4: Balancing higher frequencies

Balancing and harmonizing your higher frequencies

Following the release and clearing of lower held frequencies, your vibrational signature will be raised considerably. It is at this stage that the opportunity opens to refine the higher held frequencies within your body. While this may sound counterintuitive, you can have too much of a good thing. To put it more accurately, what you aim to achieve in this process, is balance and harmony within and without yourself, meaning you and your life. For example, the higher emotion of compassion can be out of balance if too much of yourself is given away to others with the unintended consequence of depleting your own life force. Without knowing it, you seek self-worth and validation through how others respond to your gift of compassion. In that case, worth and validation come from *doing* good rather than from a deeper held notion of *being* compassionate. The expression of compassion can be misguided as trying to *fix* someone or something or where there is a condition attached to the gifting of compassion.

Think of balancing positive attributes just as a conductor balances an orchestra. Not only does every instrument need to be in perfect tune, and every musician playing all the correct notes, the overall composition must find exactly the right balance from each section. For example, if the conductor sees a need to bring the string section into focus, he has two choices; ask them to play louder or ask the reed instruments and brass section to play softer. Each section has a vital role to play, but it must be in harmony with the others.

In this refinement process, you are guided through a set of prescribed questions to become aware of these imbalances and the need for course correction. The power of affirmations is again used to imprint new understandings and behaviours into your programming. The set of refinements culminates into 6 desired *end states* that are critical characteristics of authenticity and sovereignty: coherent (being in harmony); confident (being in your knowing); connected (being as one with all); clear (being of light and bringing light); consolidated (being unshakeable and unbreakable); and centred (being present and in your presence).

The Higher Frequency Emotions Chart *(see below)* is laid out in the same way as the Lower Frequency Emotions Chart with the exception that the six end state words are found at the top. The technique to balance these higher frequency emotions is through affirmation.

1. Using the sway, identify which end-state word you should start with (Coherence, Confident, Connected, Clear, Consolidated or Centred). If you do not get an end state word, see Important Reminder below.

2. Once you have your end state, then ask which emotion from the chart should accompany it. Identify it in the same way you isolated negative emotions, using the columns and row numbers to get to a box, and then ask which word it is within that box. Remember to resist referring to the chart as you go through this process.

3. Once you have your first emotion identified, ask if there is another until you get a NO answer. There can be as few as one emotion, but normally there are between 2 and 5.

4. Once you have your end state word and the emotions, write them all down in the order in which they were given to you.

5. For each emotion, ask if it should be directed inward (how you treat or think about yourself) or outwards (how you think about or treat others), or both.

6. Then ask if the emotion should be strengthened or suppressed.

7. Understanding these dimensions, create an affirmation statement that combines all these elements together *(see the examples following the Higher Frequency Emotions chart)*. Think of it as a command to the universe—be bold, forthright, and clear. It may take you several attempts and when you are satisfied with the statement, use the sway to measure, on a scale of 1–10, how strong the statement is. If it is above a 9, you are good to go. If not, play with the wording until it does.

8. Read the statement and say it out loud or to yourself periodically over the next day(s).

9. Check back periodically to ask if you can move on to the next end-state word. If NO, continue saying the affirmation until you get a positive response. If you are a meditator, your meditation is a perfect vehicle for imprinting this refinement. If YES, go to 10.

10. Proceed to identify the next end state word and continue this process. When you get NO to the question—do I have any more end state words to balance, you can proceed to the next stage.

Important Note. You may get all 6 end state words or just a subset of them. If you do not get any end state words, know that you may simply need more time to process the many changes to your vibrational signature. Ask your guides if this is the case and how long you need to pause. The fine-tuning process is always required following major adjustments to your vibrational signature. If it is not a question of more time required to process, it is likely that you still have either trapped emotions or energy blockages that have not been dealt with. Ask if you have any remaining lower frequency emotions to be released or cleared.

Higher positive emotions are a proven and effective way of supercharging affirmations. This is equally effective when you are reframing any situation from negative to positive. Feeling the love for a child or summoning the emotion of bliss while walking a deserted beach will deepen the effectiveness of and shorten the time it takes to imprint a new belief.

How do affirmations work?

We know that words are vibrational energies and the precise use of words and their sequencing represent instructions for encoding at the vibrational level. These affirmations imbed in your vibrational signature—and your body, mind, and soul respond accordingly. An affirmation must NOT be worded in the form of a plea, ask, or want—for such wording comes from a place of fear or scarcity. Affirmations must be worded as if already been granted to you.

HIGHER FREQUENCY EMOTIONS CHART

END STATE

COHERENT
CONFIDENT
CONNECTED
CLEAR
CONSOLIDATED
CENTERED

	COLUMN A	COLUMN B	COLUMN C
ROW 1	☐ Compassion ☐ Sympathy ☐ Gratitude ☐ Kindness ☐ Selflessness	☐ Love ☐ Empathy ☐ Thankfulness ☐ Benevolence ☐ Thoughtfulness	☐ Plentiful ☐ Conviction ☐ Certainty ☐ Supported ☐ Integrity
ROW 2	☐ Abundance ☐ Truthfulness ☐ Self-Assured ☐ Contentment ☐ Honesty	☐ Nurturing ☐ Letting Go ☐ Oneness ☐ Happiness ☐ Hopeful	☐ Caring ☐ Flexibility ☐ Inclusiveness ☐ Generosity ☐ Optimism
ROW 3	☐ Acknowledgement ☐ Acceptance ☐ Understanding ☐ Surrender ☐ Tolerance	☐ Self Esteem ☐ Patience ☐ Forgiveness ☐ Calmness ☐ Respectful	☐ Safety ☐ Secure ☐ Trust ☐ Valued ☐ Empowered
ROW 4	☐ Courage ☐ Self Sufficient ☐ Capable ☐ Worthiness ☐ Freedom	☐ Harmony ☐ Balanced ☐ Fulfilment ☐ Inspired ☐ Renewed	☐ Peaceful ☐ Lightness ☐ Radiant ☐ Creativity ☐ Vibrant

---

EXAMPLE AFFIRMATIONS

- **End State: Coherence**

  Emotions: Empathy—outward, suppress
              Accepting—outward, strengthen
              Surrender—inward, strengthen

  Possible Affirmation: I am coherent in body, mind, and soul through being less empathetic to world causes, more accepting of life's challenges and surrendering the need to control what happens around me.

- **End State: Consolidated**

  Emotions: Supported—outward, suppress
              Caring—inward, strengthen
              Valued—inwards, strengthen

  Possible Affirmation: I am consolidated in body, mind, and soul through spending less effort on supporting the interests of others and more time caring for and valuing my needs for growth.

- **End State: Centred**

  Emotions: Kindness—inwards, strengthen
              Benevolence—outwards, strengthen
              Vibrant—inwards and outwards, strengthen

  Possible Affirmation: I am centred in body, mind, and soul by being kinder to myself, benevolent towards others and vibrant in how I choose to express myself.

Summary

The Separation stage has been about self-reflection and self-discovery. It is the work so necessary for personal growth and essential to evolve into a being of higher consciousness. It has taken courage to face events, people and circumstances that have limited you. It takes strength to move from victim and blaming to taking full responsibility for who and what you are. The process demands no judgment of yourself or others. It is above all, simply to understand, to acknowledge your truth. Truth and authenticity are foundational to the rest of the journey. You and your life will no longer be the same. You not only have awakened to a power ignited within you, but you have also used this power and connection to higher guidance to be in "awareness." This awareness of who you are is key to moving from a life happening to you to a life happening from within you—life from your authentic and sovereign self.

Transformative Level 1
CONJUNCTION

"When I let go of what I am, I become what I might be"— Lao Tzu

	Calcination	Dissolution	Separation	Conjunction	Fermentation	Distillation	Coagulation
Alchemic State	Reducing (to ashes)	Suspension (in water)	Isolating (purifying)	Amalgamation (coming back together)	Interaction (of purified elements)	Condensing (reduction)	Transformation (progressive)
Journey Stage	Questioning	Resolve	Purifying	Surrendering	Practicing	Mastering	Becoming
What Happens	Acknowledgement of Breakdown or Yearning	Suspending Disbelief	Deprogramming + Reprogramming of Self	Reordering of Self	Reordering of Life	Moving from Practice to Mastery	Be-ing
The Work	Pushing the Pause Button	Connecting to Inner Guidance — Connecting to Higher Guidance	Releasing Misspent Energies — Balancing Positive Energies	Forgiveness and Acceptance of New Self	Attuning Life Structures to New Self	Manifesting from Higher Self	Body Mind Soul Oneness
Foundational Competencies	Introspection	Empowerment	Healing	Reframing	Meditation	Self Transcendence	Embodiment
Aspects of Consciousness	Seeking	Awakening	Awareness	Knowing	Self-Realization	Insightful	Enlightened
Revelation	"there is a crack in everything – that's how the light gets in"	"you are a soul with a body not a body with a soul"	"healing is the process of releasing and correcting dis-harmonic energy"	"when I let go of what I am, I become what I might be"	"mindful living is the choice to harmonize life and self"	"from seeing is believing to believing is seeing"	"be the change you want to see in the world"

Introduction

You start this stage when there is nothing more to release, nothing more to clear and nothing more to deprogram. You have rebalanced your positive emotions. The work of discovering who and what you are will continue, but know that most of the heavy lifting is done. You can have little doubt at this point that your relationship with higher guidance has led you to understanding the events and circumstances that masked your true nature and limited your potential. Awareness opens up all potential for you to become a being of higher consciousness bringing more light into this world.

In alchemic terms, this is the stage in which the separated and purified elements are brought back together—not as they were before, but in an altogether new and altered state. This is what takes place within you. There is a necessary reordering of self, taking place physically, emotionally, and spiritually. You are changed and find yourself in an altered state. The vibrational signature you once held is now much higher. As with any change, there is a period of adjustment that is required to know yourself anew. There are beliefs no longer programming you and there are new behaviours and habits you want to embrace. There is a lifetime or lifetimes of behaviours and habits you are changing, and all of this takes time to imprint as the new you. Patience and perseverance are required here more than at any other stage. You may be at this stage for a while.

For the most part, you need time to just *be* in this stage. You let things settle. You let the fine-tuning take place. You welcome an improving sense of health and well-being. You begin to see things differently and there is often heightened sensitivity and creativity emerging. This is a great time to journal, to record those changes.

But not all is positive at this stage. Change is unsettling. And it can be uncomfortable to simply be. The Separation stage was full of activity, of self-discovery while this stage is not about what needs to be done but what needs to settle; *being* a new you. And what makes things more difficult is the juxtaposition you find yourself in; there is an emerging new you but living a life you created as your former self. Your life reflects old behaviours, habits and experiences. It is like having one foot in your reordered self while the other foot is still operating in the structures of your old life. And that old life is familiar territory and there is so much appeal to seeking out the familiar rather than pushing forward.

Notwithstanding the need to push forward, this is not the time for changing your life. You are not ready. You must first consolidate the new you. Give it the time it takes to know yourself in sovereign authenticity. Simply go about your life noting where it is aligned to your new self and where it is not. You will notice and feel the disharmony in energy when you and aspects of your life are not in harmonic resonance. This is a time to invest in yourself. Know your new self. You may feel discombobulated and exhausted at times.

You may doubt you have the fortitude to reinvent yourself and your life but know this is never the case. Had that been the case, you would not have been guided in the Separation stage to your limiting programming.

You are never given what you cannot handle at one time. But here self-sabotage lurks around the corner and you need to guard against sliding back.

This stage is foremost about *states of being*. The first one is **surrendering**. Surrendering does not imply giving up or giving in. Surrendering is letting go of resistance; breathing through the changes; breathing through what is uncomfortable. Let your altered state settle. Accept that you need to be strong and sovereign. Accept that you must embrace authenticity even if it is hard. Accept that you are preparing yourself, fortifying yourself, changing life from happening to you to a life shaped by you. That takes sovereignty and a compass of truth.

Part of that sovereignty and authenticity lies in the second state of being, that of **forgiveness**. It is at this stage that all that occurred in the past as lower and limiting frequencies must now be forgiven. You must forgive yourself and others. Forgiveness is a powerful part of surrendering. Letting go of judgment is a part of surrendering. Acceptance is a part of surrendering. You accept responsibility for all things that occurred in the past and for all choices you make in the present. There is no blaming or victimhood in sovereignty.

Every negative experience or encounter was an opportunity to grow and learn. Every person who hurt you was a teacher, a gift to know yourself in all your complex dimensions. You may not have known that then, but you do now. Higher consciousness does not mean that you will no longer encounter negativity and transgressions against you. You will still make mistakes and have regrets. No, life will not be all roses; life promises contrast in our experiences. However, the big difference now is that, as a sovereign being, you become more unbreakable and unshakeable. You see these offences for what they are—a teaching moment.

You learn how to reframe your perceptions, thinking and responses. What has impeded growth is largely attributable to fear as an underlying force for self-preservation. Through higher consciousness we begin to appreciate how much fear controls and shapes almost every aspect of our lives. Fear makes us feel love as conditional and elusive. Fear makes us feel safe only when we can exert control and force. Fear makes us feel small and unworthy. Fear is limiting.

Being and feeling sovereign is not being and living in fear; it is replacing fear with trust through our power to reframe how we choose to see and respond to every situation in our lives. This is easier said than done. But even being aware that you have a choice to reframe liberates you from automatic reactions. You can choose to trust that everything happens for a reason, that you have the choice to grow and learn with every situation, positive or negative and that the universe has your back.

The higher vibrational level you now have achieved allows you to become a **healer of self**. There is a long tradition in energy medicine in understanding how to heal yourself and others through the power of intention, belief and use of energy as a healing source. The body is meant to heal itself. This knowledge is not intended to replace medical treatment but to complement what advances in science and medicine have yielded. But it does recognize that the medical field in many cases, is limited to managing symptoms. Furthermore, there is still an inability to personalize medical interventions to the very individual chemistry of our bodies at any given point in time.

This is the time to explore the power held within you to heal. You start by practicing and honing this skill on yourself. It takes time. It is a part of the investment in yourself to make you stronger. Know that this journey calls upon you to be everything that you are meant to be so that you can be that inspiration for others. You will be called upon in higher consciousness to help bring light and healing to many others and to many situations. Strength and resilience are required deep within you to take up that challenge. You are readying yourself for what is to come.

The Work

The work in the Conjunction stage has three quite different elements: surrendering to the significant shifts taking place within; forgiving ourselves and those that have transgressed against us; and the self-healing of your organs and systems.

State 1: Surrendering to the shifts

This stage of the journey is completely focused on you—using the caterpillar/butterfly analogy, this is the cocoon stage. The reordering of self takes place physically and metaphysically as you adjust to your upgraded vibrational signature. Surrendering—gracefully acknowledging and accepting the challenges that come with change, is your work. There are no instructions or techniques to master here. This is an ongoing exercise of being aware of the changes happening within you.

Seismic shifts have occurred within. Just as in the aftermath of an earthquake, one emerges to a landscape that has been greatly altered. You may discover a new-found appreciation for life, your loved ones and an altered sense of what is really important. Adjusting to this new landscape and making it your new normal takes time, a little experimentation, and some test driving.

Not only will you need to focus on becoming strong and comfortable with the shifts occurring internally, but you will need to be cognizant that they will be noticed externally as well. No longer indulging in gossip, in creating drama, in judging yourself and others, in being driven by constant busyness to guard against introspection. Stronger and healthier both physically and mentally, wiser, calmer, and more compassionate are the hallmarks of this new person that is emerging.

Some will be unconsciously drawn to you as they feel your higher vibration and your expanded and consolidated aura. While it will likely be difficult to put into words the changes that you are undergoing, it may be an opening to introduce the path you are on. This is the

Sometimes the English language does not have quite the right words to express a subtle concept. Surrendering is a word in this context, that seems inadequate. The space between love and trust is where you want to be. If you love and trust your higher guidance to always know what is for your highest good—you can stop pushing and driving forward, in favour of being pulled through your journey.

This is not easy, especially for type A personalities. We have been conditioned all our lives to make things happen. When you do find this space, you will know it and feel a great sense of release and peace.

metaphysical virus (the good kind) that draws others who may themselves be experiencing a crack, into embarking on their own journey. Be careful and judicious in your approach, and perhaps arrange an introduction to others with more experience. It is an opening you may feel compelled to acknowledge and pay forward.

Others, especially those closest to you, may have difficulty accepting the changes you have manifested, and the time and energy devoted to your transformation. A vibrational discord may be present, so trying to explain your new belief system may be quite a stretch and perhaps even deepen any fears they may have. If this is the case, it may be best to let the new you become apparent in what you do, what you say, and how you react to the inevitable stressors in life. Show rather than tell. Let them come to you when they are ready to find out more and accept that that day may never come. Your compass, your true north as expressed in your firm sovereignty, will guide you through these uncharted waters.

The Luminaries
The power and challenge of surrendering are encompassed by many spiritually inspired authors. Michael A. Singer describes this process well in his personal journey entitled, "The Surrender Experiment" and in "The Untethered Soul." See Part Seven—The Luminaries, for more information.

State 2: Forgiveness

You may be wondering why the exercise of forgiveness is not part of the Separation stage—as injustices that we have both inflicted and experienced cast heavy shadows on our body, mind, and soul. Paraphrasing Einstein, you cannot solve a problem from the same level of consciousness that created it. You had to wait for

> Forgiveness is an enormous gift to yourself. Holding grudges, anger and resentment weigh down your energy and vibrational levels. When you let go, forgiving yourself and others, you will sense a great *lightness of being*. Forgiveness = Freedom

your vibrational signature to increase to be able to address these issues, which occurred at a much lower level of frequency. This is an important phase not just for the density that it releases, but for practicing your ability to surrender and let go of that which does not serve.

Forgiveness does not imply condoning the actions that deeply wounded yourself or another—there is no doubt that there are some actions that seem wholly reprehensible and unacceptable. However, that is not for us to judge. While we delve into the past, it is not actually about the past, but what you have held onto from these transgressions. It is not about regrets, shame or assessing guilt as we cannot fix the past retroactively. We can, however, free ourselves from the density and damage of long-held wounds. This is a process, not unlike that of releasing negative emotions, of identifying those people and circumstances that created these imprints, of understanding why and how they affected your life, and of permanently releasing them.

Any act that requires forgiveness was committed from a place of fear, the need to control, or from a place of scarcity. You now understand that everything happens for a reason and that there are no coincidences. With your higher vibrational signature, you are ready to reframe these incidences as valuable lessons that help to reveal your authenticity. In fact, the shedding of this density lies in thanking our teachers and taking responsibility for our actions.

The Luminaries
The process of using your dominant and non-dominant hands to uncover insights held deeply within your subconscious is inspired by Olympia LePoint's book entitled, "Answers Unleashed." See Part Seven—The Luminaries, for more information.

The forgiveness process—Internal

1. Start with a list of the regrets that you have—in actions you took and people you may have hurt emotionally. What are the things you have repeatedly beat yourself up over?
2. Separate them into discrete categories that can be addressed.
3. For each one, recall as best you can, the situation and let any associated emotions rise up. You might feel them deeply or you

may be able to see them more dispassionately. Write down everything that comes to mind. First use your dominant hand and then switch to your non-dominant hand to activate both sides of your brain.

4. Review them both together and look for the commonalities, patterns, and insights.

5. Now reframe the conversation from one of regret and remorse to one where you see this as a gift, a teachable moment. What specifically did this teach you? How did it contribute to your growth? Did it change you in any way?

> The forgiveness process will remove the burden of long-held wounds at a vibrational level immediately. It may take your physical body and mind time to catch up though—so feeling tired and perhaps a little unsettled is normal. In fact, any time you have made a major shift, you may experience this lag. Surrender to these feelings and know that it is simply your body adjusting to its new energetic signature.

6. There is no magnet required to release this burden. Your intention to forgive, to surrender to this learning and appreciate how it added to the fabric of who you are, is all that is required. This step may be supplemented with a written affirmation about how you are now a better person after absorbing the lessons learned. If you practice meditation, this is an ideal means of helping you reflect inwardly.

If you don't actually feel that you have forgiven yourself, not to worry. The intention to forgive is what releases the density.

7. Using the sway, confirm that you can proceed to external directed forgiveness which follows. If NO, it may be that you have not identified some situations or people where acknowledgement and forgiveness of yourself are required. Be patient with this process.

The forgiveness process—External

Now that you have forgiven yourself, your vibrational level has again risen, and you are ready to take on the process of letting go of hurt and anger against those who have transgressed against us. Sometimes others hurt us intentionally, other times they may not have even been aware of their transgression. This occurred from a place of fear, a need to control or from perceived scarcity. Whatever the case, the process follows the steps outlined above with a few differences:

1. Create a list of people that you think of with a heavy heart and cause you to feel profound hurt.
2. For each one, recall as best you can, the situation and let any emotions rise up. You may feel them deeply still, or you may be able to view the incident from a distance with a degree of dispassion. Write down everything that comes to mind. Start using your dominant hand and then your non-dominant hand to activate both sides of your brain.
3. Review them together and look for the commonalities, insights, and patterns.
4. Now, reframe the conversation and write down what you learned from the incidents, and how it may have influenced your life in a positive way. *What lessons did you learn? What were the circumstances that might have influenced how you were treated? Did the situation cause you to reflect inwardly on your own role? How did this situation serve you in the longer term?* Mentally thank these people or situations for the valuable teachers that they are.
5. Again, there is no magnet required to release this burden. Your intention to forgive, to surrender to this learning and appreciate how it added to the fabric of who you are, is all that is required. This step may be supplemented with a written affirmation about how you are now a better person after absorbing the lessons learned. If you practice meditation, this is an ideal means of helping you reflect inwardly.

   For some people there are transgressions that were so horrific that genuine forgiveness is simply not possible. As long as you have honestly unpacked the incident and set your intention to forgive, this will not stop you from releasing the burden or prevent you from progressing in your journey.
6. After completing your list, using the sway, confirm that you can proceed to State 3, Self-healing. If NO, it may be that you have not identified some situations or

people where acknowledgement and forgiveness are required. Be patient with this process.

Rejoice and enjoy the incredible freedom that true forgiveness brings.

This is a good time to redo your metrics as additional density has been removed. Feel the lightness and see the changes in your biological age, overall health, and level of consciousness. (See the section on metrics in the Dissolution stage.)

The Luminaries
While many books have been written about the power and gift of forgiveness, Bill Mckenna's book entitled, "The Only Lesson" is a powerful story of this author's path to forgiveness and love. See Part Seven—The Luminaries, for more information.

State 3: Self-healing

Your vibrational level has now increased to such an extent that self-healing through directed energy will be highly effective. While the releasing of low frequency emotions, and the deprogramming and forgiveness exercises of the Separation stage ensures that no more damage is being done to your organs, there may be a need for some deep healing of specific organs that were particularly compromised. There are many forms of energy healing such as Reiki, Acupuncture, Qigong and Quantum Touch that have been used for centuries in eastern cultures—and are thankfully now becoming mainstream tools in western medicine. The technique explained here is based on the same underlying principle—that we have the innate ability to heal ourselves by firing up our own energetic powers.

Please note that self-directed energy healing should in NO way replace medical treatment—a doctor should ALWAYS be consulted on serious health issues, and your positive attitude and energy healing capabilities should be thought of as preventative or complementary.

The self-healing energy technique uses your intention as a catalyst and your hands as energy concentrators.

1. Use the sway to assess the health of each organ. Using the logarithmic scale from 1 to 10, get a score for each major organ.
2. Create a prioritized list of organs most in need of healing.
3. Standing up, place your right hand on or as near as possible to the organ. Set an intention that your right hand will draw out all toxins, harmful inflammation, bacteria, and viruses. Close your eyes and command that these harmful elements gather in the palm of your hand. Picture this happening in your mind. Spend 2–3 minutes doing this.
4. Vigorously shake your hand to release all of the toxins out of that organ.
5. Place your left hand over the same area. Now set an intention that your hand will send healing energy into the affected organ. Picture the healing that is occurring and thank your higher guidance for this healing process. Again spend 2–3 minutes on this. Summon a higher emotion to supercharge this healing. (see below)
6. This process can be done multiple times throughout the day, it just depends on your motivation and available time. Reassess periodically using the sway and logarithmic scale to monitor your progress.
7. Note that you do not have to do each affected organ serially. For example, you could have a morning and evening session in which you do 2–3 organs. You still need to do them separately, there is just no need to restrict yourself to one at a time.

Your circumstances and health are always in a state of flux—so this is an excellent technique that can be used throughout your life.

~

Doctors in China traditionally were paid to keep people in healthy states. If their patients got sick, they were not paid for treatment. This concept of focusing on prevention has opened a field of medicine known as Functional Medicine.

~

You may notice, especially when using your left hand for healing that you sway forward—this is a wonderful indication that your powerful healing energy is at work!

Supercharging Your Healing

Intensify with breath: Prepare for healing with several body sweeps of breath. Visualize bringing breath up through your feet to your head and exhale by visualizing your breath flowing down through to your heart and out through your arms and hands.

Amplify with heart energy: Tap into the frequency of love and visualize your heart expanding your heart centre. Summon and feel as deeply as you can a love energy emanating from the heart area. Bring it through the experience of loving something or someone deeply. Build that loving sensation in your heart. Know that the power of healing comes from the heart.

Guide with intention: Direct the healing energy with where or even why you want to heal. Do not worry about the how as the universe will take care of that. Focus but remain relaxed. It is not the intensity of the intention that heals but rather the intensity of the heart energy.

Putting it all together: Gather the sensation of love from your heart into your breath. Exhale out from the chest to your arms and hands with guided intention to the focus or area of healing. Send gratitude for the healing.

---

*Please note that the healing of your organs may take some time, so be patient and diligent with this practice. Monitor your progress regularly as your rising scores will motivate you to continue. Achieving a score of 9.5 or higher is **NOT** a requirement to advance in your journey. Think of this healing technique as an ongoing process and skill that can be utilized throughout your life. You learn this technique at this point as you now have the level of consciousness to do so. As your level of consciousness increases so too do your healing powers.*

The Luminaries

Self-healing is an important topic and skill to be learned. Healing can come in a variety of forms and these are all well worth exploring throughout the rest of your journey. Gaia is an important and varied source of different healing perspectives and modes. Here are some recommendations to get you started and exploring...

Quantum Touch 2.0 The New Human by Richard Gordon, Chris Duffield, PhD and Vickie Wickhorst PhD

Open Minds with Regina Meredith
A Simple Method for Profound Healing with guest Bill McKenna
Healing in the Quantum Field of Potentials with guest Dr. Joe Dispenza
Accessing Intuitive Healing with guest Jerry Wills

Inspirations with Lisa Garr
Sound Healing for Health and Happiness with guest Jonathan Goldman
Qigong's Healing Energies with Guest Robert Pong
Qigong for Healing with Guest Chunyi Lin
Awaken Your Healing Energies with Guest Deborah King

Gregg Braeden
Missing Links Season 1 Triggering Self-Healing

Healing Matrix with Dr. Sue Morter
Boosting your Auric Biofield with guest Donna Eden

Summary

Perhaps the most important change that comes with the Conjunction stage is the *knowing* as an aspect of consciousness you develop. You are in your *knowing* as the power held within you. It is an unshakeable belief in yourself as a being of higher consciousness. When you allow your authentic self to emerge, having stripped away the masks, the pretences, and the fear, you now know your true self. *Awareness* gained in the Separation stage has amplified to a *knowingness* anchored in the power of higher guidance and in yourself. There is a greater depth to knowing. You do not have to believe; you know. There is certainty. It is also a state of invariance meaning it is not conditional on circumstances and nor is it acquired from the outside in. The knowing comes from within. When you know yourself in truth, that truth has a permanence, a foundation that upholds all else.

Take the necessary time to really consolidate. As you have undertaken this journey, the universe has a plan for you, and you must ready yourself.

Transformative Level 1
FERMENTATION

"Mindful living is the choice to harmonize life and self."

	Calcination	Dissolution	Separation	Conjunction	Fermentation	Distillation	Coagulation
Alchemic State	Reducing (to ashes)	Suspension (in water)	Isolating (purifying)	Amalgamation (coming back together)	Interaction (of purified elements)	Condensing (reduction)	Transformation (progressive)
Journey Stage	Questioning	Resolve	Purifying	Surrendering	Practicing	Mastering	Becoming
What Happens	Acknowledgement of Breakdown or Yearning	Suspending Disbelief	Deprogramming + Reprogramming of Self	Reordering of Self	Reordering of Life	Moving from Practice to Mastery	Be-ing
The Work	Pushing the Pause Button	Connecting to Inner Guidance. Connecting to Higher Guidance	Releasing Misspent Energies. Balancing Positive Energies	Forgiveness and Acceptance of New Self	Attuning Life Structures to New Self	Manifesting from Higher Self	Body Mind Soul Oneness
Foundational Competencies	Introspection	Empowerment	Healing	Reframing	Meditation	Self Transcendence	Embodiment
Aspects of Consciousness	Seeking	Awakening	Awareness	Knowing	Self-Realization	Insightful	Enlightened
Revelation	"there is a crack in everything – that's how the light gets in"	"you are a soul with a body not a body with a soul"	"healing is the process of releasing and correcting dis-harmonic energy"	"when I let go of what I am, I become what I might be"	"mindful living is the choice to harmonize life and self"	"from seeing is believing to believing is seeing"	"be the change you want to see in the world"

Introduction

You are about to embark on a new phase of your journey.

You enter the Fermentation stage from your reordered state. Your vibrational signature is now a mix of much more elevated frequencies and you are beginning to re-know yourself as sovereign and authentic. The Separation stage was all about deconstructing your past, making known the *dis-ease* of body, mind, and soul you carried within, as life baggage. And after the heavy lifting of releasing and clearing what did not serve, you fine-tuned all that serves you to be in balance. And you did this through the connection and relationship with higher guidance in unleashing the power that lies within. You had to pause and surrender to these profound energetic shifts in the Conjunction stage with new understanding, forgiveness, and reconciliation of all that was, and is, to bring you to this point. All this in order to move forward.

This is the *forward* phase of the journey. How you use the gifts of higher guidance and higher consciousness are yours to determine. You have the power to open up a universe of infinite possibilities for what is to come, and both the Fermentation and Distillation stages are designed to help you do just that—expand and hone the skills of higher consciousness. There is choice here and with that choice comes responsibility.

In this stage and all subsequent stages and levels of transformation, you yield to the presence of your higher self. This is an especially important concept and distinction.

In most spiritual journeys, there is reference to the *small self* and the *higher self*. The small self is the one most in control and most habituated to navigating the outer landscape in which we live. The small self is the one that is tapped into the thinking mind and the executive function of our brains, enabling us to operate in our demanding worlds. It is the *doing* aspects of ourselves and the one keeping us rooted in our identity (the presentation of who and what we are) through which we interpret life as it happens about us. The small self is concerned with our primordial needs of safety, security and beyond that, is the citizen within the collective. We understand the rules of engagement, societal laws of the collective, what is expected of us, and what determines success and status. It also acquires information and knowledge, and values logic and the rational as the means to move us forward.

The designation of *small* in this case is the acceptance that while the small self is indispensable, it has limitations. The small self knows what it knows, seeks validation from the outside and is bound by the limitations of our sensory seen world. Its main operating paradigm is fear and the need for order, predictability, and control. It has bought into a world that keeps us from being everything we could become. It would rather patch up the cracks in our lives than embrace what is being illuminated. It keeps us focused on our needs, our survival and greed at the expense of much wider and beneficial needs of humanity and of the planet at large. The journey is about the *spiritualization* of the small self. In other words, the small self is not left behind for it always retains its indispensable acumen in the physical plane. However, the goal is vibrational alignment of the small self to the higher self.

The higher self within us has always been there. But its *felt* presence is commensurate with higher consciousness. Our vibrational signature is now such that we feel the higher self emerging in tandem with our new-found authenticity and sovereignty. It is our *truth*. Truth is unconditional. Truth is truth under any circumstance; it does not waver nor is it fear based. The higher self is the *being* within us. It is not about the *doing* but the *being* of who we are, in truth.

Your reordered state is one which is mindful of making room for the higher self to co-exist with the small self. You need to know how this new state of the higher self feels; how the energies are different; how you see and feel things from the inside-out rather than the outside in. The higher self defines who and what you are from the power source that lies within. It is not interested in the fear and control-based rules of the collective nor is it invested in the identity that others have conferred upon you. There is an alignment issue between the interests of the small and higher selves. Make no mistake, the small self does not like to share, nor does it like to give up control.

The emergence of the higher self as a promise of higher consciousness is not a straight path. Rather, it is directional and there are likely to be many course corrections along the way. You now feel what it is like when you fall off the path; when you do not invest the time in yourself, when your actions and words are not aligned to your higher vibration. You cannot always control what comes at you in life, but you can always exercise the choice in how you react. Above all, it is important to recognize and acknowledge discord within you: when you know something does not sit well; when you know there could have been a higher consciousness choice in your words and actions. This is knowing your higher self through a refinement process of reflection.

In this stage, you will be mapping out the areas of your life. This is about how you spend your time and indirectly, the value you place on different aspects of your life. It reflects the habits and patterns you have adopted in life. It becomes a composite of how you live and express yourself through life. It covers common areas like sleep, eating, relationships, physical activity, leisure time, entertainment, travel and encourages you to customize this to your circumstances. You may spend time volunteering, you may have a job, you may place value on personal and spiritual growth, you may have creative outlets.

Life is your refinement process. You get to ferment your new higher self with changes in your life. This is you, now moving forward. You are not separate from your life; you are your life, and your life is an extension of you. This is a dance between you and your life, between your small and higher selves, with the requirement to be in a relationship of harmonic resonance. You have gone through an upgrade in your programming and so too must your life be upgraded. Remember at this point, your life structures (how you spend your time) have been put in place through your old programming, largely dominated by the small self. You are reordered but your life is not. When both are in sync, the frequencies will be amplified through resonance.

In alchemic terms, Fermentation is the organic process of elements adjusting to each other in their now altered state to continue a refinement process. A change agent, like yeast, is added to start the fermentation process. The change agent here is *mindful living*. Living from that place of authenticity and sovereignty. Making room for the higher self to imprint on your life choices. This takes practice through introspection and reflection. You are guided to appreciate what parts of your life are most out of alignment: what parts of your life need to be reordered or upgraded to be in harmony with your elevated vibrational signature. It is a mindful exercise of testing the various aspects of your life against the criteria of *is this in accordance with my authentic self? Is this for my highest good? Is this aligned to my highest self*? It is about being mindful.

This can be one of the most challenging phases of the methodology as it invites a roller coaster of emotions. Changing your life takes time and sensitivity. You cannot be that proverbial bull in the china shop changing everything at once nor do you want to "throw the baby out with the bath water." There is a lot in your life worth keeping and relationships worth cherishing. One needs to proceed knowing that change can be upsetting not just for you but to others in your life. Some will be inspired by the new you and others will feel threatened. All this tests the choices you make and pace of change you exercise. It also tests how you choose to approach change. Remember that all change must come first from within.

This process of mapping your life allows you to see where the greatest misalignments lie. You create a pie chart and segment it with your life structures (*illustrated in Figure 6*). However, we were inspired to think of the pie chart as your Petri dish through the work of Bruce Lipton. His work underscores how the membrane of cells read their environment and respond accordingly. A healthy cell put in an unhealthy Petri dish will become unhealthy; the converse is true in that an unhealthy cell in a healthy Petri dish will become healthy. You are like that cell in the Petri dish of your life. Your environment must have a healthy coherence with you and you with your life. You essentially want your life structures and your authentic self to be at the same level of consciousness. This creates resonance (amplification) and resilience.

The Luminaries
Dr. Bruce Lipton is a renowned cell biologist whose work bridges science and consciousness. He is at the forefront of the new science of Epigenetics, which advocates that our fate is not controlled by our genetic make-up. See Part Seven—The Luminaries, for more information.

Know that you will experience frustration and self-doubt. You may experience *dark days of the soul* (relapses) but know that this will pass. We learn from our failures and relapses as this is an inevitable part of the bubbling up that happens with fermentation. We reframe failures and relapses to valuable lessons and the refinement process continues. One of the important competencies garnered through mindfulness is meditation. The inverse is equally true; meditation allows for more mindful living. If you have not yet adopted a practice of meditation, this is the time to do so. This is a powerful practice of connecting with your inner self.

The Work
Practice 1: Applying mindful living

We use the expression *mindful living* as a proxy for *being in the moment*. We have come to realize that so much of our daily life is on automatic pilot, often unconsciously repeating patterns, and routines without really being present with them. Being in the moment denotes the opportunity to express your highest self in the choice of your words, thoughts emotions and actions. Every choice opens up all subsequent choices. A given choice can shut down further avenues of choice or open up ever-greater possibilities. Choice denotes responsibility. You have the choice to bring in light and higher consciousness to every situation or to keep the situation in a state of lower consciousness. Keeping a situation in lower consciousness is a state of contraction where limited choice eventually closes in on itself. Conversations are shut down, views are polarized, thinking becomes rigid, systems are not capable of responding to change.

Mindfulness is the choice to bring in higher consciousness. Ironically, mindfulness is much less about how your thinking mind would react to a situation but rather how your heart would respond. The thinking mind breaks down, analyses, and strategizes how best to interpret and process a situation given known experiences. It tends to isolate and separate the elements within a situation or problem to deconstruct and then reconstruct them, conforming to known, predictable patterns and experiences. It is an intellectual exercise. On the other hand, your heart brings forth the *knowing* of a situation. Knowing is a complete, whole view. You just know.

The challenge here, is that we have long valued logic and Cartesian thinking over the knowing of the heart. We have tended to interpret a heart-centred approach as an incomplete assessment, an emotional rather than logical approach. Logic tends to be valued over emotions as an emotional response is not considered reasoned. But the knowing heart is more than emotions; it encompasses a soul connected to the wisdom of the universe. It houses the essence of our individuated divinity, our creative force.

Generally speaking, we do not trust the heart over the thinking mind. We trust science over spirituality. However, there is value and room for both approaches. The thinking mind may dominate the navigation of our outer landscape but the heart, as knowing, rules our inner landscape. When it is said that all change must first come from within, it speaks to our knowing as the key to changing our outer landscape. It speaks to our reordered selves to break free of the limitations of a life happening to us. It speaks of our inner power to effect change over forces at play in our outer landscape.

When you align life to self, it is a process and your aim here is to eliminate any discord between your inner and outer landscapes. They become one seamless expression of your highest self—thoughts, feelings, communication, and actions co-existing in beautiful solidarity. The work at this stage is road testing your authenticity and sovereignty as they are put into action through life choices.

Practice 2: Attuning your life to self

What is important to keep in mind here, is that your life is a manifestation of your creation. Your life is a series of choices you have made. Some things you may feel you have had little or no choice in, but accepting or conforming to something not of your choosing, is nonetheless a choice. Taking responsibility here is key. As mentioned above and worth repeating, you cannot always control what you are being faced with, but you always have a choice in how you respond. Furthermore, your life was structured at your old frequency and consciousness level. While you have reordered, your life is still a reflection of old patterns and habits. So, the work here requires that you evaluate the different parts of your life and develop a good sense of how each segment of your life or "life structures" lines up with your vibrational signature. If you think of your life as a pie chart with each piece representing a major aspect of what you spend your time on, you can evaluate how each segment matches up to your personal authenticity. Your external landscape (or life) can be divided into the following life structures (in no particular order).

- Health (physical and mental)
- Livelihood (job/career)
- Education (learning and expanding)
- Purpose (understanding your unique contribution)
- Creativity (how you express your imagination)
- Spirituality (introspection and beliefs)
- Relationships (family, friends, co-workers)
- Sleep/Rest
- Nourishment (what you eat, put on your skin)
- Physical Activity
- Leisure (how you use your spare time)
- Home (physical environment, comfort, safety, security, financial stability)

These have been depicted in Figure 6. If there are important parts of your life that seem to be missing—and you feel they need to be added, please do so. This should reflect how you generally spend your time.

Now that you have your life structures segmented, you can now measure how each of the categories aligns to your vibrational signature. As mentioned, your life is your Petri dish. You can only be as healthy as your environment. While there are lines drawn between each segment, the reality is that they do not represent hard boundaries. If you make a change in one, it will affect several others. For example, if you increase the amount of sleep you get, there will most certainly be a positive effect on your physical and mental health, your performance at work, and your relationships, etc.

1. Using the sway, and based on a 1–10 scale, determine the overall health of your Petri dish. Record that number.
2. For each of the segments individually, repeat the same exercise, recording the result *(see Figure 6)*.
3. Add up the scores of your individual segments and divide by the number of segments you have in your Petri dish. It should be close to your overall number. If it is not close, use the sway to determine which segment(s) needs to be rescored. Continue this exercise until you are within .5 of your overall total.
4. Now look at your results and determine in which life structures you see opportunities for alignment. For any segment it is often useful to fractal them down further to give you a better understanding of the nature of the misalignment *(see Figure 6)*. In the example provided, *Relationships* was broken down into different groups of people. The two groups with the lowest scores (the outliers) could be further broken down to specific people. This will help you zone in on the relationships where improvement will yield the most benefit to your overall score/ life—and provide uplift to other segments.
5. Be aware that simply becoming cognizant of the misalignments will energetically close the gap between your true self and this part of your life. This is less about *doing* and more about *being* in higher consciousness and having life entrain to your level of

vibrational signature. This is making room for your higher self to be expressed in the way in which you live.

6. If you feel the need to create strategies to better align this life structure, ensure that such strategies are not about fixing but bringing more clarity and light. Remember this is work of the higher self and not the small self.

7. There is no pass/fail with respect to your Petri dish. Your scores are simply indicators of where attention is required. The various aspects of your life are always in flux and this is more a process of continuous refinement through awareness and practice.

ALCHEMY OF BECOMING: CREATING YOUR PETRI DISH

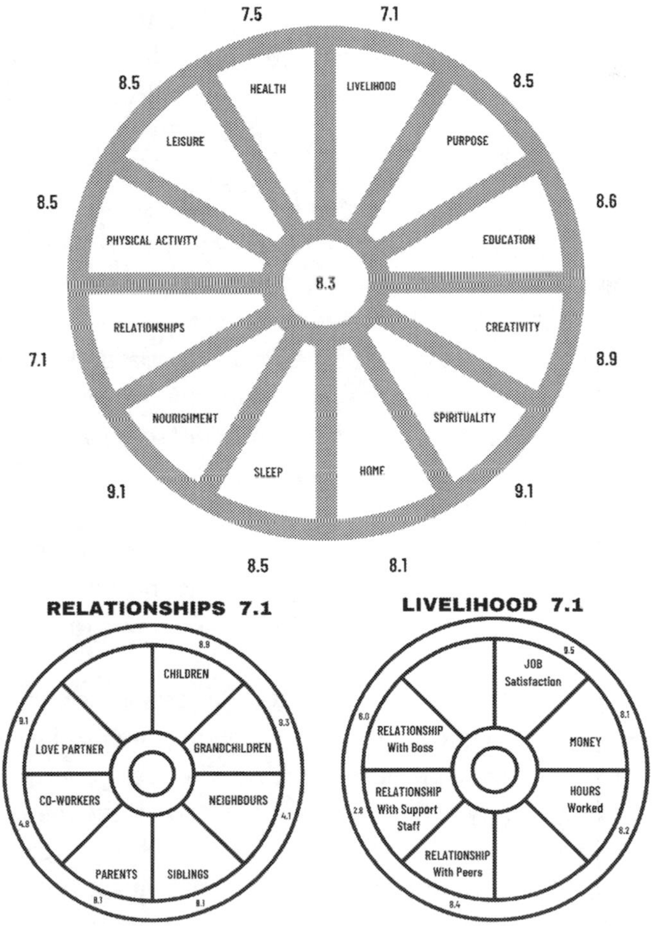

RELATIONSHIPS 7.1

LIVELIHOOD 7.1

Figure 6

Practice 3: Using power not force to effect change

Now that you have made known the misalignments in your life structures what do you do? In simple terms, you make room in your life structures for heart-centred reflections or put another way, make room for your higher self to guide the way forward. This is easier said than done. As mentioned, the small self likes to be in control. Our small self has long been calling the shots as we navigate the ever-present reality of our outer landscape. The small self does not like to give over the helm of your ship to the higher self to navigate the way forward. The small self knows what it knows and there is familiarity and comfort there. The higher self is unknown territory. You can count on the small self to bring you to familiar shores. It knows the route just fine. It has been navigating that route your whole life. But changing destinations is not the small self's forte here. Even if it thinks it would like a different destination—a welcome change—it will likely find its way back to the same old place.

How do you know who is at the helm? If your first response to a low-scoring segment of your Petri dish is to analyze it and develop concrete action plans for a course correction, you know your small self is firmly at the helm. The small self knows what it knows. It will isolate, break down the broken segment, take out the repair manual and literally create charts and timelines to force a change in direction. *I need to fix this to be in alignment with my reordered, higher vibrational self. This is what I think is wrong and this what will surely fix it.*

All of this is well intentioned and to some extent, will work. It certainly will seem satisfying. We are used to effecting change through a well thought out and executed work plan. We love to be in our doing mode.

By way of contrast, the higher self effects change through the power of unseen energy. In the Separation stage, you were able to release trapped emotions and clear energy blockages through the use of energy. You have learned to direct energy, to unleash its power to effect changes within you. You did not take a pill to effect these changes, nor did you seek medical intervention. You did this by being aware that you hold this power within you and by setting the intention to shed denser frequencies within you. You sought higher guidance acting in concert with your higher self, to systematically make known what needed to be released and cleared, to make room for higher frequencies. You are healing body, mind, and soul through the power of this guided, unseen energy.

The very same thing applies to effecting changes in your life. The reordering of your life to self is a question of the alignment of energies from self to life. Creating your Petri dish is the equivalent of making known what needs to be released and cleared in your life, to align with your higher frequency or higher consciousness. You know where the weak spots are, where you are most in need of attunement. You create the awareness and then you set the intention to upgrade that segment of your life. You affirm that intention with gratitude. You allow your *knowing* to know that what needs to align, will align. You surrender the work to the universe to make the changes your soul needs when it needs it. The small self gives over the helm to the higher self with the knowing that the navigation of your life will course correct to the vibration you now hold. You surrender the helm. The change comes from simply being in higher consciousness, not through the doing or undoing of your life.

This is not a passive process. Surrendering is never passive. Your primary job is to keep the small self from taking over. It is a constant challenge. The small self will want to take the process over. It will not understand that change can be done without great effort, discipline, and control. It will not understand that it can be done without strategies and a plan of action, without doing something, without cause and effect.

The second job is to pay attention and be patient. When the higher self sets the intention for change, it is *realized* at that moment, meaning that what needs to be set in motion energetically happens instantaneously. But you will not see the changes manifested physically for some time. One of the reasons for this is that manifestation in the physical, denser vibrational plane, lags. It takes time for material things to change whereas non-physical energy can change instantaneously. The other reason is that you may not have anticipated the changes that are in effect taking place and therefore fail to see them. Attuning life to you can be many, many subtle changes over time. And remember that the alignment you seek is directional not linear. There will be setbacks along the way. It is the overall trajectory that is important. You need to pay attention to notice the evolving changes.

Where does all of this lead you to in the struggle between the small self and higher self? At this level you will want to employ both. You may feel the need to develop a plan to make some of the changes and surrender others to the universe. The small self is making room for the higher self, but they are just getting acquainted. The trust and knowing are not yet there to give the helm over completely to the higher self to get the job done. Balance, and awareness of that balance, is what is required here. What that means is a combination of both doing and being; fixing and surrendering. Know which one is being employed and for what reasons. Pay attention. Make room for the higher self. Approach things with a knowing heart and mindfulness. Remember that all change comes first from within and that all power is held in the present moment. Stay present and pay attention to how life will reorder and align to your reordered self.

This alignment of the authentic you to an authentic life creates new patterns of behaviour, new ways of seeing things and new ways of responding. It is about paying attention, being mindful. When you practice living from your authentic self or highest self, you are less likely to slip back into your old programming. You may find yourself drawn to new experiences or to some individuals over others. You may be more discerning about what needs to be shed or let go because it no longer serves you. You may apportion your time differently, putting more attention and focus on things and people that expand or energize you as you continue to acknowledge your seat of inner power and conviction. You may find yourself choosing to eat healthier, to be less judgmental, more grateful, more compassionate, and more at peace with whom you are becoming.

These changes come not through force, discipline and control but rather surrendering to a grace held within your being. The most important thing in all of this is to be in your highest level of consciousness. This is about being the highest possible level of consciousness and entraining life to your level of consciousness.

Recap

1. Approach each segment of your pie chart with the understanding that this is an opportunity for learning through exercising yourself in higher consciousness. Reflection is important here.

2. Understand and accept what needs to be released and cleared in your life structures to align with your higher vibrational self. Say YES to the opportunity even if the change is uncomfortable or unfamiliar. Trust.

3. Resist jumping in to fix yourself or others. This is not about force (control, fear, discipline) to effect change. This is something quite different but so powerful.

4. Think about ways to bring more light into any of your life structures. This means creating openings for more understanding, tolerance and acceptance within yourself and others.

5. Set the intention to bring higher consciousness to lower consciousness areas of your life. Remember that your intentions act as a command to the universe. Exercise responsibility in the choices you make in setting intentions. Ensure that your intentions serve your highest truth, your highest good.

6. As much as possible, surrender the work to the universe. Let your higher self-take the helm and be guided by the truth and sovereignty held in your knowing. Make this not an intellectual exercise but a heart-centred one.

7. Be mindful of the power you hold in simply being in higher consciousness. Practice *being* rather than *doing*. Feel yourself as presence. Feel yourself in the moment. Feel what it feels like to give over the helm to your higher self even if it is but moments at first. That is fine. Practice.

8. Be patient. Surrender the alignment of energies to the universe. Understand that the manifestation of the changes comes with its own timing for your soul's need to learn. Like before and after pictures, try to capture the evolving changes. See them with new appreciation. Do not dismiss any change as coincidence or serendipity. Honour them as your creative force. Pay attention.

9. Do not be discouraged with what you perceive as setbacks. Reframe these as teachable moments. Remember that energy

shifts are not linear or sequential, but directional. It is the trajectory that is important.

Practice 4: Meditation

The path from the small self to the higher self is through turning inwards, shifting your sense of self from the outer landscape to the inner landscape. It is the path certainly less travelled but one you have chosen. Throughout this alchemic journey, you access that inner landscape every time you connect with higher guidance. This is *awakening*. It is not the small self that connects with higher guidance; connection to higher guidance is the sole prerogative of the higher self. The higher self knows itself as the individuated divinity that you are. And in that divinity all power is held for the fullest expression of who and what you are meant to become.

All of this is hard to wrap your head around and harder yet to believe. Yet, this is the destiny of those who journey through the alchemic stages and levels of transformation. There are many paths for those who journey, and this is but one that is offered in this methodology. But know that regardless of the path chosen, courage, commitment, and perseverance to a discipline of exploring your inner landscape, is required of you.

The practice of meditation is invaluable in navigating the inner landscape and in so doing, connecting with greater skill and ease with both your higher self and higher guidance. The practice of meditating is a skill to be learned, honed, and mastered. It is a source of wisdom, insight, and resilience beyond what can be garnered through the outer world.

Humanity is at a crossroads of great change. We are bearing witness to a breakdown of global proportions; of our institutions, of societal norms, of fauna and flora of Gaia (Mother Earth) herself, with the universal cry, "I can't breathe." But this inevitable breakdown holds great promise for those who choose to see the light coming through the crack. The times ahead will be unpredictable, unprecedented and the small self will find itself unable to navigate the unknown, and unable to see the breakthroughs that are emerging—the path forward not backwards. For these breakthroughs will be seen not through our eyes and intellect but through the insight of higher consciousness. Navigating through the breakdown will require you to be resilient, unshakeable, and unbreakable, and the practice of meditation will an invaluable companion in navigating this period.

While the physical and mental health benefits have now been well documented by the medical profession and scientists alike (refer to the many videos on Gaia that address this topic) many are initially intimidated by the whole prospect of meditation. This likely speaks to the typical portrayal of the practice as a monk sitting atop a mountain, transcending the physical body while the mind and spirit bend time and space. This may be true for those few who choose to renunciate life in the third dimension, but it is a far more available tool when viewed simply as a way to commit to your truth, to see life, problems and issues from a higher and wider perspective through the exclusive lens of your higher self.

As with the acquisition of any new skill, it takes time, practice, and patience with yourself. For some, quieting the mind is a far more difficult task than say, running a half marathon. But like training for a marathon, you start by running for short periods and gradually increasing your distance and speed. In fact, the seven stages of alchemy can be used as your framework for mastering this skill.

The seeker in the **Calcination** stage sees meditation as a means of letting in the light. Preparation for your meditation journey is critical to your success. Finding uninterrupted time and privacy from outside noise and distractions is essential. Listening with one ear for the child who may awaken, the alarms from your cell phone or for the doorbell for an expected delivery, will not allow you to go inside to that place of peace and calm. Find that time, claim your space and adorn it with things that speak to your soul.

The suspension of disbelief in **Dissolution** requires that you let go of your preconceptions and fears about meditation and be open to the promised benefits of your practice. Believe that you can master this tool.

Separation is where the real work begins as you *commit to the cushion* and commence the process of going inside, quieting the mind for just a few minutes to start, and progressively increasing that time, day by day.

It is work that requires positive intention and sustained effort. One of the fallacies that frustrates many is the belief that the goal is to empty the mind. In fact, it is far easier to reduce the busyness of your thoughts by focusing on something that is calming and inspiring. This is where the many guided meditations that are available can be especially beneficial.

In the **Conjunction** stage, your practice allows you to overcome the notion of meditation as work and instead reframe it as a necessary part of your day that you look forward to and even crave. This is the stage at which you transition from guided to self-guided meditations; consolidating your own style, how you prepare and the techniques that work for you. Meditation now becomes a form of surrender allowing your higher guidance to bring light to dilemmas or problems you are facing, or simply taking you where you need to go. You cannot always control what happens in your meditation. Find enjoyment and know that there is no such thing as a bad meditation.

Fermentation can be a tumultuous stage as it invites you to leave the cushion and incorporate the meditative mindset into everyday life. This does not mean wandering around in a trance! It does mean incorporating the mindfulness and presence that meditation demands into your life, melding with the ability to pause and respond to situations and people from your highest self. While you still will want to dedicate time each day for deep connection, it evolves to becoming a way of being.

Distillation is an ongoing stage where you continue to refine and deepen your practice. The ability to connect inwardly when the small self comes knocking, will serve you well when stressed or confused. Mastery of meditation is like golf; there is never a perfect game, and always room to hone your skills and improve your performance.

And finally, **Coagulation**—the stage at which the mindfulness of meditation becomes embodied by you, completely natural and innate. This is the ultimate goal of this ancient practice.

There are many resources on meditation, but some are more helpful than others. Choose wisely. "The Mind Illuminated" by Culadasa (John Yates, PhD), Matthew Immergut, and Jeremy Graves, is a comprehensive manual on mediation that also follows an alchemic process acquired in a series of progressive stages and levels from novice to adept. The authors write, "*While this book is a kind of technical manual, it's an artist's handbook. Meditation is the art of conscious living. What we make of our life—the sum total of thoughts, emotions, words and actions that fill the brief interval between birth and death—is our great creative masterpiece. The beauty and significance of a life well lived consists not in the works we leave behind, or in what history has to say about us. It comes from the quality of conscious experience that infuses our every waking moment, and from the impact we have on others. For life to become a consciously created work of art and beauty, we must first realize our innate capacity to become a more fully conscious being.*"

The practice of meditation is lifelong. When you stop going inwards, you stop journeying. When you stop transferring what is within to mindful living, the progression to your fullest expression of *being* cannot be realized.

The Luminaries
Culadasa (John Yates, PhD), provides a comprehension guide on meditation. It integrates meditation practices originating from Buddhist and Indian traditions along with the latest research in cognitive psychology and neuroscience. See Part Seven—The Luminaries, for more information.

Summary

It is only through the refinement process life provides that the knowing within you becomes *self-realized*. *Self- realization* refers to the fulfillment of the possibilities and potential of one's true self. It is the journey of the small self finding vibrational alignment with the higher self, and in so doing fulfilling one's potential. This is becoming everything you are meant to be as a continuous state of refinement through life experiences. In the Fermentation stage, you put your reordered self to the test of life. How do you show up in life?

Transformative Level 1
DISTILLATION

"From Seeing is Believing to Believing is Seeing"

	Calcination	Dissolution	Separation	Conjunction	Fermentation	Distillation	Coagulation
Alchemic State	Reducing (to ashes)	Suspension (in water)	Isolating (purifying)	Amalgamation (coming back together)	Interaction (of purified elements)	Condensing (reduction)	Transformation (progressive)
Journey Stage	Questioning	Resolve	Purifying	Surrendering	Practicing	Mastering	Becoming
What Happens	Acknowledgement of Breakdown or Yearning	Suspending Disbelief	Deprogramming + Reprogramming of Self	Reordering of Self	Reordering of Life	Moving from Practice to Mastery	Be-ing
The Work	Pushing the Pause Button	Connecting to Inner Guidance Connecting to Higher Guidance	Releasing Misspent Energies Balancing Positive Energies	Forgiveness and Acceptance of New Self	Attuning Life Structures to New Self	Manifesting from Higher Self	Body Mind Soul Oneness
Foundational Competencies	Introspection	Empowerment	Healing	Reframing	Meditation	Self Transcendence	Embodiment
Aspects of Consciousness	Seeking	Awakening	Awareness	Knowing	Self-Realization	Insightful	Enlightened
Revelation	"there is a crack in everything – that's how the light gets in"	"you are a soul with a body not a body with a soul"	"healing is the process of releasing and correcting dis-harmonic energy"	"when I let go of what I am, I become what I might be"	"mindful living is the choice to harmonize life and self"	"from seeing is believing to believing is seeing"	"be the change you want to see in the world"

Introduction

You enter this stage to move to a master level. All that you learned, practiced, and set into motion is now ready to be mastered. In the alchemic state, distillation reduces a substance to its essence, enhancing potency and resiliency to corrupting forces. It is the final refinement process to achieve purity.

A significant increase in your vibrational signature and level of consciousness have manifested in improving health, energy, love, compassion, sovereignty, and an overall zest for living. A solid foundation has been built for a more meaningful and fulfilling life. You have done the work to reorder yourself and taken big steps to reorder your life. The dance between you and your life is a perpetual refinement process as you now appreciate that each and every day is an opportunity for yet further refinement.

Refinement comes with honing a set of five skills and these skills become the work of this alchemic stage. And with refinement comes mastery. Mastery is the domain of the third eye, the ability to see beyond and go beyond current limitations.

The **first skill** is to *see with new eyes* and that begins with questioning beliefs that underlie your perceptions. In the Dissolution stage, you were asked to suspend your beliefs. In the deprogramming and reprogramming steps of the Separtion stage, you identified limiting beliefs and displaced them with positive beliefs. Here you question whether the general beliefs you hold in life and reflected in your life structures (Petri dish), come from a place of your truth and sovereignty. *Do they really reflect who you are becoming or are they simply a reflection of what you have been told to believe?* It is often the case that hard-and-fast belief systems adopted from our parents, society, history, and culture can limit our ability to see things differently. We are constantly trying to make sense of everything unfolding about us from the standpoint of what we believe. We tend to dismiss things that don't track with our way of interpreting the reality we hold as our belief system.

For the most part, we are unaware of our cultural and societal beliefs and of the role they play in shaping our ability to see and interpret the world around us. These beliefs can serve to expand or limit you. You see with your eyes to believe, and what you believe aligns with what you expect to see. To see beyond the current range of possibilities set for yourself, you have to change what you expect to see. And changing what you expect to see is predicated on changing your belief system. With mastery one learns that the mind must be open to new beliefs before you can see beyond what you expect to see. You seek not to confirm the same old-same old, but to expand and explore beyond your known reality. Believe wider, see wider and wiser.

The **second skill** you master is *the power to observe*. This is again the domain of the third eye which sits above your two physical eyes with the ability to reconcile duality. When you invoke the power of your third eye, you master the ability to observe. Observing offers an elevated perspective. You interpret and find meaning to life as it unfolds about you. Things happen for a reason and you find that reason, that message, that intended teaching moment for your soul. You learn to reflect and allow yourself to be curious, to explore, to take in the significance of the moment. You understand that because there is no separation between you and your life, that your life is a reflection of your soul. You created your life from choices you were given. Whether you know it or not, your first choice was to come into this reality, into this life, for a reason. Observe your life about you and you are observing yourself.

The **third skill** to be honed is *the power of the pause*. This is about the quality and choices of your interactions with life as it unfolds about you. From the elevated perspective of observing yourself, your words and actions become deliberate and natural extensions of your authenticity and sovereignty. You resist getting caught up in the fray of the moment simply reacting to events. Instead, you observe what is taking place and you choose to *respond rather than react*. Reacting excludes choice while responding invites choice. Choice allows you to initiate and respond to life from within, with wisdom and light. It is but a split-second difference between reacting and responding but in that briefest of pauses is a sacred space to exercise choice from your highest self.

Responding is both choice and by virtue of that, a creative force. There is no sleep walking through life. You have the choice to invoke higher consciousness in every situation or encounter life presents. This is the **fourth skill**. You *master being present in how you show up*; being a presence through higher consciousness. Presence is not a state of doing; it is a state of being. *You bring in higher consciousness through being rather than doing*. To give an example, reacting to something gone wrong is to jump in and fix things. The act is in the doing with a limited range of choice. Contrast doing with being. Instead of fixing, you bring in more understanding and light to a situation. Your presence as higher consciousness empowers others to see the teaching moment in the situation that has gone wrong. You offer insights and choice rather than jumping to solutions. You seek clarity through questions rather than answers. You guide rather than prescribe. It is the proverbial fishing rod that is offered, not the fish.

This form of mastery is a form of *self-transcendence,* meaning that the exercise of your inner power is gifted to others through your presence. It is not imposed, nor is there attachment to an outcome or judgment towards yourself or others. It is simply gifted from your authentic and sovereign self without indifference but also without expectation. You begin to understand that your life's purpose in whatever form it takes, must arise from this state of being. In other words, purpose comes from mastering the presence of being.

The **fifth skill** is manifesting from a state of higher consciousness— moving from a life happening TO you to life happening FROM you. It is at this stage that you avoid manifesting what you want from life from a limited range of knowns for self-serving purposes. Rather, you access a fuller spectrum of possibilities for a broader set of needs. You learn the power of *setting conditions* as outcomes rather than defining end goals. An end state or end goal is prescribed and defined. *It looks like this and only this*. When an end state is defined as the outcome you desire that end state cannot be other than a construct of how you have always thought and experienced. However, when you envision the characteristics and conditions you want to see manifested, the universe is free to select from a much broader set of possibilities and delivers an outcome for your highest good.

Mastery is accepting that with all the above skills you are co-creating the expanding universe. The choices you exercise, the actions and words you choose, create the present moment and that present moment determines the trajectory for all the moments that follow. You are contributing to universal consciousness with every thought, emotion, and manifestation. There is great responsibility in the choices you alone make as a creative life force.

Mastery is all these things working together and embodied as one. You invoke the intelligence of the third eye to challenge your belief systems thereby enabling you to see beyond your known reality. You acquire the wisdom and meaning in life from the elevated perspective of observing. Observing in turn presents choice in how you show up in life and how you respond mindfully rather than reacting to life. You begin to understand that your purpose in life is not in the doing but *being* in higher consciousness. Your higher consciousness will bring light and empowerment to every situation. You learn to manifest from a state of higher consciousness for the betterment not just of yourself but to the world around you. And you appreciate the responsibility you hold as co-creator of your reality.

This is the level at which you begin to harness the power of *insight*. The heart centred knowingness combines with a soul whispered wisdom. It is your soul that observes with the wisdom of its eternal blueprint. The knowingness of the heart and wisdom of the soul combine in a consciousness expressed as *insightfulness*.

The Luminaries

Manifesting in higher consciousness and life visioning are beautifully described in Michael Beckwith's book, "Life Visioning." These concepts are also described in Vishen Lakhiani's book entitled, "The Code of the Extraordinary Mind." See Part Seven—The Luminaries, for more information.

The Work
Skill 1: Challenge your beliefs

The work here is to go back to your Petri dish as a construct for examining your belief systems. Understanding that your life is a reflection of you, determine what the underlying beliefs are for each of your life structures.

- *Are your beliefs expectations others hold for you?*
- *Does your validation come from external sources or from within?*
- *Do your beliefs reflect your authenticity and sense of sovereignty?*
- *Is there an opportunity to see things differently?*
- *Is there an opportunity for personal growth and expansion by introducing a new possibility? (Going from the comfort of the known to the potential discomfort of the unknown.)*

By applying the questions above, you are introducing an element of risk—a necessary ingredient for growth. Shaking things up, being adventurous, being curious, getting out of your comfort zone keeps you expanding throughout life. Remember that a change in one life structure will yield benefits in other life structures.

As an example, let's apply this new lens to <u>Livelihood</u>.

A 45-year-old is on the partner track at a large law firm. Married with one child, she has been working 50–60 hours a week for the last 10 years, has developed a loyal clientele and is consistently exceeding her billable hours quota. Let's apply the questions to this fictitious scenario.

Are your beliefs expectations others hold for you?

> *My father was a doctor, my mother a college professor. While the choice was mine, I am aware that it was always expected that I would choose a prestigious profession to at least match that of my parents. I was given all the encouragement and resources required to be a top student. I never actually gave much thought to my profession and decided on law as it has a variety of specialties and I knew that it would make my parents proud.*

Does your validation come from external sources or from within?

> *I am proud of myself when I serve my clients well, particularly with my pro bono cases where I am helping people out of difficult situations. But I get a real feeling of accomplishment when I garner the praise of the partners, when I get my bonus cheque and confirmation of being on the Partner Track. My parents are proud of my accomplishments. I'm not sure I have thought of validation in any other way.*

Do your beliefs reflect your authenticity and sense of sovereignty?

> *This is a very scary question for me. I now understand that my livelihood was carefully shepherded by my parents and unconsciously by the culture in which I was raised—I was all about meeting and exceeding expectations. I don't blame my parents at all—they wanted for me what their belief system defined as success and happiness and were*

subjected to these expectations themselves. Did I exercise choice? …. not really.

Is there an opportunity to see things differently?

I am a grown woman, and I do have choices. I am the main breadwinner in my family, and they have grown accustomed to a privileged lifestyle. I now realize that shaking things up and asking what would both provide a decent living and nurture my soul would be a very good thing both for me and my family. I don't want to impose the same expectations on my son, and it might do him good to not continue living a lifestyle of complete security and privilege.

Is there an opportunity for personal growth and expansion by introducing a new possibility?

Yes! Do I really want to be a Partner in my firm and continue to just work, work, work to bring in new clients and chasing billable hours? Do I want to actually get to know my son as he grows and spend time with him? Do I want my partnership to be with my husband rather than my firm? I don't need to "throw away" my profession but I could transition to a more balanced and fulfilling life by telling my boss that I want to work 40 hours a week and do pro bono cases only. Failing that, I could heed the call of my close friend and join her in her legal aid clinic.

Just imagine how this woman's life could change by taking that risk. Applying authenticity and sovereignty to this life structure turns validation from outside-in to inside-out. Consider how many of her life structures would benefit from the change she can now see.

While it may not be necessary to go into this much detail on every one of your life structures, apply the same lens of thinking to each of them to challenge your belief systems and open up to new, albeit somewhat risky possibilities. With mastery, one learns that the mind must be open to new ways of seeing before you can contemplate new possibilities.

Skill 2: The power of observing

Whatever actions or strategies you have chosen to implement (as a result of aligning yourself to your life structures) observe how they play out. Reflect on intentions you have set, on the meaning of how life unfolds, what opportunities present themselves, and what messages the universe is sending you. Each day is an opportunity to know yourself at a deeper level and to exercise the choice of your interactions. Observe how you give meaning to life through your presence, how you can change the dynamics of a situation by what you choose to say, do or not do. How has a person or situation been a teaching moment for you?

Intuitiveness comes with observing and reflecting on life. We come to see patterns playing out, we feel shifts in energy, we pay attention to synchronicities, we become good at reading people and situations, we develop a knowing with the help of higher guidance.

Skill 3: The "Pause"

The pause is that sacred space that allows you to think before you respond or react. You become the observer of you, giving yourself space to reflect. When you are confronted with a question or a potentially uncomfortable situation, rather than reacting unconsciously (and perhaps reverting to your old programming), the pause is a split-second opportunity to internally ask the question—how would my best self respond? That briefest of moments allow for calm deliberation resulting in the best possible response to be offered. For example, an immediate reaction might be "Well that's just ridiculous" but if you can pause and reframe from your highest self it might look like "interesting … that's a perspective I hadn't thought of." This reframed response allows for openness and learning as opposed to a conversation ending judgment. It is easy to forget and slip up, but your inner dissonance will immediately let you know when you have—and better prepare you for the next opportunity.

When you invoke that sacred space, you are using your observational power to step outside your feelings and emotions and invite in all possibilities. You shift from using your two eyes to see what is in front of you, to observing with your third eye to see what might be. In that moment you are making a conscious decision to change the trajectory of all that follows. Understanding that every choice will impact the future is a great responsibility but so empowering at the same time! It is the power of creating rather than reacting. This is the mastery of mindful living—of comprehending at all levels that you are the creator of, and accountable for your life and how it evolves. Each and every decision you make, the words you choose and the actions you take carry great importance in how your future unfolds.

Skill 4: Emphasis on "Being" rather than "Doing."

Life is a series of unfolding events, obligations, pressures, and responsibilities. The to-do lists are endless, and we can often feel overwhelmed. We can get so caught up in what needs to be done that we leave ourselves behind in the *doing* of life. Much of what we do are repetitive tasks performed daily which only adds to the propensity to go through life on the automatic pilot of our habits and behaviours. We forget to be truly present in our lives, to be in the moment rather than planning the next task. We keep up but leave ourselves behind. And the more we do, the more we expect of ourselves.

This is where it gets difficult. It is the discipline of *being rather than doing.* Being present for others. Really showing up. It is the practice of self-awareness but not just in those quiet, alone, meditative moments. It is being aware of your presence in motion, in life, in groups, on the go. It is the choice to bring light and higher consciousness to every situation and encounter through being authentic and sovereign. It is the choice to voice compassion when others would rather judge; the choice to not go along to get along; the choice to be truthful when avoidance of truth is far easier, the choice to let others be heard and validated over your own needs, the choice to refrain from drama and gossip.

This is all easier said than done and you can start small. Carve out an activity or encounter with someone for a finite (and short) period of time. Set the intention to be present as your higher self for that time no matter what transpires. Keep that awareness of yourself as if you could see yourself being filmed. Afterwards reflect on whether you observed a difference in the quality and outcome of the activity or encounter.

Skill 5: Manifesting in higher consciousness

In the previous Fermentation stage, you deconstructed how you spent your time using the Petri dish, to ensure that your life and self are operating on the same vibrational plane. In step 1 of this stage, you applied the lens of your long-held beliefs to allow you to re-imagine your life from your authentic self. In this step you take your Petri dish to a whole new level.

The life structures within your Petri dish do not change, but the question asked of them evolves from *how can I improve the overall health of my dish?* to *how could I re-create this dish to reflect the life I want and help raise the consciousness of others?* This reimagining of your life underlies the whole theme of this level—the shift from *Life Happening TO YOU, to Life Happening FROM WITHIN YOU.*

Before you start with this exercise, an important consideration is how best to express this reimagined life. Creating a picture of what you want is quite challenging as we are constrained by what we know, our history and experiences. What if there are amazing possibilities that you simply cannot imagine because they are outside of your frame of reference? We don't know what we don't know.

The solution to this lies in what Vishen Lakhiani (Mindvalley founder and author of "The Code of the Extraordinary Mind") refers to as mature wanting vs. immature wanting. This is perhaps best explained through examples. Immature wanting expresses our tangible and often material driven desires such as a high-income job, a big house in a desirable neighbourhood or being able to run a marathon in under 4 hours. They represent end states—a tangible goal that falls within your known frame of reference. Mature wanting specifies the *conditions or characteristics* that underlie what we want.

To take the example of the house that we want, we could specify:

- ☐ the exact neighbourhood
- ☐ 4 bedrooms
- ☐ 3 bathrooms
- ☐ a front porch
- ☐ large kitchen with new appliances
- ☐ double car garage
- ☐ sits on 2 acres of land

> Setting defined end goals for what you want in your life limits you to known experiences.
>
> Setting the conditions around what you want in your life allows for an infinite array of possible outcomes.

What if this want was expressed in another way?

- ☐ a safe and well-maintained neighbourhood
- ☐ enough bedrooms and bathrooms to comfortably accommodate my family
- ☐ a garage large enough to accommodate our vehicles and bicycles
- ☐ enough land to accommodate a garden and outdoor living space
- ☐ good Feng Shui
- ☐ a dwelling that makes us feel safe, comfortable and is welcoming to friends and family

In the first instance, we have a picture in our mind of what that house looks like, and the more specific that image is, the fewer possibilities exist that meet those criteria. *We limit our possibilities by our known experience.* In the second instance, we are defining the conditions that you want from a home, and *the possibilities now expand beyond our known.* By outlining the conditions or characteristics, we could find a house that better meets our needs and exceeds our expectations.

When you create the characteristics that you want to achieve in each of your life structures and put them out to the Quantum Field, the universe is now free to select from infinite possibilities and delivers an outcome that is for your highest good—one that you may have never thought possible. This is co-creation. This is also a wonderful example of switching from *head based* to *heart based* manifesting; gratification coming from inside rather than from external measures or societal standards.

For each of your life structures apply the question for each category to identify the conditions you wish to achieve. Let's look at some other examples of how to put this into practice by showing the differences between immature and mature wanting.

LEARNING	
Immature Wanting	Mature Wanting
To get my MBA by the time I'm 30	To be led to resources that will expand my horizons and raise my vibrational signature
To learn how to play bridge and become a master	To use leisure activities to enhance my ability to learn and improve my memory
To get my certification in X by December 31	To become more knowledgeable about Newtonian and Quantum physics
To become a Reiki Master	To enhance my knowledge of and ability to perform energy healing
To read 2 books every month	To be led to books that enhance my spirituality

LIVELIHOOD	
Immature Wanting	Mature Wanting
To be in the top 10 in my field	To be a respected expert in my field
To make>$150K per year	To feel fairly compensated
To be a Vice President	To feel recognized for my contributions
To be granted stocks	To feel recognized for my contributions

To enjoy what I do	To provide positive value to the world To provide positive value to our customers To be energized and inspired by my work To wake up each morning eager to get to work To work with like-minded individuals To be valued for my leadership and expertise To feel that I am making a difference in the world

You can hopefully see the shift from external to internal validation in these examples. Mature wanting is less about how you are perceived by others and more about how your life activities nourish your body, mind, and soul.

Your work is to re-create your Petri Dish and express your wants as the conditions you want to achieve in each area of your life. This may take some time and several drafts, but it will help you to really think about what you want from life, how it serves to support your spiritual growth, and how you can transcend your ego to serve the greater good.

Skill 6: Putting It all together

You have now been introduced to the 5 Master Skills of this first level of alchemic transformation: challenging your beliefs to see with new eyes; observing from an elevated perspective rather than just seeing; honouring the sacred space of the pause to create what comes next; understanding the power held in being rather than doing; and manifesting from setting conditions for outcomes rather than settling for limitations of the specific and known realms. Each of these is powerful in its own right and can be mastered as discrete skills. However, they also hold amplified power when used together synergistically. The following is intended to illustrate how they came together in a particular case of a woman journeying through the Distillation stage. This is Julie's story.

In reflecting on her Petri Dish, Julie felt the need to examine one of her life structures which represented her artwork. While Julie has a successful career, she also spends serious time on her artwork. Julie is a self-acknowledged perfectionist and only feels comfortable when in control of every situation. By extension, her artwork is a form of high realism. She is very accomplished and sought after by galleries for the exceptional interpretative realism of her work. Her considerable talent is undeniable.

One of Julie's journey challenges has been to find fulfillment and validation of her worth from within. Her father was abusive and often violent, leaving her determined to be nothing like him. She spent her youth and adult life helping other people and only felt happiness when she was able to make everyone around her happy. She only saw her worth, her goodness (as the antithesis of her father) through the eyes of others. She was there for everyone but herself. However, the needs and wants of others proved relentless and it became increasingly difficult for her to meet the expectations she herself set. She was depleted but did not know who she was or what she really wanted in life without the role of fixing others. The inevitable crack appeared in her world when she could no longer keep up.

Skill 1: *Having come to the Distillation stage, Julie now understood that even her artwork was something she did to please others and to find validation. The high form of realism reflected life around her but not within her. In challenging her belief in her artwork, she was able to see that she did not enjoy it.*

Skill 2: Rather than a creative outlet, it became work needed to be done to gain the recognition galleries could potentially offer. Even more discipline and control would be needed to satisfy the commitment galleries would expect of her. She was observing herself as unfulfilled and unhappy and getting in deeper. Her artwork was no longer something she looked forward to.

Skill 3: This realization took a new-found sense of sovereignty and authenticity. Julie realized that her art form ought to be an expression of herself—how she felt about the subject she was committing to canvass regardless of how others see it. It needed to be more free-flowing and allowing more interpretation by the viewer. Therein lies the choice in a reflective pause. She had choices by letting go of what she believed would garner recognition. She had the talent to express herself in more creative and fulfilling ways.

Skill 4: Her new belief was that her artwork, as an authentic expression of herself, should reflect her as a presence rather than aiming to be technically perfect in the doing of her art. The departure point is completely different. Her presence, her creative uniqueness, not just her skill, should be evident in her work.

Skill 5: Julie set about outlining the conditions for manifesting a new reality for this life structure. The conditions she chose reflected the desire to be fulfilled through the creation of her art. Her art was to be an authentic expression of herself, meaning that validation and worth should come from within.

However, one of her conditions for manifesting this change was that the merits of her artwork should be reflected in the monetary value assigned to them. Although her artwork had been praised, the monetary value offered by galleries would not compensate her for the hours of work required to do a piece. Upon reflection, her insistence on monetary worth was based on a general resentment that she was prone to being exploited by those around her. The condition revealed a deeper held belief. Julie realized that it was not really others who were exploiting her, but that she was giving away her power. She only saw herself through the eyes of others. Julie had been addicted to the praise and validation others bestowed on her.

In the end she let go of the attachment to a monetary outcome in favour of surrendering that to the universe. Rather than fear and the desire to control the outcome, Julie had to trust that a more soul-oriented expression would yield its own rewards. It was by consciously applying these skills that Julie was able to acknowledge the need to grow through this understanding. The beliefs she held about her artwork were formed in lower consciousness. Having elevated her consciousness, Julie is on a journey to heal and repair lifelong patterns with the insights gained. There was also the recognition that these beliefs were not limited to her artwork but permeated throughout her life structures. A change in one would lead to many others...

Summary

To create a more fulfilling life, there is a requirement to do the work. That work is a refinement of your life; how to live life in congruence with your small self and higher self in vibratory alignment; how to express that alignment through the experiences you seek, the growth you need to evolve and the contributions you make. In reordering and reimagining your life, be mindful that the work must balance the needs of the body, mind, and soul. It is a journey of body, mind, and soul becoming, transforming and you cannot leave one behind.

Your physical body is no less important than the mind and soul. You are meant to fully embrace life and attend to the body as temple for your soul.

We are gifted with a powerful mind, a thinking mind capable of limiting or expanding us; a mind that serves best when we are mindful of the choices we make. Being mindful allows the mind to be inclusive of heart centred knowingness and soul whispered wisdom. The knowingness of the heart and wisdom of the soul are one in an aspect of consciousness expressed as insight, as to see within.

All the work you have successfully completed with the goal of uncovering your authentic self, of purifying, of creating resilience and potency has, perhaps somewhat ironically, also led you to a place where you can go beyond yourself—to self-transcendence. It is only at this point in your journey of *becoming* that you can now turn your attention to the world around you. The opportunity is to use your unique gift of *being* to bring light to others, simply through your ability to observe and respond with higher consciousness. In this state of *being*, your presence brings light, openness and new possibilities to every encounter.

Transformative Level 1
COAGULATION

"Be the change you want to see in the world" — Ghandi

	Calcination	Dissolution	Separation	Conjunction	Fermentation	Distillation	Coagulation
Alchemic State	Reducing (to ashes)	Suspension (in water)	Isolating (purifying)	Amalgamation (coming back together)	Interaction (of purified elements)	Condensing (reduction)	Transformation (progressive)
Journey Stage	Questioning	Resolve	Purifying	Surrendering	Practicing	Mastering	Becoming
What Happens	Acknowledgement of Breakdown or Yearning	Suspending Disbelief	Deprogramming + Reprogramming of Self	Reordering of Self	Reordering of Life	Moving from Practice to Mastery	Be-ing
The Work	Pushing the Pause Button	Connecting to Inner Guidance / Connecting to Higher Guidance	Releasing Misspent Energies / Balancing Positive Energies	Forgiveness and Acceptance of New Self	Attuning Life Structures to New Self	Manifesting from Higher Self	Body Mind Soul Oneness
Foundational Competencies	Introspection	Empowerment	Healing	Reframing	Meditation	Self Transcendence	Embodiment
Aspects of Consciousness	Seeking	Awakening	Awareness	Knowing	Self-Realization	Insightful	Enlightened
Revelation	"there is a crack in everything – that's how the light gets in"	"you are a soul with a body not a body with a soul"	"healing is the process of releasing and correcting dis-harmonic energy"	"when I let go of what I am, I become what I might be"	"mindful living is the choice to harmonize life and self"	"from seeing is believing to believing is seeing"	"be the change you want to see in the world"

Introduction

In this final alchemic state, the transformation from a base element to precious metal is revealed. In nature the fully formed butterfly emerges from the cocoon to take flight, fully transformed.

From ordinary to extraordinary, this is the journey of body, mind, and soul as you have shed negative energies in favour of positive energies and the creation of a sovereign, authentic you, living your truth. You had the courage to question your life as defined by others and the resolve to step out of conformity. You went through an intense understanding and purification of what held you in density so you could welcome in higher frequencies. You learned the precious gift of surrendering to the often-turbulent shifts taking place deep within as you awaited the emergence of a reordered self. And in your sovereignty and authenticity, you first practiced then mastered a life in necessary alignment to your new vibrational signature. This is becoming. Not a final state, but one that continuously evolves. You are *en-light-ened* as in welcoming greater light and lightness as embodied in your presence.

This has been a process of breakdown to breakthrough. A process repeated throughout nature to regenerate and to evolve. Evolution is just that—breaking down to shed what no longer serves to transmute to a more powerful, resilient form to thrive in an evolving environment. As beings of energy, we are either contracting or expanding. And expanding is surrendering to and then embracing the unknown, the unfamiliar. It is BE-ing as to be in motion.

You pushed that pause button of your own volition and you made a life-altering decision to connect to your higher self and through your higher self to higher guidance. And now you know you are never alone or unsupported. The guidance is always there for your highest good. Through that guidance you are healing body, mind, and soul as indivisible in this continuing journey to enlightened consciousness.

And even at this last of the 7 stages, we never cease BE-ing.

The Work
Theme 1: The power of words

Words carry frequency and that frequency holds information. Every word, every number and every geometric symbol holds a unique frequency. Words are foundational and we often use them unconsciously and without intention. Jim Self, in his book, "A Course in Mastering Alchemy," states that words as vibrations are fundamentally more important than words used in language. Think about the power of mantras. By aligning ourselves to the words we speak and think, we create the opportunity to experience and receive the vibrations they hold.

Barbara De Angelis in her work, "Soul Shifts" expresses the same point in a different way. Words sequentially strung together with intention (as exemplified by this manual), do two different things because they contain two types of content: informational and vibrational. The informational content of words is designed to impact your mind with ideas, concepts, and explanations that provide you with new understandings. The vibrational content is a transmission of coding designed to provide an alchemic experience. In other words, by merely reading the words, there is a frequency of transformation encoded within. You are not just informed, you are transformed. Once you understand this, you are much less interested in works that merely inform. Each of the authors referenced in this manual has been selected for the quality and indeed brilliance of their work to not only inform but transform.

The same holds true for how you speak. The spoken word has a frequency developed over time through association with intention. The Lower Frequency Chart is comprised of negative word frequencies while the Higher Frequency Chart contains words of higher frequencies. Your choice of words is a reflection of your vibrational tone. You have a vibrational signature and a vibrational tone, both unique to you. Just as people project a vibrational signature, so too do they project a vibrational tone through the choice of words used to convey a thought. The same thought can be expressed as hurtful or helpful depending on the calibration of one's choice of words. Overall, a person's tone can be hesitant, sad, angry, or defensive, or on the other hand, engaging, joyful or inspiring. There is a correlation between the calibre of one's vibrational signature and vibrational tone.

Theme 2: Embodiment

The work in the Coagulation stage is centred around the theme of **Embodiment.** This is the stage where you express your authentic self as one—as a body, mind and soul working to express itself as a unified entity. You will be first introduced to the "Seven Living Words" as characteristics that we aspire to embody; and then to three transformational themes that, once fully embraced and absorbed, will form the basis for future spiritual growth.

The "Seven Living Words"

This description of the Seven Living Words is adapted and slightly modified from Jim Self's channelled work "A Course in Mastering Alchemy." Your personal quest throughout the levels of this transformative process is to embody these Seven Living Words in perfect balance within you. You become or personify these words, hence the *living* designation. These also correspond to the Chakra centres. They are:

- **Sovereign**—this is about being in dominion of you and by extension of your life. This is understanding who you are, knowing your worth and loving yourself. Validation comes from within. You cannot always control what happens in your life, but you can control your response to any situation. You are the seat of your power. (Root Chakra)

- **Joyful**—this emotion comes from within. It is different than happy which is usually a response to something or someone on the outside of yourself. Joy comes from a place of deep feeling of peace and self-love. Just say the words joyful and happy out loud and you will note the difference in the vibrational tone. Happy is light and airy, fleeting, and joyful has a deep, lingering vibration. (Sacral Chakra)

- **Commanding**—this is the attribute of soft, confident power that lies within. It is closely tied to Sovereignty as the place in which your willpower is seated. This is a quiet power, never forced nor imposed. It is not about the need to control nor does it ever come from a place of fear. It comes from a place of strength and will and never from weakness. (Solar Plexus Chakra)

- **Knowing**—this is a deep feeling of trust and certainty. The ability to interpret any situation from a place of knowing. It is not an intellectual knowing as much as it is a vibrational knowing. The more you are in your knowing, the more you explore the unknown. The courage to go beyond your knowing to the unknown comes from the foundation of being deeply in your knowing. Courage and knowing come from the heart. (Heart Chakra)

- **Gracious**—this is the attribute of expression. It is what and how you project yourself. There is a flow to grace rather than harshness. It softens without diminishing strength. It is a voice of the Buddha, where words are spoken with intention and actions are deliberate in their conveyance. Your projection is a reflection of all that lies within. (Throat Chakra)

- **Masterful**—this is the power to not just see but observe. And to observe is to see beyond; to integrate and reconcile what is observed from a higher perspective. You observe the interconnections of all that you encounter, the oneness of the creative forces. Masterful is the designation of skills fully embodied. (Third Eye Chakra)

- **Presence**—this is a felt presence; the self as exemplified through your physical and auric fields. It is how you show up to yourself and others. It is the oneness of body, mind, and spirit. Your presence reflects your vibrational signature. (Crown Chakra)

Instructions for the Seven Living Words

At each level of transformation, you will be guided to one of these seven words. Whichever word you are guided to is the one you most need to develop at this time. The objective here is to embody these seven words in complementary and harmonious balance. As you get a word, it is the one most out of balance with the others. Each of these seven words must be in vibrational alignment with each other to be operating as a unified, harmonious field of energy.

1. Write each of the 7 words down on separate pieces of paper (one word per paper). Shuffle the papers and place them face down. Keeping them face down, number them from one to seven without looking at the word. Ask your guide if it is word number 1 or 2 or 3, etc.

2. Once you have your word, the next step is to determine what attributes of this word best align to you and to the frequency of the word. Go to the *Higher Frequency Emotions Chart* (see Separation stage, Step 4) and ask which word, from which column and row will help strengthen this Living Word within you. Repeat the process until

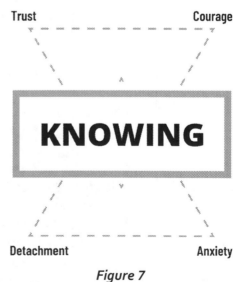

Figure 7

you have two guiding higher emotions from this code. Draw a triangle and place the Living Word at the bottom of the triangle with the two higher frequency emotions at each of the top corners of the triangle *(see Figure 7)*. You now have a powerful image upon which to imprint on your mind with intention. Reflect on the dynamic interplay of the three words. Each will reinforce the other as complementary and resonating frequencies.

3. Repeat this process using the *Lower Frequency Emotions Chart* (see Separation stage, Step 1) to determine which emotions threaten to undermine realizing the full power of your designated Living Word. Place the two lower frequency emotions at either bottom corner. Look for the dynamic interplay of the three words *(see Figure 7)*.

4. Now you have two triangles; one which is a key to understanding what draws in power and the other, which is key to understanding your vulnerability to embodying the power of the living word.

5. Remain mindful on a daily basis of what brings strength and power to your word and what can compromise your embodiment of that word.

Theme 3: Oneness

There is no separation. There is no separation within you. You are humanity and divinity intertwined in the dance of life. You and your life are held in a frequency of your making. You are not separate from the actions you take or the words you speak or the beliefs you hold. You are unique, individuated divinity connected to one universal consciousness. But not only are you connected to universal consciousness; you are creating that consciousness in tandem with the expanding universe. Consciousness is the creative force that underlies ALL that is.

This is a difficult concept to understand. The closest analogy we have in our three-dimensional experience is the World Wide Web. Think of the World Wide Web as immaterial (somewhere in the cloud) analogous to worldwide consciousness. We, as individuals, and in the collective, are creating the Web with every interaction we take. Every time we look something up, we give power to that site (the more hits, the more profile). Every time we add content, we shape and expand the Web as a reflection of us. The Web is us; it is our creation. And it has a frequency, a consciousness that mirrors our collective level of consciousness.

It holds negative energy in the form of hate and hurtful material and it also contains the best of what humanity offers. It holds the memory of every past interaction, is active in the NOW and manifests the future from infinite possibility. We as the observers will determine the future manifestation of the Web as congruent with the attention and focus we project to it. It reflects our thoughts, feelings, and beliefs and to a great extent, it reinforces them, as we tend to seek out what we hold as familiar and true. But it also holds the exciting and inspiring brilliance that draws us to the leading edge of insights and discoveries. And its expansion is limitless.

So as beings of higher consciousness, we need to take responsibility for what we can uniquely contribute to collective consciousness. We are a microcosm of the macrocosm. We are the *wayshowers* of elevated consciousness. And remember that higher frequency has more power than lower frequency in all dimensions of reality. Higher frequency will entrain lower frequency to move up; such is the power we hold.

Our physical experience in this 3-dimensional world anchors us in a persistent perception of separation. Our physical senses are highly tuned to boundaries and contrasts to distinguish and help navigate this dimension. But oneness is the only true reality as viewed from a much greater height or in the case of quantum physics from the very smallest of particles. The work here is to see beyond the limitation of our senses and embody the concept of oneness.

Theme 4: Sovereignty and authenticity

This first level of alchemic transformation has been from experiencing life happening TO YOU to life happening FROM WITHIN YOU. The essence of this paradigm shift was in uncovering your inner power as a creator force. You took power back to realize your sovereignty to be in dominion of your life. And to be sovereign is to be authentic. Authenticity is the seat of sovereign power. Authenticity is foundational to the progression to higher levels of consciousness. You must get this right. Authenticity and sovereignty are intertwined. You can only be as sovereign as you are authentic. You live your truth in sovereignty. It is not someone else's idea of truth, or someone else's pronouncement of your worth or of your validity. You take on the responsibility to know and define yourself from the inside-out. There are no excuses, no blame, nor victimization. It must be all you. The coherence you are striving for is harmonizing your inner landscape to your outer landscape. Life by you and as a reflection of you.

It is not easy to maintain authenticity in a culture that values conformity, is highly judgmental, drawn to drama, and above all, is fear and control based. In fact, it is exceedingly difficult. It is far easier to go-along to get-along. We love to belong to a tribe of like-minded individuals. And here too we have a beautiful community; a tribe of those awakened to higher consciousness. But even in this tribe we must honour inclusiveness, the absence of judgment and understanding and compassion for all. Higher consciousness must never be mistaken for being above anyone. We are all here by choice and there are lessons to be learned by each of us in honouring our purpose no matter what level of consciousness we hold.

We are not here to fix others or to determine that they need fixing. Rather, we are here to illuminate the way forward for those who are seekers. Those who seek will find us. And when they do, we empower all who seek to be on a path to their own awakening. It does not have to be this journey or this methodology; there are many paths. But we are here to support each other as we courageously embrace the unknown and unconventional.

Summary

You have arrived. Your first level of transformation has come to fruition. You now have the skills and frequency to be the change you want to see in the world. This has nothing to do with imposing your will or your beliefs on anyone. The change you want emulated comes from within. You are a being of light with the power to illuminate. Exemplify the change. Be felt as higher frequency. Do not await change in the world to provide a window for change; you are the doorway to change the world.

๏๛

Transformative Level 1
CONCLUSION

Consciousness as the prime directive

The prime directive of this journey as imbedded in the methodology is the attainment of higher consciousness. All healing of body, mind, and soul comes with progressive states of higher consciousness. So too is there an urgency to uplift and heal our world in higher consciousness. Today's intractable issues can only be addressed through the individual and collective expression of ourselves in higher consciousness. Our survival and that of the planet is dependent on this. It is our evolutionary call.

As one goes through each step of the instructions, as you now have, it is easy to lose the thread of higher consciousness, as the purpose of this methodology. Given the many beneficial changes happening within us, and the challenges inherent in reordering ourselves and our lives, we can lose sight of the fact that all spiritual paths must lead to knowing ourselves in higher consciousness. But rest assured, your vibrational signature as the reflection of your level of consciousness continues, even now, to quietly elevate in the backdrop of the journey. The changes, at once subtle yet profound, are being manifested in the physical and non-physical realms that you are.

This is after all, the alchemy of *becoming everything you are meant to be*. And what you are meant to be is individuated divinity as your unique and divine expression in higher consciousness. You now understand how it was possible to experience the transformative process of this methodology as uniquely yours and yours alone. You were empowered from within and guided from above. You released and cleared low frequencies in an order personalized to your experiences, your life circumstances. You then welcomed higher frequencies, again in a precise order and amplification required for the level of consciousness you now hold. You are refining the skills to be resilient as a *being* of higher consciousness. You know yourself in truth and as sovereign. Life is happening from within you.

This is a life-altering accomplishment. Not just your life, but LIFE. We are each co-creating this universe as it unfolds. As daunting as that seems, we are further reminded of our responsibility in helping to shape the trajectory of humanity.

We are also reminded that we live in an extraordinary time. For the first time in great numbers, we are conscious of our consciousness. We are conscious of evolutionary choice. Evolution as conscious choice, not chance. There are many among us, whether inclined through science or spirituality, that believe we are at a precipice. We will choose to devolve or evolve. And the operative word here is *choice.* It is no one's choice but ours; no one's accountability but ours. *Ours,* means the choice resides with me and you; it must. Stop for a moment to take this in.

If you are not evolving in consciousness, you are devolving. If you are not expanding, you are contracting. Your choice to evolve and expand means the ramification of that choice reverberates endlessly. There is a power held in the vibration of a positive choice that changes all it encounters.

We are not to dismiss the power held in one to effect great change. We are assured that the actions of one become an attractor force for many. This is a creative force not constrained through conventional thinking that presumes change can only be accomplished by many or through the hierarchy of inspired or domineering leadership as we have known it. Quite the contrary. Barbara Marx Hubbard, in her book "Conscious Evolution," contends that small grassroot islands of higher consciousness in a sea of chaos can jump systems and structures of instability to a higher order of consciousness, freedom, and connectivity. It is through synergistic networks of those predisposed to positive action and higher resonance that we can avoid the collapse of our life support systems as foreseen by many.

This sounds ominous but it need not be. We are being given a gateway, a planetary opening for higher consciousness that is unprecedented for the unprecedented times in which we live. Systems and structures, we once thought permanent and immovable are collapsing at an incredible speed. Nevertheless, it is precisely in times of great change and instability that the greatest possible change can occur. And the breakdown we are witness to is counterbalanced by the breakthrough of the many finding their path to higher consciousness. It is in higher consciousness where the reknowing and recreation of systems, structures, as well as the conventions that underpin them, must take place. It is in the phenomenon of non-linear, exponential interaction of innovations and solutions, that spontaneous self-organization occurs. It is neither forced nor planned but rather *emerges*, enabled through the alchemy of the right ingredients spontaneously interacting with the change agent of higher consciousness.

This *emergence* made possible with islands of higher consciousness, requires something else—connectivity. A connectivity through innovative media platforms that highlight the newsworthy, not what is breaking down, but what is working. A megaphone for breakthroughs and successes to be replicated, built upon, and advanced. Such platforms would act as stimuli to awaken creativity and connect ideas. Remember the invariant law that we cannot solve a problem at the same level of consciousness with which it was created. In lower consciousness we are drawn to the drama of the broken—broken hearts, broken systems, broken people. The innovative solutions never reside in what does not work but is their reconceptualization of that which is possible in a spirit of collaboration, not competitiveness.

We are at this critical juncture, this precipice of devolution or evolution. We are losing patience with ourselves. There are now many cracks and we must choose whether the way forward is in patching them up or following the light that has been let through. In a sense it is a time of reckoning. We must acknowledge that we are witnessing the inevitable dismantling of what we *miscreated* in our politics, our economy, the media, systems of governance and social and educational structures. Much depends on how we respond to these challenges and the invitation of higher consciousness to guide our choices as we move forward.

Aspects of Consciousness

There are aspects of consciousness imbedded throughout the methodology. The aspects of consciousness are seeking, awakening, awareness, knowing, self-realization, insight and enlightened. These aspects are loosely tied to the seven alchemic stages and are depicted in the Level 1 chart. Their depiction is not intended to be interpreted as the evolution from one state of consciousness to the next but simply co-existing as dimensions of consciousness. In other words, we do not progress out of one to the other so much as we carry one dimension forward into the other. Each aspect reveals something different about consciousness and the journey towards higher consciousness. At each stage of the alchemic journey, we are gifted with an insight into a particular dimension to explore and nurture.

In this way, each dimension is both seeding an aspect of consciousness and describing its ultimate fulfilled state. For example, the state of awakening is both a beginning and an end. You are awakening at the onset of the journey and fulfilled as *the awakened one* in higher consciousness. You are always in a process of awakening. What follows is but a brief description of these aspects of consciousness.

Seeking (Calcination)

Is there more to life or have I got more to give to life? A *spiritual homesickness* is at the essence of *the seeker.* The beginner's mind, humble and malleable and ever expanding, ever searching. The dimension of consciousness that seeks ever deeper truths. It is the path to self-discovery that is lifelong. It is the continuous search for meaning and purpose. It is also the quest to vibrationally align the trinity of body, mind, and soul through the spiritualization of all three. To be a *Seeker* is the one answering the universe's call to travel further and deeper.

Awakening (Dissolution)

Awakening to the vast potential of all that lies within. This is the essence of *the awakened.* It is the initiation of one's spiritual path and the soul's cry for freedom. It is the ability to see the illusions of this world through a malleable mind. You understand that nothing external can bring you happiness and fulfillment, and no one can fix you other than yourself. You awaken to the power and resolve within to forge your spiritual path. In fulfillment, *the Awakened One* achieves a higher state of being and becomes a wayshower for those still seeking.

Awareness (Separation)

To know thyself is an essential part of the spiritual journey. It is the aspect of consciousness that is about self-discovery meaning to be aware of our beliefs, thoughts, feelings, habits and behaviours. It is being deeply aware of how you interact with life, how you have been shaped by your experiences and how you attract the experiences required for your soul's growth. You cannot change your beliefs, behaviours or habits without first being aware of what lies deep within the subconscious as limiting programming. It is this awareness of what needs to be released and cleared that allows you to elevate your vibrational signature. The *One in Awareness* is in recognition of their internal landscape with the understanding of the truth of who they are, what they are and how they serve.

Knowing (Conjunction)

Knowing simply is. There is a fundamental difference between believing, having faith, and knowing something to be true. Believing means you have accepted a truth and having faith implies a belief that is unprovable. Knowing is a heart-centred certainty that goes beyond believing. You do not have to believe, you just know. It is not an intellectual knowing but a felt knowingness founded in truth. It is unshakeable. Knowing anchors consciousness deeply within. *The One Knowing* needs no outer authority and has the power to influence, transform, and enhance through their conviction and presence.

Self-Realization (Fermentation)

Self-realization is the fulfillment of one's full potential. It is the essence of becoming everything you are meant to be, through the lessons that life brings. Spiritual grazers or dabblers fail to embody spirituality and to live life in that realized authenticity. Self-realization is a gradual process of unfolding and sustained mindfulness. It is rarely linear but a spiral of unfolding transformation, refined through the ebb and flow of life. Indeed, it is life's lessons that provide the opportunity to be tested, and self-realized. To be fully self-realized, both the small self and higher self are required to be in vibratory coherence and complementarity—each performing their necessary functions in accord with each other.

Insightful (Distillation)

Spiritual insight is the second sight of the third eye. The third eye sits above our two physical eyes and from its elevated perspective offers observation and soul whispered wisdom. You observe what others can only see. It is the result of seeing beyond what our senses alone can perceive, the inner nature of things revealed, the divine within all creation. It is the perception of the wholeness of a thought or situation and the deep understanding of the connection and interdependence of all things. The one who is *Insightful* sees the patterns of creation, beyond the illusionary nature of time and space. This aspect of consciousness is often referred to as intuitiveness but there is a distinction. Intuitiveness is the ability to understand a situation immediately, without the need for conscious reasoning. It is formed through the instantaneous capture of knowledge, experiences, and memory—and as such is subjective. Insight is objective as it comes from the observation and understanding of the interrelationship and interdependence (cause and effect) of patterns, that in turn leads to a profound revelation, producing that *aha* moment.

Enlightened (Coagulation)

Enlightenment is often understood as the ultimate manifestation of consciousness—as in you have arrived at the end of your path. However, as an aspect of consciousness, it is more helpful to view this term simply as a state that brings progressively more light to your path. In this way, it is understood as directional and not a goal. It is to be aimed for rather than reached. Bringing in more light implies an understanding of our true nature as *beings of light*. There is both light and lightness in the concept of higher consciousness and in the concept of becoming. The one who is *En-light-ened* enjoys the path lit as they walk it.

Consciousness as Vibrational Credibility

All aspects of consciousness reside within you. There is nothing missing inside of you. This mosaic of attributes is at the ready, ready to be a source of spiritualization, of guidance throughout your journey. Initially you may understand them intellectually as something that one should aim for. However, over time they take on more meaning as the alchemy transforms a superficial understanding to an embodied, felt state. Each aspect is discrete yet incomplete. They form an indispensable part of the whole of consciousness. And in the alchemy of their interaction with one another, the body, mind, and soul are transformed. There is both a vibrational alignment and vibrational credibility when consciousness is at the core of your truth. You are the living presence of consciousness through your thoughts, words, emotions, and actions—reverberating endlessly into the universe.

PART THREE

APPLYING HIGHER GUIDANCE
TO EVERYDAY LIFE

APPLYING HIGHER GUIDANCE TO EVERYDAY LIFE

Introduction

While experiencing the wonders of the 4th and 5th dimensions, you have developed some pretty amazing abilities and tools, the most powerful of which is being able to connect with higher guidance. Higher guidance is available to you 24/7; is eager to serve, and has your highest good as its prime directive. And having mastered the art of the neutral mind, it will unfailingly provide you with honest answers no matter how profound or mundane the question (as long as it is framed to elicit a yes or no answer). Now if anyone had suggested this was possible before you started this transformation, you would surely dismiss the notion as simply too good to be true. But true it is, and you have this amazing compass by which to guide your way. And your way is still playing out in the 3rd dimension—that of everyday life with all its comfort, beauty, stresses, frustrations, and Newtonian constraints of time and space.

A question that naturally arises is whether this power can be used to ask about the future. The past is known, and the present is unfolding based on your current decisions. The future exists as possibilities in the Quantum Field, based on the choices you make in the NOW. Your will, as exercised by your choices, cannot be tampered with by anyone or anything, and it is that which determines the future. Each thought, decision, word, emotion and action you take is a trajectory for what happens next. The future is what *you* make it to be. This is life happening from within you. The connection with higher guidance ensures that decisions made in the present will have the best possible ramifications for the future.

Our days are made up of a series of never-ending decisions ... what to wear, eat for breakfast, the roads to travel to work, the groceries to buy, books to read, lectures to attend. All those little ones mixed in with bigger ones like *should we have another child? Is this the right career for me? Does this relationship support and nurture my soul?* Quite dizzying if you stop and think about the incredible daily array of possibilities we have before us, and the consequences of making a choice that does not serve our overall well-being.

And the right choice for some may be the exact opposite for others. The concept of *individuated divinity* as discussed earlier, speaks to the fact that you are entirely unique. No one has or will ever have your individual blend of abilities and characteristics, nor your singular mix of genetic markers, biology, and chemistry. One of the downsides of our modern reality, resulting either from a lack of understanding, marketing, or simple practicality, is that we are bombarded with information that suggests that we are all alike. *This diet will work for you, everyone should take this supplement every day, this product will make your wrinkles disappear, this food will make you healthy, this kind of exercise will make you strong and energetic.* In fact, because of our innate uniqueness, we all need different things at different times.

You have entered the realm of customized well-being. What you eat, what supplements you take, what you put on your skin, and even what kind of exercise is good for you, can now be tailored exactly to you. How can you make this happen? Simply modify Nike's tagline of "Just Do It" to "*Just Ask*".

To illustrate how powerfully and simply this can be done, Diane and I are happy to share with you how we have incorporated higher guidance into our daily lives. There has been much laughter when even we, after having debated the pros and cons of a specific approach ad nauseam, finally stop when one of us says ... why don't we *just ask?*

Please note that these suggestions are meant to empower you to take more responsibility for your overall well-being and in no way replace or override the advice of medical professionals.

Application 1: The food we eat

What we ingest by way of the calories we consume plays a significant role in our overall health, and there are a plethora of books, articles, videos, blogs, and websites dedicated to this subject. When the latest diet fad is promoted, we rush to buy the book only to find that while it works for a period of time, it's simply not sustainable and any lost weight is more often than not regained. Off to the shelves to gather dust and remind us of our apparent lack of discipline. But what if ... you could determine exactly what your body needs when it needs it?

Your body loves diversity. In fact, under the umbrella of the growing field of Functional Medicine, the microbiome of your gut is becoming a fascinating field of study and all indications are that the diversity of the healthy microbes in your gut plays a huge role in your overall physical and mental health. And what fuels this healthy diversity? A healthy and diverse diet. Kale, a wonderful dark leafed plant that is full of nutrients and fibre would be a welcome addition to any plate, but if it was all that we ate we would eventually suffer from malnutrition. One of the challenges we face is that we are creatures of habit and tend to eat the same food all the time. How different is your grocery list from week to week? A great place to start diversifying is to first determine how healthy the items in your cupboards and refrigerator are for you. Use the sway and the 1–10 scale to determine if there are any you should remove from your grocery list, and which ones are keepers. The next time you go to the grocery store, pick out a few items such as fruits and vegetables that you have never tried, and see how you react (sway) to them. Keep measuring different offerings and start building your own personalized, "life force diet." *We don't know what we don't know.*

And speaking of shopping, when you are selecting a new item or brand, a handy skill to perfect is the art of "fake reading" those tiny ingredient labels. What you are really doing is waiting for the sway to tell you if this is a yes or no purchase. You can rely on the strength of the sway to indicate its relative life force for you or ask if it is above a 9 on a 1–10 scale. Note the difference between organic and non-organic products! If we are shopping together, I may find a product that sends me flying forward while that same item will elicit a negative response from Diane. Making recommendations to others based on what works for you just doesn't make sense. We are all different.

Once you get home with your carefully selected items, the real fun begins. What you eat and when you eat can be optimized as well, *you just need to ask.* Your guides know exactly what you need given the state of your systems, biology, and chemistry at any given time. When opening the fridge to pick out a snack, ask if this is what you should be eating. You will be amazed at the results, especially when you get a yes to that piece of chocolate cake. (The soul needs sustenance too.) Sometimes you will get a series of nos no matter what you select—which means you actually don't need anything! Of course, you can ignore your higher guidance, there is no judgment here. As a side note, when I first started doing this I was directed away from any and all sugar, including fruit. I was an acknowledged sugarholic which was playing havoc with my pancreas and I had to completely detox. It lasted 6 weeks at which time I was able to slowly introduce back a limited amount of fruit, dark chocolate, and a few other indulgences. If this direction had come from anyone else but my higher guidance, I would not have had the discipline to follow through. When you have this kind of belief, making changes to lifelong habits becomes remarkably effortless. My cravings disappeared as did 10 lb of unnecessary weight. (True confession time... I never did give up my cherished glass of wine—I think my guides knew that this was the line in the sand).

It may sound like a lot of extra work, but it becomes very natural and the benefits to your health and waist line give you the incentive to make it a regular part of your life. *Just Ask.*

Application 2: The supplements we take

The same goes for supplements, perhaps even more so. Much shelf space is dedicated to vitamins and supplements and there is great variability in the quality and quantity of ingredients in each. To get started, measure what is already in your cabinet for overall value to you. When you are in the supplement aisle in your pharmacy, identify those that your body wants by picking them up, connecting and waiting for your response. (Remember to read those labels carefully ☺.) This can take time, but your newly enhanced intuition may help direct you to particular ones. Each morning, before you eat breakfast ask if there are any vitamins you need to take on an empty stomach (collagen and iodine are a couple that work best for me after fasting). Repeat that exercise after you have eaten as well. You will be directed to the ones you need at that point in time, and the quantity of each. Some days you may be asked to take many, other days none at all. Over time, once you have corrected an imbalance or altered your diet, you may not need some of your supplements. Its wisdom is uncanny and almost like you are having daily blood tests to determine what your body needs. If it's a grey day in the middle of winter, I will be directed to take 3000 mg of vitamin D. If it's sunny and I'll spend time outside, none at all. *Just Ask.*

I am writing this during the first wave of the coronavirus (Covid-19) outbreak, and I noticed a dramatic increase in the amount of vitamins C, D and Zinc I was being directed to take. It may be that for me, they are protective factors against the virus, but remember that it's what I need, not necessarily what you need. *And if your doctor has prescribed or recommended a supplement heed that advice.*

Application 3: Skin and hair care

Your skin has a microbiome of its own. And it too loves diversity. Using the same face cream every day is something that is quite common, as is loyalty to certain brands. Perhaps not as dramatic as the Kale example but putting the same product on our skin each day may eventually decrease its efficacy and ignore other needs. So why not diversify your portfolio? We have adopted the practice of having three of everything—toners, serums, creams (face and body) foundation, sunscreen, etc. The initial investment to triple your line-up may be a little daunting, but it will not be more expensive overall as your products will last 3 times as long. You will, however, need more space! The same thing goes for your cleansers and shampoos. Using the sway, find ones that register above a 9.5 for you, and keep exploring the many options available. Once you have your new array of products, ask which ones you should use each day—and notice the variability in combinations that are recommended.

I can't tell you how many people commented on my improved appearance once I adopted this strategy! The days of recommending products to others are over for us. We have learned that what is a 9.5 or above for one, can be below 5.0 for another. *Just Ask.*

Application 4: Physical activity

There is no doubt that your body benefits from movement and from weight-bearing exercise. In fact, it loves it. There are as many exercise options as there are diet books and not all are tailored to your needs. Again, here is an opportunity to use your powers to determine what your body needs on any given day. You may need a brisk walk followed by a bodybuilding class, a Hatha yoga workout, or a Jazzercise session. A useful way to approach this is to create your own chart, similar to the Lower Frequency Emotion chart with columns and rows and fill them with exercise options. As we generally gravitate to what we are comfortable with and what we do well, we subconsciously choose these modalities over others that your body is in fact in need of. If I am doing a class, before we start, I look at the instructor's body to get an idea of what muscle groups are going to be emphasized. If that instructor has a particularly great upper body, be prepared for your arms and shoulders to be sore the next day. It's human nature. Using a chart and the sway will help stretch you (pun intended) in ways that will better serve your overall well-being. Your body temple loves diversity.

Another somewhat overlooked aspect of exercise is related to whether you identify as an introvert or an extrovert. The differentiating factor here is *how* you replenish your energy. Extroverts are often described as the life of the party. Their outgoing, vibrant nature draws people to them, they love attention and being at the centre of gatherings. They thrive off the interaction and are energized by it. On the other side are introverts. They typically are characterized as more reserved and while they may engage in many social activities, they need time away from others to recharge their energy. Most people seem to be a complicated combination of both, and every gathering benefit from a good mix. Being aware of your tendency is especially important when choosing your exercise options as one may in fact drain your energy as opposed to replenishing it. Many of my best holidays have been spent travelling through various countries aboard a bike with a guide and a small group of people. I strongly identify as an introvert and enjoy meeting new people, but when I'm peddling, I much prefer to be in my own head rather than keeping up a steady stream of conversation—for me that's exhausting. I was directed to a daily practice of Jason Quitt's "Egyptian Salute to The Sun" postures to replenish my energy and strengthen spiritual connection, whereas Diane, who is more on the extrovert scale, uses Donna Eden's 7-minute daily routine when in need of an energy boost.

There is not a lot of literature dedicated to this concept as it applies to exercise, but when trying out new options, note what effect various forms of exercise have on your energy levels. Your higher guidance will know what works for you and steer you accordingly. *Just Ask.*

Application 5: Reading and other leisure activities

You can read for pleasure and relaxation—momentarily losing yourself in a good mystery or historical fiction can be great for relieving stress and resetting your mood. The same goes for TV programs and movies, all wonderful pastimes when pursued in a balanced way. When you are reading or watching video programming for learning, this is where your guide can help optimize your knowledge acquisition and time. Diane makes great use of her guides in not only choosing the books, videos and authors that informed this journey and her spiritual growth, but what sections of the material contain the messages and information most needed at that point in time. When choosing a book to read, you can ask how it rates on your 1–10 logarithmic scale—it can help you quickly decide if it's a good use of your time and energy. What we have learned is that once again these are very individual, and that your rating may change over time. Sometimes you are simply not ready to easily absorb the content and vibrational frequency of the material, other times it's exactly the right thing at the right time. *Just Ask.*

There are so many ways that you can use your power to connect to enhance your daily activities. What has been outlined here are but a few of the possibilities. What is critical is developing a neutral mind when asking for guidance. Your earlier experiences of identifying negative and positive emotions by using columns, lines, and numbers, is a perfect way of experiencing the *feeling* of the neutral mind and the freedom that comes from not being attached to the outcome. If you are in an emotional state, overly tired or stressed, it will be difficult. A brief meditation to clear your mind in advance is very helpful and you can always limit your biases by creating charts of possible answers and using the sway to hone in on your answer.

Practicing the sway in these practical ways is a necessary pathway in the development of your intuition. Some may feel that they actually don't need the sway to get their answers, but we strongly encourage you to use it. The developmental stages of an infant are instructive here. A baby may be able to go from sitting to walking physiologically but skipping the crawling stage has been proven to have negative consequences as those movements are important in developing left brain/right brain coordination. Over time and as your vibrational signature rises, you may be able to use your intuition as effectively as the sway but practicing this technique will only enhance this possibility.

And you are free to heed your higher guidance or not. We are not perfect and far from consistent—our imperfections are a launching pad for growth. You will never be punished, admonished, or judged; those actions are simply not in the lexicon of our higher guidance. Experiment and enjoy your powers with a sense of lightness. Use them to reexamine how you can improve your Petri dish in other areas of your life and bring a little more of heaven to earth.

Karen Diguer

PART FOUR

THE INVARIANT LAWS

THE INVARIANT LAWS

The alchemic methodology as presented is underpinned with what the guides refer to as invariant laws. Invariant laws are truths that are universal and timeless in their application not only to the methodology but everything beyond seen and unseen, known, and unknown. Each author, the luminaries of this work, was aligned vibrationally to these laws and as such, these laws underpin their contributions to planetary higher consciousness.

These spiritual laws support the prime directive of transcending current levels of consciousness. They form a backbone of integrity to the work and the progression of understanding and acceptance. They appear here in no particular order of importance. This is because there is none required, and their relevance will be understood in a pattern unique to those who awaken through this methodology. They do appear here, numbered, but only for ease of reference.

Law 1—Empowerment. Supporting the prime directive of raising consciousness is the notion of empowerment. Everyone, without exception has the innate ability to raise their consciousness through intention and will. There is to be no dependency on anyone or anything to embark on this journey of becoming. The methodology is intended to be self-guiding and for those able and willing to journey. There is no judgment attached to any choice.

Law 2—Connecting to higher guidance is your source of empowerment. Higher guidance is something you tap into. It is a relationship to a force far greater than us, far greater than the limitations of our thinking minds. This guidance is available anytime, anywhere with no conditions or judgment. It will provide answers to your questions framed to provide what your soul seeks and needs at that moment. It is non-interfering meaning that you must ask. It is the law of request. It is a trust you develop over time and it becomes embodied over time in the form of intuitiveness. It is the source of your knowing.

Law 3—We are gifted the power and responsibility of will. Will is of the highest order and an essential life force embodied in our spirit and in every breath we take.

Law 4—Body, mind and soul are indivisible. The methodology is designed to apply higher consciousness to all, to awaken all, to heal all and to nourish all, that being body, mind, and soul. Each has different requirements to come into alignment; meditation for the mind, energy practices for the body and reflection time for the soul. There is no fixing here from the outside. The work is within, done at the energetic level and the results are felt physically, mentally, and spiritually.

Law 5—This methodology is not about renunciation of life. It is about embracing life to its fullest, to experience all that life has to offer in its array of contrasts. We learn from every experience and every experience is our teacher in growth.

Law 6—*As simple as can be, but no simpler* underpins every stage and process within the methodology. It is work and understanding reduced to its simplest form.

Law 7—We cannot heal or make whole from the same level of consciousness that created the dis-ease or separation of body, mind, and soul. We can manage the symptoms but true freedom from suffering, from our brokenness, must come from the purview and power of higher consciousness.

Law 8—Everything is vibrating energy. No matter how solid something appears it is frequencies of energy in vibrational accord. No matter how unseen it is, such as thoughts, emotions, and information, they are nonetheless a form of energy.

Law 9—Energy is encoded information. There is no empty space and space is not empty. The universe itself is *in-formation* and encoded with information which we can learn to tune into as we do with tuning into a radio frequency.

Law 10—Energy is always in motion, the law of flow. We are either expanding or contracting through the choices we make.

Law 11—We each have a *vibrational signature*. It is our unique radio station emitting its own frequency. Our vibrational signature is made up of a combination of lower and higher held frequencies as a reflection of our consciousness state of body, mind, and soul.

Law 12—Energy is everything and connects everything. Boundaries between objects are illusionary. We and our lives are not separate. We are connected to every other living and inanimate structures of our planet. Our planet is connected to every part of the cosmos.

Law 13—We are co-creators of an expanding universe. We are collectively creating the universe with every thought, emotion, and action we express throughout our lives. We matter. Think of it not unlike how we are forming and expanding the World Wide Web whether we just look at it or interact with it. Even just looking at a site, empowers it. We hold great responsibility individually and in the collective.

Law 14—The law of choice. The universe holds infinite possibilities and within the realm of possibilities, we exercise choice in the encounters and experiences that shape our lives. Every choice is an opportunity for the soul's growth. We cannot always control what comes our way, but we always exercise choice in how we respond. The choice is to meet the encounter in the frequency it holds or to uplift it vibrationally by nature of our response. The higher self is never a victim.

Law 15—The imperative for the soul's growth. The soul is eternal, and the soul has a purpose. Each soul houses the blueprint for its growth, meaning its spiritualization and expression as individuated divinity. The journey of becoming is awakening to the soul's purpose.

Law 16—Time, as we know, and experience it, is illusionary. It is a reality of the 3rd dimension and our challenge is to accept that power only truly exists in the NOW. The NOW is the only "time" of infinite possibilities at our disposal.

Law 17—Consciousness is the force driving evolution. We are meant to evolve as beings of consciousness and our survival as a species depends on this. Evolving consciousness is aligned to the evolutionary force of the cosmos. For the first time, we, in great numbers, are conscious of our consciousness. We are aware that consciousness is evolving. Evolution is a choice we now exercise.

Law 18—Everything that has been created can be re-created to be in alignment with its true nature. Divinity is the true nature of all that is of creation and there can be no exclusion to this in the physical and non-physical realms.

Law 19—The law of miracles. A miracle is a wonder that defies the beliefs we hold. It is the action of creator forces beyond what is in the known realm of science. You can experience wonder without science and to do so will elevate your frequency. Everything can and will be explained scientifically once science is released from denser frequencies.

Law 20—We are individuated divinity. That divinity is expressed in *who we are* as unique expressions of the creative force. There never has been nor will be another expression of us. That divinity is expressed in *what we are,* as expressed in form and in *how we serve* as beings of consciousness.

Law 21—Our purpose is to be the highest expression of our individuated divinity. Purpose is not in the doing of life but of being a presence of high consciousness. This is inherent within the journey of becoming. We become not the expression of our small selves but the expression of our higher selves in the service of raising consciousness from our presence of simply being.

Law 22—It is through the transmission of energy that transformation occurs. This is not a methodology of will power or self-control, nor is it a journey premised on guilt or fear. It is not a journey of the should dos but the journey of why don't I? We let energy do the work, but work it is. The intention to raise consciousness, to raise our vibrational signature must be there, coming not from a place of fear but from a place of belief and knowing. It is the work of discovering who you are in order to become.

Law 23 — "As above, so below; as within, so without." This is the law of correspondence. The higher our consciousness, the deeper we can travel to uncover our true divinity and through that divinity, our purpose. All change must first come from within. As within is reflected in what lies without. Our lives are our individual and collective creation through the exercise of choice. If you want to know what lies within someone, look at their lives and choices.

Law 24—The law of intention. Intentions are more powerful than wants, wishes, or hopes. Intentions release a force that honours the noble effort and purity of ideals coming from the higher self. It is the basis of manifestation.

Law 25—Manifesting comes with its own rules. Manifesting is the command to the universe to bring something into *realized* form. It is an ask. It must not be in the form of a want, thwarted want, or plea, for these come from a place of fear and scarcity. Nor can it come from a place of indifference. Manifestation must come from the place of the already realized. This means that you envision the ask as already granted, already realized in your gratitude to the outcome.

Law 26—Mature manifesting comes with accessing the infinite possibilities held in the Quantum Field. When you manifest from your known parameters, you will manifest from known possibilities. Specificity narrows the field of possibilities. Alternatively, when you choose to manifest from a set of broad conditions around outcomes, you broaden the range of possibilities to beyond your known field of experience. Something far greater can emerge to serve your soul's needs.

Law 27—The law of attraction. Energy of a certain frequency attracts and entrains like frequencies. Our vibrational signature radiates outwards and will attract like vibrations. Low vibrational signatures will result in lower densities of life happening to us. We can be fated to repeat negative experiences and influences in our lives even as we are unaware of these life patterns. Such patterns are well established in our subconscious behaviours and habits which draw us to experiences and people within a familiar context. The inverse is equally true. A high frequency will attract positive, inspiring experiences within our lives. In such cases when we encounter a lower frequency situation, we learn to refrain from reacting from a like frequency. We understand we have the choice to respond and reframe the situation in higher frequency.

Law 28—Everything can be known anew and re-created in higher consciousness. There is no permanence other than consciousness. In order to create something anew, you must strip it of it worth, its history, meaning and value. This is *Unmanifesting*. To re-create ourselves from higher consciousness, we must unmanifest our negative past imprints, our cultural dictates and beliefs that no longer serve. Everything is malleable. Everything is in transition.

Law 29—We are eternal souls within a body. Our form has no permanence, but our consciousness does, and we come back over lifetimes of consciousness held in different forms.

Law 30—To release something, it must be known or acknowledged. The methodology is a means to shed negative and misspent energies held within us. But to do so is a process that must make these negative imprints known to us before they can be released and replaced with higher frequency imprints.

Law 31—Within the methodology you are never given anything you are not ready for or cannot handle.

Law 32—The answer to every problem lies in the problem.

Law 33—The cycle of breakdown to breakthrough permeates all life force. We have to break down, to unmanifest before the breakthrough comes. Energy spins as in a vortex of expansion and contraction, of breaking down to breaking through in renewed energy.

Law 34—Alchemy is the process for transformation through a continuous cycle of breaking down to breaking through.

PART FIVE

LEVELS OF TRANSFORMATION—
OVERVIEW

LEVELS OF TRANSFORMATION—OVERVIEW

"It's your road and yours alone.
Others may walk it, but no one can walk it for you." — Rumi

The cycle of breakdown to breakthrough is just that—an ongoing cycle of transformation. As a being in motion, you are always becoming. You are knowing yourself in greater truth, greater love and in progressive mastery of self, as purpose. There are levels to this journey. Each level is a transmission of information and frequency that allows for higher levels of consciousness. It is a choice to journey yet deeper within to attain yet higher levels of enlightenment. "As above, so below." Each level builds upon the preceding one. The levels act as spiritual foundations supporting progressively higher alignment of body, mind, and soul as indivisible and individuated divinity. And as with any foundation, integrity is key to strength and resilience.

The alchemic methodology is that key to integrity. The guidance will not be there for the next level if you are not ready. It is a form of protection. The learnings, healings and transmissions of frequency must be fully embraced and embodied at one level in order to proceed to the next. And once embraced and embodied, it is your intention that opens the door to furthering the journey.

The choice to travel deeper and further is not for everyone. Know that achieving the first level is an incredible accomplishment in its own right. For many there may not be the need to go further and, in that case, know that you have journeyed and journeyed well. For others, they may be guided to await a different phase in their life to undertake a deeper journey. No matter: the journey awaits all those who seek. There is no right or wrong; there is no judgment.

As we have come to understand this, there are 4 levels of transformation as channelled thus far *(see Figure 8)*. They are all levels to becoming for this is a journey of discovering who you are meant to become. A level is one pass through the 7 alchemic steps. These 7 steps are repeated in sequence, albeit with different themes and greater understanding and skills to be mastered with each level. The levels are as follows:

- **Level 1 transformation**—From Life Happening to You to Life Happening from Within You
  <u>Theme</u>: You as truth (living in authenticity and sovereignty, a place of inner power)
- **Level 2 transformation**—From Life Happening from Within You to Life Happening Through You
  <u>Theme</u>: You as love (understanding love and creation as frequency channelled through you and expressed by you)
- **Level 3 transformation**—From Life Happening Through You to Life Happening as Enlightened by You
  <u>Theme</u>: You as light (in service of elevating situations to states of wholeness)
- **Level 4 transformation**—From Life Happening as Enlightened by You to Life Happening as You
  <u>Theme</u>: You as realized individuated divinity (full expression — "Being of Divinity")

ALCHEMY OF BECOMING: LEVELS OF TRANSFORMATION

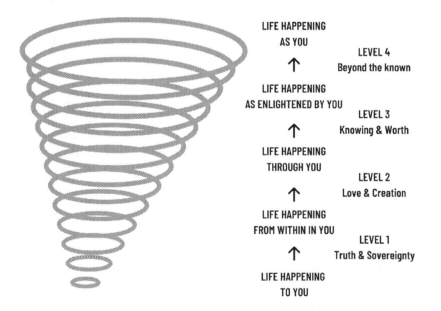

Figure 8

The characterization of the levels is an adaptation from the brilliance of Michael Beckwith's book, "Life Visioning". Michael's four levels of consciousness were also incorporated in "The Code of the Extraordinary Mind" by Vishen Lakhiani. Both works provide powerful insights into visioning progressive levels of consciousness from one's vantage point. In other words, what your life looks like as you achieve higher levels of consciousness.

While the content here is different and drawn from numerous sources, it remains consistent with Beckwith's overall characterization of levels. The methodology in "The Alchemy of Becoming" uses the alchemic formula of transformation to systematically bridge from one level to the next. The methodology also adds specific themes that run through each level. Each level demands its own book, and the following is intended to provide but a brief introduction.

Level 1: From life happening to you to life happening from within you

Level 1 is the subject of this manual. This is the level where we break free of the limitations of the third dimension. The third dimension is the level in which we acquire the skills to navigate the world around us. We learn to conform to the norms and expectations of this outer landscape. In the collective we work together to establish the rules of conduct that govern our lives. It is a world of hierarchical structures and conditionality. You are worth something if ...; you are loved if ..., you are considered to be an upstanding citizen if.... It is both collaborative and competitive and mastering the rules of engagement is necessary, even essential to one's survival.

The glue that binds is, for the most part, fear and control based. There are the forces of love, trust and freedom but these are all conditional on a solid foundation of deterrent based governance. To this point in our evolution, it is primarily fear that has ensured our survival. Conformity is the price most of us gladly pay for the illusion of the safety and security that it provides.

We have learned in the collective to live in periods of harmony. However, we tend to be suspicious of the unknown, more comfortable with those most like us and often quick to judge. We are tolerant to the extent we do not feel threatened. We are often made to feel small and powerless particularly in a patriarchal society which has valued equalitarianism in words more than in action. Some have been more adept at mastering this world and certainly on a global level, there are signs of progress. However, we accept the fate of those less fortunate; inequality is simply a fact of how things are. In essence, we find ourselves as both survivors and victims. There is a measured peace in this acceptance and coexistence.

This is the characterization of life happening TO you. You bob and weave to keep your head above water. We often live at the edge of stress, of busyness, of the need to be doing and acquiring the next thing that promises happiness and fulfillment. We live for the moment but never in it. For those that press that pause button long enough to question and reflect on the meaning of life, on their purpose, a path opens up. They become seekers of themselves.

There are many paths. This is but one. This journey begins with the transition of *life happening TO you* to *life happening FROM WITHIN you.* The world of limitations becomes unlimited possibilities. You connect in a real way to higher guidance and you are literally guided step-by-step towards higher consciousness. You reinterpret the world from within; you ignite a power within; you take back power you long ago gave away in fear and compromise. This is the alchemic transformation of finding yourself in authenticity and in sovereignty over the dominion of your life. The journey of becoming starts with understanding **who you are in truth, unmasked.**

There are many learnings to be acquired at this level. The most important is that everything is energy expressed as frequency and that all frequency is encoded with information. You learn to tune into your unique frequencies expressed as your vibrational signature. All aspects of this journey happen at a frequency level. You heal body, mind, and soul at a frequency level. You set intentions as frequency and you manifest your life from frequency.

The sovereignty you acquire is from reordering yourself first and then your life from the inside-out. You begin to validate yourself from within rather than relying on external sources to establish your worth. You understand why and when you are aligning with fear rather than discernment or trust. It is a long and arduous process to replace fear with trust or discernment, but it certainly begins at this level. The laws of transformation demand that you must come to know and acknowledge what does not serve, what needs to be "unblocked" before change can happen. Only then is there a choice to transform through setting a specific intention to do so. This is one of the invariant laws of this journey.

The changes do not happen overnight but change you will. And if the level of your frequency changes so must your life be in accord with that new frequency. There must be resonance. You will find yourself letting go of things that no longer serve you while embracing new experiences. You will find yourself attracting new and welcome possibilities into your life in line with your elevated vibrational signature. Life will seem less happening to you as you are manifesting it from within. It does not mean that you will be able to control everything that happens (as much happens from collective agreement), but you can choose how you respond ... and the choice in responding (rather than reacting) comes from sovereignty and the quality of response comes from authenticity.

Focus of Physical Healing: organs of the body
Level of Consciousness: 350 + (Hawkins scale of consciousness)
Theme: you as truth (authenticity and sovereignty)
Chakra Focus: Root, Sacral, Solar Plexus (the lower chakras as seats of sovereignty, truth and will)

Level 2: From life happening from within you to life happening through you

You begin again with a beginner's mind willing to be a seeker of deeper knowledge and truth. And yes, you have to suspend your belief systems yet again to remain open and malleable to new understanding and skills that await this level.

This is the level of **love and creation** as channelled and expressed through you. This is awakening to a new concept of love. Here love is not a sentiment, emotion, behaviour or connection to an individual; it is a frequency. The frequency carries the information to infuse all creation with love. Your vibrational signature is elevated through this alchemic process to be in alignment with the high frequency of love, as an expression of consciousness. "I am in my frequency of love" is stating the intention that aligns and indeed activates the higher frequency of love.

The choice here is to create from a frequency of love. So, what does this mean? In level one we learned the difference between reacting and responding. You react when life is happening TO you. But when life is happening FROM WITHIN you, from your place of sovereignty and authenticity, *you respond with conscious thought and intent.* It is the merest of pauses, a sacred space where choice enters the equation. The same principle applies to level 2 in the difference between doing and creating. Instead of going through your day in a state of doing, you create from a place of conscious love. You elevate the state of doing with creative intent. Everything you do is an expression of self; every expression of self is an opportunity to create with purpose and intent. This is a choice to infuse the frequency of love in how you express yourself and by extension, what you create in expression. It brings meaning to everything you express; your words, your actions, your interactions. Love as frequency is a creative cosmic force in its own right.

Love as a sentiment is but an aspect of that cosmic force running through you. It is a powerful, uplifting emotion in its focused attention. But you cannot find love anywhere but inside of you. You can find a relationship, but you cannot find love. Love is about cultivating your inner connection to the divine and to the ultimate field of love. When two people have a relationship, they are each accessing that love from their own individual sources.

As Barbara De Angelis states, "A relationship is not the same as love. Love is a vibrational field of sublime, life-enhancing energy. A relationship is a vehicle through which you can experience love. Love doesn't come from the outside of your life in. Love comes from the inside out. Love isn't something we can actually 'get' from anyone else. Love is its own source."

Love exists at lower frequencies but here it is in the domain of the ego, of the small self. Its expression is often conditional and possessive, mired in the need to control and in the fear of loss. All this from a lack of abundance from within. The quality of love you are able to express is dependent on its life force frequency from within you. And the same goes for what you create.

You create at all frequencies. Your thoughts, vision, ideas, sentiments, words, and actions are all expressed creations. When you look at what you create, you can ask yourself whether it was created from a lack of abundance or from fear or the need to control or from the confines of culture and history. You can ask whether your relationship with love and creation keeps you small as in *I only like this, I only eat this, I only like to do these things, I only like those types of people and places, I only see beauty in this and not that.* There is comfort in defining your boundaries, your edges, but it can keep you small—you know what you know, you are what you are, in your limitations.

Love at a high frequency is all inclusive. You can no longer hold the frequency of love for someone and not another. You cannot hold this frequency for one culture over another. When you say, "*I prefer this,*" it is a statement of discernment. It means you are open rather than closed as a mindset and world view. That is progress. To say "*I prefer*" is to acknowledge in truth that you have experienced a broader range and you live life larger. The edges are not hard. What you prefer may expand and change with time and exposure. And you give worth and meaning to a broader spectrum of life. This is about your *breadth of being* and *breadth of creation* which gives you *presence*. You don't just occupy space; you fill that space with your presence—life happening through you as presence.

The *through you* is important here. This is an inspired level of frequency meaning that what you express in love and creation are not forced but comes through you as emanating from a force field of inspiration. More and more, you find yourself *in the zone*. It can feel effortless like you are being uplifted and resistance dissipates. When you speak you did not know you would or could have thoughts so eloquently expressed and on point. You were not exactly aware of what you were about to say. Somehow the right words simply flowed. Or when you write, thoughts as if by divine intervention, simply appear and you can hardly keep up with getting them down on paper. Creative endeavours such as art, music, inventions, and all that you create are somehow uplifted and hold a frequency of inspiration; works created through inspiration which have the power to inspire right back at you. Such is the power of the love frequency.

This level of transformation is about discovering and entering into a powerful relationship with your own infinite field of love; a limitless vibrational field of creative energy. It is the source of all creation. What is created in love will hold the frequency of love.

You can only journey here in sovereignty and authenticity. You can only experience the sacred space of presence from a place of your truth. Thus level 2 is only possible once level 1 had been embraced and embodied. You journey deeper in level 2 to heal deeper systems within your body, mind, and spirit. You release negativity held deeper within and you invite in higher frequencies aligned with love and creation. You unblock, unlock the resistance to aligning with the frequency of love. This cosmic force is channelled through you. Your vibrational signature becomes one of love. As such, life happens through you as your *creative* expression of love.

Focus of Physical Healing:
Connective systems (musculoskeletal, lymphatic, nervous, circulatory, respiratory, integumentary)
Level of Consciousness: 500+
Theme: you as love (love and creation as expressed by you)
Chakra Focus: heart and throat (the seats of expression)

Level 3: From life happening through you to life happening as enlightened by you

Once again, the choice is to begin anew with a beginner's mind to travel yet deeper to further your reach. There are big transitions between levels, and you must be ready to suspend even deeper held beliefs and have the resolve to move out of the known to the unknown. And you must be ready to serve for this is a level where you, as you, are called to be in service.

The purpose of being awakened is to become a wayshower; to forge the path so that others may follow. Knowing yourself in sovereignty and authenticity paved the way for you to express yourself in the frequency of love and to infuse what you create with love. Level 3 is the alchemic process to claim the next octave of frequency allowing you to change the world because you are changed. When you work in high frequency, the power you hold to transform, to heal, to re-create, to re-know something as renewed, is gifted to you. That is what is meant to be *in service*.

This is life enlightened by your presence, by your being, and enlighten here not only means to bring in light as in *to illuminate* the truth of something, but to *lift it from a lower to higher frequency*. You make it lighter. Each of you comes with the ability to transform the world through your encounter with it. You are literally lifting your world in vibratory accord through your presence, intention, and witness to what you observe. You set the intention to align it in higher vibration and it will be enlightened through your intention. It is less about the law of attraction as it is the law of refraction. You become sensitized to the needs of the community or the world itself. You become a tuning fork for your vibration and because your vibration is always an expression of yourself, it is aligning everything that it encounters to its requirements for evolution.

Here your Petri dish no longer depicts just the structures of your life but the systems of the world. The compartments become those of health, education, justice, economic, technology, politics, governance, environment, science, social media, arts, etc. And these exist (are expressed) at all levels of life from the impacts on you, your household, the community you live in, to a regional view, to a country-wide perspective, to hemispheric and ultimately worldwide. The object here is to *realize* them in the same frequency you hold within you as authentic, sovereign and from love and abundance. So how is this done?

This is the domain of the third eye—the ability to see, re-perceive and give meaning, form and voice to a new world view held in freedom from fear and control. It is observing the structures, constructs and systems that govern us, reconceived and evolving as whole and wholesome. You allow the frequency to do what frequency does. You realign the systems or seed them into the higher frequency. There is no proselytizing nor force required. The energy does the work. This works across borders, across cultural lines, religions and languages. Intent is intent. Intention is above the limitations of the physical world.

This understanding of being *in service*, requires your continued commitment to your spiritual journey. You must be prepared to release deeper held negative emotions and attract more powerful attributes to raise your vibrational signature. You no longer just affirm them, you claim them. It is not the small self that has the power to transform the world through the expression of itself. This must come from the higher self and from the knowing and worth that you are Divinity, meaning a creation of Source. Individuated Divinity. It is more than a commitment to being a good person doing good in the world. That is laudable in its own right but this is not what this is about. This is about holding the highest possible level of consciousness that, in itself, will serve to transform the world as you encounter it and envision it.

You will be joined by many others who are becoming awakened in every field of endeavour. And in the collective, all is amplified. In the collective there will be a shift of emphasis from focusing on what does not work to the potential of what could work when viewed from the higher held consciousness of synergistic collaboration. This is so powerful. Synergy is what creates connectivity and connectivity is what creates collaboration, not competition. This is not about a new movement for world change in the conventional sense but an attractor force that spontaneously creates connection, amplification, and order from disparate parts. It is energy as a force of creation.

You know that everything is vibrating energy and that everything is connected, and that energy is encoded information. Energy operates within and outside of the limitations of time, space, and matter. Your added understanding here is that everything is malleable to thought and transitory in nature. To conceive of something in higher consciousness, whether in your life or out in the world, is to view it first with a neutral mind, free of its history and worth.

The governing law here is the *law of unmanifest*. To conceive something with a neutral mind, you must first see it free from its history, its meaning and it's worth. History should not forever bind something in meaning and worth. All that is known and named is a shared narrative, a collective agreement to a landscape that we share and collectively give worth to. This is true whether we are talking about something as physical as a table or as conceptual as a government; in each case we have named them as such and agree in the collective to their respective form and function. And all that is known and named is transitory in nature; the table was once a tree and will eventually become firewood and a government once was simply an idea that became an ideology for the people it serves. The point is all constructs, structures and systems be they government, health, financial, education, food supply system, environmental management, etc. are all ideas we collectively agree to and give meaning to. We have to understand that everything is malleable no matter how solid or immovable it appears. The very fabric of reality is malleable to thought. How you perceive anything gives power to the object of your perception.

You cannot conceive of something presented as new if your investment in the old is paramount. When you un-invest in the meaning and worth of something, you observe it with a neutral mind and that gives it the potential to be transformed. All structures and systems hold consciousness which means they hold information, and they house power. The power they hold is a reflection of the level of consciousness in which they were created. At their core, most were created from the perceived need to exert control, predictability, stability, and self-preservation. There is a choice here to reconceive them in higher consciousness. To do this you must acknowledge the potential of any structure or system to be re-conceived in a new foundation of truth and love. Potential is first known in the higher octave or frequency and then made manifest.

So, the process of stripping away history, narrative, worth and investment to understand something as malleable, is to unmanifest it. To see something and release your investment in the outcome or ideology is to simply see it with a neutral mind. You then conceive a new relationship to it in higher consciousness. What could it look like? How could it serve all of humanity?

We find ourselves on the cusp of great change. This is a time of reckoning. We are being held accountable for what we have created; that which we attach meaning to and invest in and that which we neglect and ignore at our peril. This is not a question of some judgmental force at play; it is a question of sustainability in evolutionary terms. It is a time when the conventions and structures we thought would always preserve our known way of life, for good or bad, are being challenged and in some cases, imploding. Systems we thought would always be, will fail. But all of this holds the potential for making itself new. This is a period of grand breakdowns paving the way for breakthroughs of imagined possibilities from a place of higher consciousness. And the really good news is that there is an unprecedented rise in consciousness across humanity. It is like a rising tide where we are all being lifted. It is a new era of world consciousness, of a world awakening like we have not seen before.

These two things—the breakdown of systems and the rise in consciousness—allow the possibility for unprecedented transformation of our world. And here we are not talking about incremental change but transformative change only possible from a place of higher consciousness. Einstein said that it is not possible to fix something from the same level of consciousness that created it. The key to transformation is to reconceive what is broken, what no longer serves, from the vantage point of higher frequency. A frequency of creativity not held in fear and scarcity but in truth and love as we acquired in levels 1 and 2.

That is where we need to start the reimagined life. That is the potential it holds. And this understanding that all things, all systems, all constructs are vibratory and interconnected is the starting point for all transformation. What is conceived in higher consciousness, will hold the frequency of higher consciousness. If we are of our highest consciousness, what we create through our presence, through our encounters with the world and through the potential we hold to enlighten the world in vibratory accord, will manifest.

As you can see, this is not a level for complacency. Every generation confirms the world they live in. This level creates the awareness that will support the next generation in a new realization of what it means to be human and exist as your divine self. How you choose to serve in this regard is not about doing or necessarily advocating for change. It is being that tuning fork of vibration held at your highest level of consciousness.

Bringing in more light, more love, more synergy to every situation and every person. Intention and frequency changes everything.

The small self is not abandoned here. The small self is an aspect of who you are, what you are and how you serve and is indispensable to navigating the physical plane in which we are expressed in form. But what happens is that the small self is now aligned to truth, love, and light, and it is the re-identification of the small self in vibratory alignment to the higher self that transforms the world. In this way, we understand ourselves both as operatives of the physical realm and as operatives of higher consciousness beyond the physical. Both aspects (small self and higher self) in vibratory alignment collaborate to bridge the physical and non-physical realms.

Never underestimate the power held within each of us to transform the moment we stand in and in so doing change the trajectory of every subsequent moment. Like the butterfly effect, we may never fully appreciate the gesture that changed the evolutionary course of humanity.

Focus of Physical Healing: regulatory systems (digestive, endocrine, urinary, reproductive)
Level of Consciousness: 700+
Theme: you as light (life as enlightened by you)
Chakra Focus: third eye

Level 4: From life happening as enlightened by you to life happening as you, as divinity

This final transition in physical form is life happening as you, as a conscious evolution of individuated divinity. In essence we **prepare to *become* an evolved human species** of higher consciousness. This is an entirely new chapter in the evolution of mankind. So, first some context.

The essence of the creation and expansion of the universe is consciousness. The story of evolution has always been the relentless pursuit of higher consciousness. We are the first in great numbers to know that we are evolving; the first in history to know that we can impact our evolution through our thoughts and actions. The arrow of evolutionary time has taken us from chaos to increasing order, from simple to increasingly complex organisms through a continuous cycle of breakdowns and breakthroughs. The planet has gone through several mass extinctions and the birth of new species following extinctions. We are at an evolutionary shift point; a shift point to potential devolution or evolution. So, this story of evolution now takes on a new twist of choice...

For the first time in our history, we are conscious of our impact on evolution. Not only that, but we are also conscious of our consciousness. Consciousness, once the domain of the very few intellectuals, mystics, or prophets throughout recorded history, has now become mainstream (or at least closing in on mainstream). One only has to look at the proliferation of yoga studios, the growing practice of meditation, the amount of spiritual material and media platforms now available, the rise in energy medicine and Eastern practices to see this startling trajectory over just the last few decades. The awakened are not measured in the few but now in communities.

So not only are we conscious of our consciousness, but we are also conscious of the evolution of our consciousness within ourselves and in the collective. As Barbara Marx Hubbard put it, we are "conscious evolutionaries". There is a growing understanding, even within the scientific field, of a cosmic evolutionary impulse guiding us towards higher consciousness. This awareness has profound implications. Evolution was once the domain of chance; it is now the domain of choice. Awareness and choice bring great responsibility. We are no longer bystanders or victims in evolutionary terms. We are co-creators of the universe and consciousness itself. Through choices in consciousness, we will either no longer serve its evolutionary purpose (and become extinct) or we will transmute to a new evolutionary level; an evolutionary leap of mankind held in higher consciousness.

In level 3, we, as wayshowers, acquire the power to reimagine and reconceive of structures and systems through unmanifesting them of their histories and worth and honouring the essence, the truth of their potential to be realized and serve in a plane of higher consciousness. In this fourth and final level, the power of transformation is turned back towards ourselves, turned inwards as we now unmanifest ourselves in order to re-imagine ourselves transmuting, emerging as a more evolved species. We unmanifest the small self; we take away its history and worth and reconceive it as the divinity held in the higher self. The small self cannot transform; it holds on to what it knows. We release the force of the small self to yield to the power of the higher self to realize us in divine form. It is the action of becoming; of discovering who we are meant to become. The alchemic process of becoming. We become the full expressions of ourselves as a call to the evolutionary process.

Enough of us have to do this. Enough of, meaning not all but a percentage of the awakened among us. There is a tipping point that occurs through something called *spontaneous self-organization* or *emergence*. In scientific terms, when enough non-linear, local interactions occur, the initial disordered, unconnected parts spontaneously self-organize to become a wholly decentralized, robust, and self-determining system. There is an emergence of a new system from seemingly unconnected parts. This is the premise here. Enough of the awakened around the globe, in every field of endeavour, in every discipline, will spontaneously self-organize through the consciousness field.

The very re-creations of systems and structures by the wayshowers of level 3 become vibratory attractor forces in this consciousness field through which all of awakening humanity can ultimately reconceive of itself as new and emerging. Build it and they will come. Forge the paths, build the bridges for others to follow. What this means is that if the systems and structures that serve us are reconceived as whole and wholesome, in their truth and through foundations of love and abundance, the frequency they hold will create a resonant coherence and align all those through which they serve. In essence, we create a new narrative, a new understanding of who we are and what we are and how we serve as this emerging species. It becomes a meme of new belief, of a new culture through a planetary awakening. We become the evolutionary story of the higher self taking over where the small self left off. That is the evolutionary leap. The understanding that we are all connected through one consciousness expressed as individuated divinity.

We have to choose to evolve. The code to this evolutionary leap to an evolved form of humanity is already within us. But we must turn it on, so to speak, by consciously choosing to evolve to the unknown. We have the power at this level to genetically turn on the evolutionary impulse held within every cell within us. As Barbara Marx Hubbard said "It is choosing to say yes to that impulse."

Focus of Physical Healing: foundational coding, cellular and genetic make-up
Level of Consciousness: 900+
Theme: you as realized individuated divinity (full expression — "Being of Divinity")
Chakra Focus: crown

The Quest for Consciousness Capital

The prime directive of this methodology, as is for all spiritual paths, is to create higher levels of consciousness and in so doing, to create what we are calling *consciousness capital*. Consciousness as a new form of capital. The capital you draw upon in your journey of becoming.

The four levels as described are an invitation for the attainment of higher consciousness. They are progressive. It starts with you. You become the change others seek and in so being, you attract those that seek what you have. They may not know it or be able to express it, but the divinity within them is always seeking greater truth. It is of *being* in higher consciousness that you acquire the capacity to uplift all that you encounter. Your resonance is felt. And it is that uplifting vibrational resonance embodied within you, that acts as an attractor force. Without effort, simply through being, you gift the power of your resonance held as capital. But it is also self-capital you draw upon for your own continuous refinement of becoming—becoming all that you are meant to be. It is an endless cycle of building and gifting your capital reservoir of consciousness; higher consciousness, not in an end in itself, but in service of what being in higher consciousness brings forth to you and your life. Building self-capital as a reservoir is the work of level 1.

Successive levels are about understanding the power of that capital through its expression in truth, love and light and its application beyond you to the *us* and *we* of the collective. It's the capital we need to address today's intractable issues and to prepare for those to come. It is the capital needed to change the course trajectory for humankind. The premise is that it is only through the attainment of higher consciousness that the problems created at lower levels of consciousness can be addressed. Consciousness capital is the currency of our future and the Philosopher's Stone of our age.

Our concept of capital has evolved over time. We think of financial capital as investments that earn a higher return than the capital's cost. With social capital, we expand that notion to include assets like public libraries, parks and museums that strengthen communities not so much in financial terms but in evidentiary outcomes. Human capital is the investment in people designed to increase productivity and loyalty in the workplace. Development capital applies to global humanitarian needs addressing the plight of poverty and environmental disasters. In all these cases, the investment in capital has a multiplier effect that attracts investors given the promise of greater dividends be it for business, societal or humanitarian needs.

We are certainly a kinder, more benevolent species than we were a thousand years ago. We have evolved and we will continue to do so. We accept that our well-being is tied to the well-being of others. We are prepared to invest in ourselves, our tribe and even tentatively beyond that. This means that we are prepared to contribute to something greater than ourselves, with the caveat that our individual needs are not unduly compromised, and in fact are met. But the quest for our well-being, individually and collectively has come at a price. Our presence, as a footprint on this planet exacts a cost greater than the benefits we leave behind. We are running a continuous and accelerating deficit with each successive generation. This is not intentional, and we do try to correct this imbalance but we pretty much fail to accept the price it inevitably incurs. Our relationship with the ecosystem that is our planet, is in decline.

But this is not just a reckoning of our past lapses. The future will hold untold possibilities with scientific and technological advances which will increasingly pose difficult moral and ethical challenges. Just because we can do something does not mean we should do so or are collectively prepared for the ramifications and accountability of such advances. We need only think of the issues currently inherent in the manipulation of digital information, algorithms underlying social media platforms, and advances in AI (artificial intelligence) as well as

designer genetics (eugenics) to appreciate the potential undersides, particularly if these are not addressed with collective higher consciousness at the helm. *Simply put our well-being is likely to be seriously compromised if our capabilities outpace the maturity of our consciousness to anticipate and manage tomorrow's ethical dilemmas.*

Our notion of what constitutes well-being must stretch well beyond ourselves to include all that is, seen and unseen, known and unknown. If that sounds laudable but impossible, it is—at least at lower levels of consciousness. No amount of discipline, force, threat, or inspired leadership is likely to change the course trajectory to the degree and urgency that is required. The real question is why? For one, our ability to accept each decline as the new normal is quite astonishing. We adapt. We rationalize. We deny. We carry on. However, the greater truth may be that we simply do not have the capacity. As long as our world view is one of fear, scarcity and greed, we are in a zero-sum field of energy. This means that for every good for someone or something there is a corresponding cost or loss for someone or something else.

A world view of abundance cannot co-exist with a world view of scarcity. And the world view of scarcity is held as our current level of consciousness. If we elevate our level of consciousness, so too do we uplift our world view from fear and control to one of abundance and gratitude. Abundance is collaborative, not competitive. It seeks the inherent truths in the diversity and uniqueness of expression of who we are and what we are. Abundance is about seeing the wholeness, the interdependencies and synchronicity in the world around us and the alignment of ourselves and of our creations to that reality.

At its essence, this is the quest for consciousness capital as a new world and planetary view. It is the premise and promise of a vastly different trajectory for humankind through the innovations, inspirations and desires for a new world order. The capital in consciousness capital is a currency in the form of a global living reservoir of those awakened, of awareness, of high consciousness, inviting collaboration and harmony not only amongst ourselves but with all other living species and nonliving forms that inform and shape the planet. There is alchemy in the collective, an exponential power, an emergence of a higher order. This can only be acquired through a journey of becoming the highest possible level of consciousness available to us, individually and collectively. The higher perspective of elevated consciousness allows for clarity and purpose; the re-knowing of what has been created in lower consciousness and the necessary consciousness maturity we need for the future.

PART SIX

STEPPING STONES TO GREATER UNDERSTANDING

STEPPING STONES TO GREATER UNDERSTANDING

In many ways, the journey is like travelling to a foreign country in which you share the same language, but the dialect is different. Words you are familiar with, take on a different meaning and then there are expressions you've never heard—a total fabrication of the locale you happen to be in. The customs often appear a bit strange too, sometimes quaint but difficult to navigate. You find yourself looking for a guidebook to help bridge the two worlds. And the two worlds to be bridged are science and spirituality. This is that guidebook. There are concepts and terminology that you have to get your head around. And while there are many excellent reference sources, the following is intended to provide a brief introduction to the ones that serve as stepping stones to your understanding of the journey. Further exploration of any or all, is highly encouraged.

Energy

"If you want to find out the secrets of the universe, think in terms of energy,

frequency and vibration" — Nicola Tesla

"Everything is energy and that's all there is to it. Match the frequency of the reality you want and you cannot help but get that reality. It can be no other way. This is not philosophy, it is physics."

—Albert Einstein

Frequency, Vibration, Vibrational Signature, Resonance

First, the science...

Absolutely everything seen and unseen, living, or inanimate is a form of energy. Most energy in the universe exists beyond the limited range of what we can pick up with our 5 senses. We think of energy as heat, electricity, wind, or fuel for our bodies in terms of caloric intake. But even the most solid of things around you such as a table or chair is made up of energy. All things in the universe, even objects that appear stationary, are constantly in motion, vibrating, oscillating, and resonating at various frequencies. Energy is always in motion, contracting or expanding as wavelengths.

Energy is measured in terms of its frequency and the frequency is displayed as wavelengths. The greater the energy, the higher the frequency and the shorter the wavelength. Lower, denser energy has a lower frequency and longer wavelengths. As frequency rate increases, matter becomes lighter and lighter.

All objects have a natural frequency or set of frequencies at which they vibrate. When you pluck a guitar string, the sound it makes is a vibration or when you blow air over the top of a pop bottle, the air inside will vibrate. Your vocal cords vibrate. Frequency is the rate of vibration.

We all vibrate energetically at a particular frequency. The body itself is composed of different systems which are made up of tissues and organs which are made up of cells, which in turn are made up of atoms. Atoms are made up of subatomic particles (quarks and photons) that are energy without physical structure. In thermodynamics (the study of energy transfer) we are considered to be an open system meaning that we exchange energy with our surroundings. For example, we take in chemical energy in the form of food and do functions in our surroundings such as walking, moving, and breathing which radiate heat.

We are also comprised of energy fields such as an electromagnetic or auric field. This field consists of multiple bands of energy called auric layers or auric fields, that encompass the subtle body, connecting us to the outside world. A special form of photography is able to take pictures of the auric field. In the 1930s, Russian scientist Semyon Kirlian and his wife, Valentina, invented a new photographic process that involves directing a high-frequency electrical field at an object. The object's pattern of luminescence—the auric human energy field—can then be captured on film. Contemporary practitioners are using this photography to show how the aura responds to different emotional and mental states, and even to diagnose illness and other problems. Medical science is now using a heat aura, as well as other imaging processes, to show the different aspects of the body's electromagnetics.

How this relates to the journey

We are a container or vessel of energy comprised of our physical body and the metaphysical properties of thoughts, emotions and feelings, memories, etc. Our vessel includes several electromagnetic fields, some of which extend beyond the physical form such as the auric field. Our thoughts, ideas, feelings, emotions are energy without physical form. What we think, how we feel and the emotions we process and express are in a form of frequency. Feelings of gratitude, peace and love have a higher frequency than feelings of shame, anger and hate. Healthy tissue and organs have a higher frequency than those that are compromised or diseased.

At any point in time, you are this composite of frequencies both higher and lower. You have a set point or vibrational point correlating to your unique set of frequencies. This vibrational set point we refer to as your *vibrational signature.* Think of yourself as an antenna with your own personalized radio station which is

transmitting incredible amounts of information about who you are, what you are and how you are interfacing with the world around you. That is your dial on the radio tuner. All frequency carries information.

The journey is empowering you to first connect to your radio station or more precisely to the information which is being transmitted. You tune into your unique radio bandwidth. This is awakening to an understanding of yourself from the inside-out as opposed to the outside in. Then the journey is empowering you to elevate your frequency. *So why would you want to do this? And how is this done?*

Because we are an open system and everything is connected, higher frequencies attract like frequencies. This is the law of attraction. It is real. An interesting phenomenon occurs when different vibrating things or processes come into proximity: they will start to vibrate together at the same frequency. They sync up or entrain in a way that can seem mysterious. This is described as spontaneous self-organization. What this means is that your life syncs up to your vibration. You attract a field or plane of frequencies commensurate with yours. If you are dense, what you attract in life will be fear-based. If you identify as a victim, you will be one.

Resonance also applies here. When you take two tuning forks and you strike just one, the other tuning fork will start to vibrate as well, even though it has not been struck. Not only will the two tuning forks vibrate but the vibration created by the resonance factor between the two, will be more powerful. The "syncing up" actually amplifies frequency. Fear will attract and amplify fear while love will attract a like frequency of love and it too will be amplified.

When your vibration is elevated, you live and create in a higher vibration plane and elevated field of consciousness. Life becomes a continuous source of inspiration. Trust and benevolence replace fear. There is peace and freedom in that.

This seamless interface between you and life is reinforced through our understanding that everything and everyone is connected throughout the universe by energy. There is no real separation. Separation is an illusion, albeit it a persistent one, inherent in our 3-dimensional plane. We see and feel boundaries that define objects as forms and the forms are further defined by the space that appears to separate one object from another. However, if we could see energy as pixels, we would understand that all that we see and feel and all the space we cannot see or feel, is all vibrating energy. There is no separation in reality.

The methodology of this journey is transformation at the level of energy and frequency without physical form. The way to elevate your vibrational set point is to identify, separate and release lower, dense frequencies from the mix. Once space is created, higher frequencies are welcomed in and you reorder yourself and your life at a new elevated plane of existence. Physically and emotionally, you heal as you welcome light within. Transformation here is not an intellectual exercise or one of will or control. It is not a hardened should do/must do scenario. It is one of grace and surrender. You shift at an energetic level.

The formula here is intention to shift followed by an awareness of what needs to be shifted; what needs to be released followed by the release; what needs to be added followed by your intention to receive. This is most important. The awareness or knowing is key to transformation at this level. This is why there is a code for both lower and higher frequency emotions.

The emotions must be identified, named, if you will, with a context of the event or experience which has led to the need for their release. You cannot transform what is not known or acknowledged. Here we are in the Quantum world where everything happens in the relationship between the observed and the observer. (See below "Newtonian and Quantum Realms.")

The takeaway concepts

1. Everything is energy
2. We all are connected through energy
3. Energy is measured in frequency
4. All frequency carries information
5. Separation is an illusion
6. Thoughts, ideas, emotions and feelings are frequencies of energy
7. We have a "vibrational signature"
8. The journey serves to elevate your frequency
9. The transformational shifts occur at and through the release and attraction of energetic frequencies
10. You cannot transform what is not known or acknowledged

Consciousness

"... *consciousness isn't something we have;*
it is what we and the world are"
— *Jude Currivan, Astro Physicist*

"*The evolution of evolution: from unconscious to conscious choice"*
— *Barbara Marx Hubbard, Futurist.*

First, the science...

Consciousness is universally described as an awareness of self; the ability to self-reflect or to know about yourself.

The topic of consciousness has a long history of controversy that goes back at least 400 years. René Descartes in the 1600s postulated that consciousness did not seem to be physical as it could not be observed, nor could it even be described. He concluded that it must be made of immaterial that does not abide by the laws of nature but bestowed by God. The mind and the body exist as separate entities and interface at the pineal gland. This has since been referred to as Cartesian duality.

Freud divided human consciousness into three levels of awareness: the conscious, preconscious, and unconscious. Each of these levels corresponds and overlaps with Freud's ideas of the id, ego, and superego. The conscious level consists of all the things we are aware of, including things we know about ourselves and our surroundings. The preconscious consists of things we could pay conscious attention to if we so desired and is where many memories are stored for easy retrieval. Freud saw the preconscious as comprised of thoughts that are unconscious at the particular moment in question, but easily retrieved, through recall. The unconscious consists of things that are outside of conscious awareness, including many memories, thoughts, and urges of which we are not aware. While these elements are stored out of our awareness, they are nevertheless thought to influence our behaviour.

More recently, David Chalmers, an Australian philosopher and cognitive scientist, termed the issue of consciousness as the *hard problem*. There is nothing in modern physics that explains how a group of molecules in a brain creates consciousness. The beauty of a sunset, the taste of a delicious meal, these are all mysteries to science—which can sometimes pin down where in the brain the sensations arise, but not how and why there is any subjective personal experience to begin with. Furthermore, nothing in science can explain how consciousness arose from matter. Chalmers speculated that if you had a doppelgänger that was a zombie, a brain scan would not be able to detect the difference. In other words, as Descartes postulated, consciousness is not made of ordinary physical atoms. He and some of his contemporaries have put forward the notion of *panpsychism* that consciousness is a fundamental property of reality as is time and space. Everything is consciousness. The planet and the universe itself are consciousness.

But this idea even goes further as a concept called *Biocentrism* which combines the fields of biology and physics. Consciousness is creating the universe; we are creating the ever-expanding universe through our consciousness. It is a simple but amazing concept; life creates the universe rather than the other way around.

Our thoughts, beliefs, experiences, and evolution itself are creating the universe as we go along. Think of it like the Worldwide Web. We are creating this cloud of information each and every second globally as we interact with the web. Even just looking at the web changes it, let alone adding or manipulating information. It is expanding exponentially and ultimately the information it holds, reflects our state of consciousness.

In summary, while science is very divided on the subject of consciousness, there are an increasing number of scientific leaders in all fields including physicists, biologists, psychologists and futurists who believe that consciousness is somehow the very fabric of life and that science cannot be thoroughly explained without taking consciousness into account. In great measure this has been propelled through the advances in quantum physics.

For these scientists, consciousness highlights the oneness of all creation by revealing the energy essence of all that exists, seen or unseen.

How this relates to the journey

Consciousness is the essence of the journey. The journey is the discovery of whom you are meant to become. How you come to know the truth of who you are, what you are and how you serve (how you were intended to express yourself).

There is a correlation we do not quite understand as yet between the level of frequency and the level of consciousness. Higher levels of consciousness correlate with higher levels of frequency. What we do know is that higher levels of frequency and consciousness interact with each other to receive and emit light. More recently, the study of biophotons shows that we, along with all living things are made up of tiny low intensity particles of light frequency. Information is stored in these light particles within DNA and serves to communicate effectively with cells. The stronger the emission of the light frequency, the healthier the organism. The electromagnetic energy that the cell emits and receives is the life force that governs molecules. We are quite literally beings of light each radiating a very vital life force.

When we say higher levels of frequency and consciousness receive and emit light, light here means increased health in a physical and emotional context. In a spiritual connotation, higher frequencies and the associated light brings greater illumination of your authentic self as a way to live in sovereignty. It means expressing yourself as love, it means knowing your worth and serving from a place of worthiness and ultimately it means the *realized self as our higher self.* This higher vibration takes us beyond the limitations set for us and by us.

Consciousness is a progressive state of being. David Hawkins in his seminal work, "Power vs. Force" developed a consciousness scale with a numerical range between 0 and 1000 *(see Figure 9).* This scale serves to stratify the expressions of consciousness from the lowest (shame, guilt) to higher forms of love to enlightenment. He measured the world consciousness level at 209 and believed that those born at a particular level would live out their lives at that same level. He believed the knowledge did not exist to transcend your "consciousness lot in life". We now know that not to be true.

This journey through its methodology is designed to do just that; transcend the levels of consciousness. It is just one of many paths happening globally that is accelerating the rise in consciousness. We are living in extraordinary times of a great consciousness opening. We are the first in humankind in significant numbers to be aware of the evolution of our consciousness. Consciousness is the driving force behind evolution (and everything and everybody as creation, is of consciousness).

We are conscious of our consciousness. The evolution of evolution is consciousness.

The urgency inherent in this journey, in the methodology, is, as a species, to raise consciousness. We have a responsibility to the highest possible evolution of our humanity to raise the vibrational level of consciousness. Evolution is an unrelenting force of creation. As a species our survival until recent times, has been predicated on fear and control. The civilizations and societies we have built are the exercise of structures and laws to ensure collective conformity through behavioural deterrents. And while there is argument that this has served us well in our survival as a species, it is our collective humanity that will propel us forward. Reframing ourselves from a species of fear, mistrust, and the belief in scarcity to a species of truth, love and abundance is what will guarantee our continued evolution.

This is rooted in the concept of *universal consciousness*. We are all part of one universal consciousness evolving in tandem with the universe, which is itself, conscious. We are in effect, a microcosm of the macrocosm. We are individuated yet connected; we contribute uniquely to a greater or collective consciousness shaped by us. Jude Currivan expressed it this way, "Comprehension of the unity of consciousness doesn't imply homogeneity. Instead, it gives greater meaning to our personal sense while celebrating the diversity of our collective human experience, allowing us to perceive the profound purpose of all lives."

The takeaway concepts

1. The field of science cannot be fully explained without taking consciousness into account
2. Consciousness is the essence of the journey
3. Consciousness is a measurable and progressive state within the journey
4. The urgency is to raise consciousness at both the individual and collective levels
5. We are individuated yet connected in consciousness

MAP OF CONSCIOUSNESS
Developed by David R. Hawkings

The Map of Consciousness is based on a logarithmic
scale that spans for 0 to 1000

Name of Level	Energetic "Frequency"	Associated Emotional State	View of Life
Enlightenment	700-1000	Ineffable	Is
Peace	600	Bliss	Perfect
Joy	540	Serenity	Complete
Love	500	Reverence	Benign
Reason	400	Understanding	Meaningful
Acceptance	350	Forgiveness	Harmonious
Willingness	310	Optimism	Hopeful
Neutrality	250	Trust	Satisfactory
Courage	200	Affirmation	Feasible
Pride	175	Scorn	Demanding
Anger	150	Hate	Antagonistic
Desire	125	Craving	Disappointing
Fear	100	Anxiety	Frightening
Grief	75	Regret	Tragic
Apathy	50	Despair	Hopeless
Guilt	30	Blame	Evil
Shame	20	Humiliation	Miserable

Figure 9

Newtonian and Quantum Physics

*"Those who are not shocked when they first come across quantum
theory cannot possibly have understood it."*—Niels Bohr, *Essays
1932–1957 on Atomic Physics and Human Knowledge*

First, the science...

At present physicists have two separate rule books to explain how the
universe works—classical Newtonian physics and Quantum mechanics.
It is a clash of incompatible descriptions of reality. Generally, one rule
book applies to large objects and the other rule book applies to very
small particles.

Newtonian physics

Newtonian physics was developed by Sir Isaac Newton in the 17th century. His view was that events are mechanistic and deterministic in nature. What this mean is that the laws governing the universe are continuous, orderly and predictable. The past will determine the future. So, for example, if you throw a ball with the same force, velocity and trajectory it will land in the same spot every time. Every cause matches up to a specific, local (discrete) effect. As we know, Newton accounted for the force of gravity and all things it dominates such as orbiting planets and the laws that govern the movement of all objects. His understanding was that the world operated separately from us and that all events occurred locally meaning as a discrete event in one place. There is no relationship between the observed and the observer. Whether you witness something or not, the behaviour of the event will not change. As a theologian he believed that God created these laws and set the universe in motion to run indefinitely as clockwork. His laws of physics still apply in great measure today and have been instrumental in our scientific developments including putting a man on the moon. Basically, they are still relevant in our slow moving, large object reality of the world we can perceive with our senses.

Newton put forth the notion that things unfolded in the same way regardless of where you observed them from. This held true until Einstein came up with his famous theory of relativity where speed and location do make a difference. For example, a one-meter ruler will stretch if you are running with it or travel with it on an aircraft. The infinitesimal amount of additional length (of the ruler in this example) has been proven with advances in scientific instruments. Both Einstein and Newton agreed that the speed of light is a constant (does not change under any circumstances) but time and velocity do vary, and this known as the space-time variable. That is because light is a physical property, so it is a constant whereas speed and space have no physical attributes and therefore are considered as variables. Newton viewed space-time as unchanging whereas we now know that space-time is dynamic and changing in line with gravitational forces and velocity.

Quantum physics

None of the above applies to the realm of the very, very, small. Quantum deals in the subatomic world. Atoms are the building blocks of everything in the physical universe. Atoms are made up of a nucleus surrounded by a large field containing one or more electrons. The field is so large compared to the tiny electrons that it appears 99.999999999999% empty space. This is hard to fathom but the relationship of the nucleus to the atom would be an equivalent relationship to a basketball being played on a court that was 25 square miles in size. The electrons circling the nucleus are even a smaller scale wherein the electrons would be the size of a grain of sand in this basketball analogy. A grain of sand in 25 square miles of "empty" space. But the space is not actually empty. It is made up of a vast array of energetic frequencies that make up an invisible, interconnected field of information. This is the Quantum field or the zero-point field.

Electrons that move around in that vast field behave in a completely unpredictable manner, not subject to the same laws that govern matter in the larger universe. They can be there one moment, disappear the next and reappear in a completely different place. It is impossible to predict when and where they will appear. This is because, as researchers have since discovered, the electrons exist simultaneously in an infinite number of possibilities and probabilities.

And in the case of the Quantum world, there is a relationship between the observer and the observed. Remember that in Newtonian physics whether you observe something happening or not, it does not make a difference to the event. It happens independently from the observer. Not so in the Quantum realm. It is only when the observer focuses his or her attention and looks for something that the invisible field of energy collapses into a particle we know as the electron. This is known as a *Quantum Event or Quantum Superposition*. But as soon as the observer looks away, the electron disappears back into the field. In other words, the electron cannot exist until we observe it or give it our attention. The "Double Slit Experiment" on YouTube is a fascinating demonstration of this phenomenon.

The other remarkable phenomenon is called *entanglement*. In Quantum physics, paired particles remain connected so that actions performed on one affects the other, even when separated by great distances. In other words, you can separate photons (photons make up particles) miles apart and if you tickle one, the other will be likewise tickled. This transfer of excitation (a more scientific word than tickled) between the photons takes place at least 10,000 times the speed of light, possibly instantaneously, regardless of the distance. Time and space do not appear to exist in this realm. More recent experiments have managed to beam photons from one location to another à la Star Trek "Beam me up Scotty." The phenomenon of entanglement so riled Albert Einstein that he called it "spooky action at a distance."

A universe in-formation

So, two very different worlds, Newtonian and Quantum with different rule books and what appears to be a clash of incompatible descriptions of how the universe operates. The cosmologist, Jude Currivan in her book, "The Cosmic Hologram", provides a way in which to reconcile these two realms. She explores how information is physically real and more fundamental than energy, matter, space, or time. Meaning everything in the universe is energy and all of energy is encoded information. Information is at the centre of creation and this universe is unfolding as in-formation. There is an intelligence imbedded in the information that underlies creation and all of the forces manifested by energy, seen or unseen. She explains how Quantum mechanics and Einstein's theory of relativity can be reconciled if we go deeper in our understanding of energy-matter and space-time as complementary expressions of information.

Furthermore, she contends that it is consciousness that connects us to the many layers of universal information making us both manifestations of and co-creators of the expanding universe. In essence what Currivan is putting forth is that the universe is expressed as information and the laws of physics must be restated in informational terms. All energy is encoded information, the expanding universe and evolution are *in-formation* and that consciousness is the divine intelligence that underlies it all. Energy=information=consciousness

How this applies to the journey

Setting the stage

As physical vessels, we experience life, by and large, in the Newtonian world of large objects conforming to the laws of gravity with deterministic and predictable outcomes. Our senses are honed and operate in a limited range to allow us to navigate a 3-dimensional reality. There have always been some among us with an expanded range of sensory capability allowing such individuals to see or feel energy or have paranormal faculties such as remote viewing. They have always been the wayshowers to other dimensions of reality. It's rather refreshing that we no longer burn them at the stake!

Indeed, we are lending credence to these phenomena through advances in scientific instruments and projects (think large hadron collider—CERN) which are exploring the mysteries of the Quantum world of the tiniest particles and their role in the creation and unfolding of the universe beyond our 3D reality. It is an exciting time.

When we journey, we enter the non-physical realm of frequency in the non-physical fifth and sixth levels of dimensions of the quantum. We have established that the transformative process is driven by frequency shifts. For example, the release of trapped emotions is the release of dense levels of unwanted frequency. All frequency contains information. This targeted frequency contained the information of the negative emotion from its type (which emotion), to when, where and how it was acquired and how it manifests within the body. In identifying the emotion to be released, you access the information contained in that frequency. You had to access it and set the intention to release it.

Accessing the Quantum realm

We access the quantum through awareness as consciousness. It can only be accessed in the NOW. The present NOW is the only doorway in. As Joe Dispenza advocates, you try to leave YOU behind. You are not accessing this realm with your senses. The extent to which you access this field as YOU—with your sense of identity, belief systems and history (your personality), the more you narrow the possibilities to a limited field of what you know; possibilities in line with your experiences, habits and personality. If you can take your attention off your specific identity, in place and time, the more you have access to the full spectrum of possibilities. You move from just the possibilities of the known to the possibilities of the known and unknown. This is what some call the zero-point field made up of nothing but invisible frequency carrying information as consciousness.

This is the realm of our connection to spiritual guides. They communicate by and large with us through this realm. When we have this neutral mind, when we stop thinking, stop being somebody, some place, some time, we connect. But it takes the shift of our attention to pure awareness. It is a practice that becomes easier over time.

This is also the realm of manifestation. Dispenza reminds us that we are creatures of habit and conformity. We fall into the same patterns every day and our futures look very much like our past. When we do this, we are collapsing the infinite field of possibility into the same familiar pattern even as we wish for or expect a different future. If you focus on the known, you get the known; if you focus on the unknown, you create a possibility for a new experience. You also create resiliency in the face of new experiences. You tend to go forwards rather than retreat to life patterns that are familiar, even if unwanted.

This is the realm of choice. You enter the Quantum Field in the NOW and the future is but infinite possibilities. The infinite possibilities collapse to whatever you put your attention on. Your attention creates the next moment and all subsequent moments derive from that one. It's like a film reel where each frame is discreet, representing the present moment, and the one that follows is a discrete choice among many simultaneously available to you.

This is the realm of the observer. When you are only operating from your senses, you are collapsing the realm of possibilities into the limited range that corresponds to your senses. When you are only seeing with your eyes, you react or respond from what is patterned from the neurological connections already linked in your brain. When you observe through a state of awareness, you are observing from the third eye, beyond the senses, which permits greater choice in creating the next moment rather than the next moment being a patterned reaction.

This is also the realm of the law of attraction. Since our emotions and beliefs impact the field of possibilities, what we put out into the Quantum Field we attract back. By attracting back what we mean is that once again we collapse the infinite field of possibilities to a compatible frequency to what we put out there. If we fear, we will attract what makes us fearful; if we send out gratitude and feelings of abundance, so shall they be received.

This is also the realm of energy healing including remote healing. The science is proving what healers and shamans have long known. Space and time do not exist in this realm and everything is entangled. The healing energy carries the exchange of information through intention to heal, regardless of distance between healer and the one being healed.

This is the realm of the interconnected. The universe is innately coherent and unified where everything is interconnected and informational in nature. There is no separation.

The takeaway concepts

1. Newtonian and Quantum physics operate by a different set of laws which science has yet to reconcile
2. In the Newtonian world, life as we experience it is continuous, orderly and predictable
3. In the Quantum world everything is probabilities and possibilities
4. In the Quantum realm there is a dependent relationship between the observer and what is observed
5. Time and space do not appear to exist in the Quantum realm
6. Energy as frequency contains information; consciousness underlies all information
7. We access the Quantum or zero point field through awareness as consciousness
8. We access the field in the present NOW
9. The zero point field is made up of nothing but invisible frequency carrying information as consciousness.

10. This is the realm of manifestation through the choice of what you set as intention and therefore what you put your attention on

◈

From Genetic Determinism to Epigenetics

"The moment you change your perception is the moment you rewrite the chemistry of your body. Belief underlies our biology" — Bruce H Lipton

Until fairly recently, the field of biology was governed by the principles of Newtonian physics wherein physical mechanisms determined how the body functioned. The body was thought to be controlled throughout its lifespan by the DNA and the genetic programming that gives you the eye and skin colour you were born with. In other words, you were born with an inherent code that determined your physical characteristics, growth, predisposition to disease and ultimately the quality of your health. Disease was thought to run in families, and you were either born with good genes or bad ones. This is called genetic determinism.

First, the science...

All of this changed with the advent of stem cell research, the evolving understanding of quantum physics and one unconventional biologist, Bruce Lipton. Lipton was a pioneer in stem cell research in the late 1960s which proved to be key to unlocking the fundamental understanding that the cell membrane reads its environment and will react according to the information held in the surrounding environment. Prior to that it was thought that the nucleus of the cell held the intelligence. Lipton demonstrated that it is the membrane of the cell which in fact operates as the cell's brain. Lipton was able to clone a single embryonic stem cell into 50 thousand cells and divide them up into three Petri dishes, each containing a different culture. The cells, having just one parent, nonetheless had different outcomes: the cells in one Petri dish became bone cells, the second became muscle cells and the third became fat cells. Rather than being genetically programmed, the cells evolved in response to their environment. Three different cultures, three different outcomes.

Lipton's revelation led to the understanding that we are essentially a skin covered Petri dish containing 50 trillion cells. And each of those cells is responding to the body's built-in Petri dish culture in the form of blood that sustains the cells. Our brain acts as the chemist creating and adjusting the blood culture to provide the information required by the cells for proper functioning and regeneration. But the brain, as chemist, is taking its cues from our beliefs and emotions. In other words, the brain creates a chemical cocktail to support the beliefs and emotions we hold. If we are positive and happy, what is pumped into our blood will be chemicals like dopamine, oxytocin, serotonin, and growth hormones, all designed to produce vitality and a general sense of well-being. When we are fearful, it is stress-related hormones such as cortisone, adrenaline and inflammatory agents that are introduced into the blood to help gear-up for the danger or stress environment we are sensing. So that which we believe and the emotions we hold, determine the nature of the chemical release providing the instructions to our cells. Our health is predicated on the proper interpretation by the brain of our physical and emotional environment.

There is an inherent feedback loop here. If we feel physically vital, if our gut is healthy and supporting the bacteria and fungi we need for a robust immune system, that information is fed back up to the brain as an "all systems OK" signal. No need for the stress chemicals. In other words, there is a constant communication flow from every cell to the brain and from the brain back to every cell through the blood stream. Rather than a genetic determination of the cell's role and functioning, the cell is constantly reading information and adapting to the environment as required to maintain homeostasis.

From victims to masters

Genetic determinism saw us as victims of our genes when in fact we are masters of our genes. This new field of biology is called *epigenetics* ("epi" meaning above genetics). This changes everything. We have the power to rewrite our genes. Our genes do not cause disease, but they can correlate to disease. Under harmful conditions the expression of certain genes can lead to disease. But under supportive conditions, the same genetic factors will rewrite themselves to align to the supportive environment.

That environment is our lifestyle; what we eat, the environment we live in and the relationships and community that supports us. But overriding all of this, is our belief system. We see this in the placebo effect. We can be given a sugar pill and it will prove effective if we believe it to be so. Some call it the power of positive thinking and so it is. But the *nocebo* effect is equally powerful. When we are told (and believe) that procedures or medications will have negative side effects, worsening symptoms often appear even though no medical intervention was administered.

If our environment is stressful, negative and our lifestyle poor, the vibrational frequency created by such conditions will impact the health of our cells and organisms. Less than 1% of disease is now thought to be caused by genetics as opposed to being correlated with disease.

In a fight/flight mode the body suppresses the immune system, constricts blood flow to the brain and heart, preferentially pushing it out to our limbs to outfight or outrun the danger. This is so powerful that stress hormones are given to transplant patients to sufficiently suppress their immune systems from rejecting a foreign organ. All of this worked wonderfully when we had to outrun the proverbial tiger for a few minutes. However, in today's 24/7 stressful environment, such unrelenting suppression of our immune system is causing havoc. A compromised immune system cannot effectively combat disease or opportunistic organisms such as viruses. Furthermore, you cannot be in a growth mode at the same time the body is investing its energy in the immune system. Only one can function at any one time. And here growth mode means the everyday requirement to generate new cells and organisms within the body.

Unfortunately, we are programmed to be fearful. It is our default setting. At least 70% of our thoughts are negative, fear-based, and self-limiting. And the worst of it is that, for the most part, this programming is buried deep within our subconscious. Lipton argues that we remember little from birth to age 7 because a child's brain is made up of theta waves which are very close to a state of hypnosis. That fear-based programming is literally absorbed by a child and sets up lifelong patterns. Ninety-five percent of our functioning is controlled by the subconscious mind so our ability to change our beliefs with our conscious minds is limited. When we think, it is our subconscious programming that takes over. That is why you can drive somewhere and not know how you got there.

The good news with epigenetics is that the science accords with taking back our power. The work though is changing our belief system. When we fall in love, our belief system changes almost instantly; our world changes instantly. Love is that powerful. The world in that moment is heaven on earth. Everything seems possible and wondrous and we feel expansive, open and generous. We are at our best. The quest in the end is as Lipton says, the *forever honeymoon*, which is only possible when we reprogram from fear to love.

How this applies to the journey

The journey is about discovering who you are meant to become. And who you are meant to become is about unleashing the power that lies within. We long ago abdicated our power to heal by believing that only doctors could cure us and that prescription drugs were always the answer. The pill cures all or at least manages the symptoms. There is a time and place for medical intervention and we are grateful for its rightful place. But that does not mean abdicating our power to be wholly and consciously in charge of our health. And that health is of body, mind and soul ... indivisible.

The journey brings home the power we have given away. We systematically release what distorts and blocks energy. We are divinely guided to identify limiting beliefs about ourselves in order to replace them with empowering beliefs to live by and express through elevated consciousness. We heal ourselves and others by simply "being" who and what we are meant to be.

The journey uses the analogy of the Petri dish to describe the interface of ourselves to our life structures. We are that cell in the Petri dish of life. There is no separation between the self and the way in which we express ourselves; in the choices we make, the words we use, the relationships we honour, the experiences we treasure. We create the culture that supports us in life.

The takeaway concept

1. We are not victims of our genetic makeup
2. Cells are not genetically programmed but respond to their environment
3. The environment is governed by our belief system
4. Our belief system is primarily formed in childhood by others
5. Our belief system is programmed at the subconscious level
6. Most programming is fear-based and self-limiting
7. We are capable of changing our belief systems through the methodology
8. We are capable of taking power back in healing body, mind and soul

The Body's Nine Energy Systems

"By studying energy anatomy.... you will be able to read your own body like a scripture and take the edge off the sensation that you are looking blindly into empty air for information" — Caroline Myss

As Donna Eden says, "The body is designed to heal itself." For centuries, and throughout numerous cultures that understanding led to a description of subtle energies that support and animate the physical body known as "Qi" or "chi" in China, "prana" in the yogic tradition, "ruach" in Hebrew, "ki" in Japan, "baraka" by the Sufis, and "oreda" by the Iroquois. The body's energies are not just a force that causes your body to function, but an intelligence that orchestrates all biological functions. When all of the body's energy systems are brought into harmony, your body flourishes.

Balance is a pivotal concept within energy medicine and all systems move towards a state of internal stability and harmony with other systems. However, all activity and interactions with our environment impact this balance so there is a constant fluctuation, much like we observe in blood pressure readings. The amount of solar radiation hitting the earth's surface and the phases of the moon have long been known to influence behaviour of planetary energies and of ourselves. More recently new scientific instruments can now detect how your thoughts impact what is referred to as the subtle energy systems of the body. The energies of other people and animals also impact our own energies and mental state. Rooms also have an energy of their own, another long-held belief in the art of Feng Shui.

Rupert Sheldrake, a researcher, proposes that there is a morphic field of resonance which carries memories and accounts for the idea of mysterious telepathy-type interconnections between organisms and of collective memories within species, accounts of phantom limbs, how dogs know when their owners are coming home, and how people know when someone is staring at them. Many biologists and researchers are exploring similar concepts such as water and food holding information and memory. Donna Eden herself can detect the subtle energy differences between two similar-looking apples, one organic and the other not. Much of this is still highly controversial in the scientific domain but remains a valid if unproven line of enquiry and research.

Donna Eden contends that we are a constellation of energy systems and that there are at least nine such systems within the body that work together, below the threshold of our awareness. They are the meridians, the chakras, the aura, the electrics, the Celtic weave, the basic grid, the five rhythms, the triple warmer, and the radiant circuits. The blending of these systems may be harmonious or jangled. They may contain blockages, or the energies may be running backwards or simply be weak and contain vulnerabilities.

About the Meridian System

In the same way that your arteries transport blood throughout your body, meridians carry energy—thus they can be thought of as your *energy bloodstream*. They affect every organ and all physiological systems including the immune, endocrine, respiratory, skeletal, lymphatic, nervous, circulatory, digestive, and muscular systems. The functions of the meridians are to provide life force energy and metabolism balance, as well as to remove blockages and regulate the rate of cellular renewal. Their unimpeded flow is critical to the health and vitality of your body. If blockages do occur, they will impede the healthy functioning of the organs and systems they support and are often a precursor to disease. The ancient healing modality of acupuncture identifies key points on the meridians near the surface of your skin and stimulates the flow of energy with the use of fine needles.

Twelve of the 14 meridians are constructed in a chain that serve different organs and systems. They are:

The Spleen Meridian
The Heart Meridian
The Small Intestine Meridian
The Bladder Meridian
The Kidney Meridian
The Circulation-Sex Meridian
The Triple Warmer Meridian
The Gallbladder Meridian
The Liver Meridian
The Lung Meridian
The Large Intestine Meridian
The Stomach Meridian

The other two meridians share characteristics of radiant circuits (see below) and are designed to allow energy to flow into and out of the body. They are:

The Central Meridian
The Governing Meridian

The health and balance of your meridians are in a constant state of flux, reacting and adjusting to physical and emotional inputs. As with all the energy systems described here, they can be cleared and balanced at the physical level (see Donna Eden's "Energy Medicine—Balancing Your Body's Energies for Optimal Health and Vitality"), or at the vibrational level which is the primary focus of this book.

About the Chakra System

According to Anodea Judith, the chakra system is a seven-levelled philosophical model of the universe and refers to spinning spheres of bioenergetic activity. A chakra system is a centre of organization that receives, assimilates, and expresses life force energy. Chakra patterns are programmed deep within us as the embodiment of spiritual energy on a physical plane. They are said to have a location in the body and, as energy, contain information that helps us interpret and meld the outer to inner worlds.

The lower chakras are closer to the earth and relate more to physical matters of our lives such as survival, movement, and action. The upper chakras represent the metaphysical realm and work at the symbolic level of words, images, and concepts. Metaphorically, the chakras relate to the archetypal elements: root is earth (solid and dense); sacral is water (formless and fluid); solar plexus is fire (radiating and transforming); heart is air (soft and spacious); throat is sound (rhythmic and pulsating); third eye is light (illuminating); the crown is thought (the medium of consciousness).

Together the chakras describe the polarities of heaven and earth, mind and body, spirit, and matter. These polarities are a continuum of sorts, moving from a denser vibrational state to higher, subtler, and freer forms of vibration. There are seven levels in the chakra system, and they are often represented by the seven colours in the rainbow. The slowest and densest vibration of visible light is red and thus is associated with the root chakra and the fastest and shortest vibration of visible light is violet and thus is associated with the crown chakra. Each of the in between colours (orange, yellow, green, blue, indigo) represent the chakras as visible light. As one learns to heal the chakras within us, we become the *Rainbow Bridge* as a link between heaven and earth.

Chakra means wheel or disk. As Judith says, the word disk is particularly apropos, given its association with a common storage unit of programmed information. In this analogy the body is the hardware, our programming is the software, and the Self is the user. Our operating program was written long ago and passed down through DNA and genetic coding. We have a program for sexuality, power, love, communication, and survival, as well as others. However, what activates any computer system is electricity and, in our bodies, this is energy or simply life force (chakra, chi, ki, or prana). Thus, you can have a well-functioning program, but you cannot activate it, or fully activate it, if there is a block of the energy pathway.

The energy or life force pathways run vertically from the crown to the root and from the root to the crown. Hence life force runs between two poles or polarities. When energetic contact is made through the body, it is referred to as *grounding*. Grounding is the solid contact we have with the earth through our legs and feet. It is rooted in the solidity of the material world. Grounding makes us feel safe, alive, centred, and rooted. At the other polarity, consciousness comes from the embodiment of the spiritual world and when properly connected to the body, makes consciousness tangible and effective. We are literally plugged into this life force current and just as we plug into a radio, we can tune into the different channels that are our chakras. Chakras become channels, receiving and broadcasting at different frequencies.

Judith explains that soul and spirit are expressions of these polarities. "In my use of these terms, I see soul as tending to coalesce toward the body, leaning toward form, attachment and feeling, whereas spirit tends to move toward freedom and expanded consciousness. Soul is the individual expression of spirit, and spirit is the universal expression of soul. They each connect and are enhanced by the other."

The polarities create both a downward flow and an upward flow. The downward flow is the flow of manifestation. When we take thoughts and turn them into reality, we go through each of the chakras from crown to root; we think them, visualize them, name them, give meaning to them, give them purpose, create them and give them form.

The upward flow is the pathway of liberation from the density of the material world to ethereal consciousness. The current of liberation takes you from density to less restricted states; water is less defined than earth; thoughts are less specific than words.

The basic premise within the chakra system is that we need to find balance within the polarities; too much liberation and we become aimless dreamers; too focused on manifestation and we fail to grow and expand. The union of opposites is what creates limitless possibilities. The union of polarities is what is called the sacred marriage or sacred space. Judith says that it is the metaphoric source of conception, a word that implies both the birth of an idea and the beginning of life (thought and form). We have too few such words in the English language to give expression to the sacred space which embodies the full spectrum.

Chakras also have two currents that run horizontally as both receptor and expression currents. If we are unable to receive a particular kind of energy, the chakra will atrophy and become further limited in its functioning. If we are unable to express a particular energy, there is a form of repression of the functioning that occurs. Damage to the current can be both vertical and horizontal. Childhood traumas, limited beliefs, cultural conditioning, and even physical and emotional injuries can all cause blockages to the flow of the chakra currents. The manifestation of blocked energy is very often displayed in either excessive or deficient behaviours. For example, a bully who compensates for insecurity exhibits an excessive third chakra. On the other hand, a person who feels powerless and avoids conflict, exhibits a deficient third chakra.

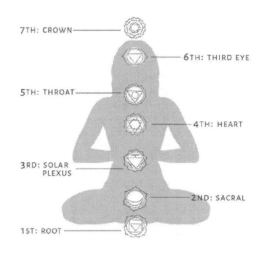

Each chakra houses an identity that emerges and shifts as we mature through life. The first chakra (root) is known as the physical identity and its job is self-preservation. The second chakra (sacral), is our emotional identity and its job is expanding the experience of the body through the interpretation of emotions which in turn, connects us to the flow of the world around us. The identity of the third chakra (solar plexus), is our will and its job is self-definition. Much of our judgment comes from this chakra as we assess what we do as good or bad. This is the ego identity.

Social identity is the domain of the fourth chakra (heart), also known as the persona. It is the personality created to interact with others and its job is self-acceptance. Self-acceptance is often a sense of validation and worth garnered from outside of ourselves. As we raise our level of consciousness, we learn to shift this identity to one of inner sovereignty of our worth.

The fifth chakra (throat) is the centre of creative identity and its job is self-expression. Initially we learn to express our own creativity through ego, and higher forms of consciousness allows us to express our personal contribution to larger systems. Self-expression in this more mature manifestation leads to self-transcendence.

The sixth chakra (third eye) expands into an archetypal identity where the individual "I" is seen as an event in a much larger story. We experience self-reflection in the larger system. We are aware of the evolution of our consciousness and the archetypal role we play in relating to things and greatness beyond ourselves. At this level we get involved in causes that go beyond serving our immediate and limited needs.

The identity of the seventh chakra (crown), is universal identity and its job is self-knowledge of the divinity within. The more our consciousness expands, the more we transcend the small self and limited world to embrace the unity of all life and all creation. At the outer extreme of this chakra, individuality is transcended and absorbed into the larger field of the divine. It is the realization of universal identity. This does not deny the reality of the smaller identities but sees them as part of the integrated whole.

We must consolidate our identities at the lower levels before we can sustain larger identities. Each chakra and each identity support the ones above it.

About the Aura

The aura is a multilayered field of energy that surrounds your body that is sometimes referred to as a *biofield* or *subtle body*. This field of energy emanates from within you and can be thought of as an interface between you and the external world. Your auric field functions as both an antenna and a filter, picking up information (energy) and bringing it into your chakras, while sending energy from your chakras outwards. You can think of it as a protective layer that parses and filters information from the external environment, blocking the negative and welcoming the positive. As you develop the ability to sense subtle energies, you may be aware of negative energies trying to make their way into your aura and participate in the conscious act of discarding them. Your aura contains much information about you, your intentions and vibrational signature. This is picked up by others and is often the first impression that others unconsciously register. Often you can feel a person's vibrational signature—a high frequency serving as a positive attractor force and lower frequencies sending feelings of caution and negativity.

Auras have different sizes and strengths, and are sensitive to the environment, thoughts, physical and mental health to name a few factors. Many sources cite an average auric field size of seven feet surrounding your entire body, but as your level of consciousness increases so too does the size of your field. Your aura can also be measured in terms of its strength. Some may have very leaky fields of disorganized energy and the specialized cameras (Kirlian photography) that can detect auras, also reveal gaps that can be signs of distress of some sort. The more sovereign and higher your frequency, the larger and stronger your auric field. Kirlian cameras have also confirmed the presence of 7 layers in your aura that appear to be loosely affiliated with the 7 chakras. Each of these bands is connected energetically to different parts of your physical and emotional body and are thought to work together to coordinate the massive amounts of information entering and leaving your presence.

About the Electrics

The electrics are not an independent energy system like the meridians or chakras, but move through the systems like water, performing the functions of connecting and coordinating all the imbedded electrical frequencies throughout. The electrics then, connect all the systems to facilitate whole body healing. The Celtic weave and the five rhythms also fall into a similar category of being "separate from, yet part of," the labyrinth of energy systems in our physical and etheric bodies. Donna Eden describes various electric points in the body that send signals throughout the energy systems to restore order and balance, the most powerful being the pair of points or indentations at the base of the skull (known as the headache points). As with any of the energy systems, blockages can be removed at the vibrational level using the techniques described in the Separation stage.

About the Celtic Weave

The body's energies flow in multiple patterns, spinning, twisting, and crisscrossing throughout. These patterns or weaves have been depicted throughout history in different cultures. The Tibetan energy ring, the yogic version of two curved lines crossing seven times to encase the chakras, and the caduceus of serpents intertwined around a staff used by alchemists and as a symbol of modern medicine, all draw their inspiration from the motion of a dynamic infinity sign. These are the powerful threads of energy that bind all the energy systems together, and that creates a unified resonance amongst them.

While each person's energy signatures are unique, the Celtic weave (as named by Donna Eden) is a common denominator. It allows for the coordination between the brain and the body; the right hemisphere controlling the left side; the left hemisphere controlling the right. It is thought that the double helix strand of DNA is the prototype for the Celtic weave as an energy system. It unifies the 14 meridians to work in harmony with each other and can be thought of as an information highway (think of all the cloverleafs of underpasses and overpasses allowing for the easy flow of access and egress of traffic). Low energy can often be traced to energy patterns not crossing in this weave pattern and can be remedied with specific exercises. Blockages in this system will prevent the free flow of energy throughout and manifest in low energy and poor health.

About the Basic Grid

The basic grid can be thought of as the infrastructure for your energy systems. Picturing it as the steel girders that are linked together horizontally and vertically as the backbone of a tall building, is useful in depicting its appearance and function. These grid like energy lines, house the chakras and function within the energetic body—i.e., they do not interface with the external environment. They are there to support the functioning of all your energy systems, so if something happens to the basic grid, all other energy systems lose integrity—they are literally operating on a shaky foundation. The grid is made up of 64 patterns, 8 of which are major branches. If a branch is compromised or healed, its tributaries are similarly affected.

According to Donna Eden, the main function of this grid is to act as a shock absorber for severe trauma—protecting the body, soul, and psyche as best it can from devastating occurrences. While the basic grid can absorb much of the impact, it appears that it has an immediate or short-term role in preventing catastrophic events such as a heart attack or stroke. In the longer term, if the basic grid is compromised the grid lines pull apart and can disturb the optimal functioning not only of your energy systems, but your organs and other physiological systems as well. Here an analogy to a building that has been built to withstand earthquakes is particularly relevant. The building remains intact during the earthquake, but tiny cracks emerge, and joints are loosened that must eventually be repaired. The event and its details of trauma are stored in the grid and recalling them may cause painful memories to surface. Know that if you do uncover uncomfortable memories, you are ready to process them.

About the Five Rhythms

The five rhythms again are not a separate energy system but one that is interwoven through all others that leaves a vibrational impression on your personality traits and overall health. These rhythms have ancient origins and were mapped by the Chinese as *the five elements of life*. They are comprised of the four seasons; winter, spring, summer, and autumn; and of the four transitions between the seasons encapsulated into one—Indian summer. Each of the seasons is paired with an earth element and parts of the body:

Winter—water—kidney/bladder
Spring—wood—gallbladder/liver
Summer—fire—small intestine/heart and triple warmer/circulation/sex/pericardium
Indian summer—earth—stomach/spleen
Autumn—metal—lungs/large intestine

We are born into a primary rhythm and often have secondary rhythms that are the seasons immediately preceding and following it. They are an indication of your essential characteristics or personality traits and are dynamic in their balance as you go through life with all its ups and downs. Your vibrational signature is influenced by your rhythm and you will likely relate more easily to those with a similar profile.

As with your chakras, there are specific characteristics of each season that need to be in balance—too much of one and too little of another can lead to lower levels of consciousness, health, and vitality. Understanding your unique rhythm, its traits and signs of imbalance are valuable tools for ensuring overall health.

About Triple Warmer

Triple warmer is a hybrid system that functions both as a meridian and a radiant circuit (see below). Its primary function is to protect you by regulating your immune system—keeping it on constant alert for attacking toxins, bad viruses, and bacteria—anything that is a threat to your body. Triple warmer networks all the meridians and the organs they serve and can conscript resources from all but the heart meridian for a heightened immune response when needed. In addition to the radiant circuits, it also works closely with the hypothalamus gland which controls body temperature and the fight or flight response. Anything new that enters your body is considered by triple warmer as a threat that must be guarded against. An obvious example is when a donor organ is transplanted into the body, the immune system must be suppressed chemically to let that organ function in its new environment.

It seems that triple warmer is a bit of a slow learner and has not evolved at an equal pace to the introduction of new modern threats that our bodies must deal with on a daily basis. Like the new organ that is considered an enemy, so too are the plethora of environmental toxins, polluted waters and even cosmetic chemicals that have become part of our reality. The meteoric rise in allergies, autoimmune diseases (where your immune system goes into overdrive and attacks healthy cells) and immune deficiency disorders (where your immune system becomes so overwhelmed that it literally shuts down) are a direct result of this rapid introduction of these new threats, and the inability of triple warmer to keep up with distinguishing between friend and foe. Walking the fine line between overprotection and under protection is triple warmer's job, and it is a challenging time for this energy system. We can do everything possible to allay this by eating organic and non-GMO foods and using cleaners, cosmetics and beverages that have as few harmful chemicals as possible. In addition to ensuring that your energies are flowing in a crossover pattern and clearing energy blocks, Donna Eden has several methods for either calming or strengthening this energy system.

About Radiant Circuits

There are ten radiant circuits that include the belt flow, penetrating flow, left and right bridge flows, left and right regulator flows and the four meridians that double as radiant circuits. Their functions are to regulate blood supply, antibodies and nourishment and are associated with the spleen. Triple warmer and radiant circuits are alike in the way they physically distribute and balance energy, not being confined as meridians are, to specific pathways and directions. They can radiate to, between and even jump over these pathways to efficiently organize a physiological response. However, they are quite different in terms of their strategies. While triple warmer activates an attack on an invader—radiant circuits would rather achieve a peaceful solution through diplomacy. They are the advance guard, ensuring that all systems work together for the common good—trying to prevent the need for forceful intervention.

Donna Eden describes the radiant circuits as *psychic circuits* as they respond to our energetic thoughts, ideas, beliefs and words more than any other system. The symbiotic relationship between your thoughts and radiant circuits are harbingers of your physical and mental health. The effectiveness of your immune system is then strongly aligned to your thoughts; your chemistry follows your thoughts.

How this applies to the journey

Our energy system is a complex organism whose components operate synergistically in an effort to promote free flow and maintain equilibrium. With optimal flow and balance come health and vitality. There are many things that can compromise this delicate balance; most notably emotional and physical traumas that often are buried subconsciously. Getting to the root cause of energetic blockages and releasing these impediments is the focus of the work in the Separation stage. But life goes on, throwing new challenges our way each and every day, so a regular practice of moving energy through our bodies is a crucial component of maintaining well-being. There are many vehicles for doing this, and as we are all so unique in our chemical, biological and temperamental makeups, that is a very good thing!

Understanding where you lie in the spectrum of Introvert to Extrovert is valuable as it is an indication of how you re-energize and find your energetic balance. Some modalities and exercises are more attuned to introverts and others for extroverts and you will need to find the ones that best suit you. Many eastern practices have become mainstream and it is easy to find classes, books, tutorials, and videos for everything from all forms of yoga (especially Kundalini as its focus lies in moving energy up from the lower chakras) to Tai Chi and Qi Gong, Egyptian Postures of Power, etc. In fact, all forms of exercise, including simply walking and running, move energy and your natural instincts facilitate this. Have you ever wondered why your right arm moves in tandem with your left leg while walking or jogging? This is nature's way of encouraging the crossover energy patterns your body needs to maintain vitality. Donna Eden's life work has been in teaching how to keep energy systems strong, and her book "Energy Medicine—Balancing Your Body's Energies for Optimal Health, Joy and Vitality" is an encyclopedia for ongoing maintenance and self-healing.

Not only do you have physical ways of optimizing your energy system, but equally important are the metaphysical tools. Indeed, the focus of this journey is on unleashing the power you have within. The powerful mind/body connection is a proven and potent method of self-healing, whether through meditation or such modalities as Reiki or Quantum Touch.

Find what works for you. Explore and try out new and different approaches. Rely on your own intuition and higher guidance to find the best vehicles for maintaining this crucial component of your well-being and spiritual growth.

The takeaway concepts

1. Our body's energy systems are a complex array of interconnected pathways and circuits that communicate with each other
2. The unrestricted flow of energy in these systems is a requirement for optimal health
3. We can remove blockages at the vibrational level and keep them flowing through tracing circuits and manipulating pressure points

PART SEVEN

THE LUMINARIES

THE LUMINARIES

In the introduction, I mentioned that perhaps the uniqueness of this methodology is in connecting the brilliance of so many of today's spiritual thinkers and seekers of higher consciousness across a vast array of disciplines and of their genius. The world is grateful for their contributions as they illuminate the way forward for us all. This methodology was channelled through me, gifted to me, as another way to showcase their insights in such a way that you can connect the dots through a synthesis of their works or partial works. I was led to each of these authors in a curious sequence that was necessary for the development of the methodology and my own process of surrender and journey. The authors and their works listed here are those most pertinent to the first level of transformation. The sequence, however, is not important for those who choose this methodology as a means of guiding their own journeys. You will find your own sequence of teachers that speak to you. Some will undoubtedly be from this list, but you will also be led to others in line with your needs.

I also mentioned that I was often led to particular chapters or even pages within their works as it seemed important to highlight areas of particular significance. In other cases, I was to slightly modify or add to the insights without compromising the foundational concepts. I have done so with the greatest care and respect. All of this to say that the following references include an acknowledgement of the way in which these individuals and their works specifically contributed to this methodology. Everyone listed here is well worth reading or watching as many have complemented their considerable body of work through videos and interviews.

The Gaia and Mindvalley media platforms are of great importance to connecting the growing community of spiritual seekers. I will be a lifelong subscriber to Gaia and in particular to whatever Regina Meredith produces. Regina's interviews are discerning in integrity, well researched on her part and her deep respect for those she interviews attests to the name of her program, "Open Minds". There are also a number of series on Gaia well worth watching from beginning to end.

I would also add that there is value in accessing these works more than once. I found that each author deepened my understanding and appreciation of their works after I had read several of them once-over and then went back to reread or rewatch each one. You appreciate the connections, dimensions, and angles as you put them together as pieces of an intricate, wondrous puzzle. What is most satisfying, and validating is the complementarity of the works and the consistent underpinnings of messages.

Your personal journey will be greatly enhanced through all these suggested voices and platforms along with others you will undoubtedly be led to in this growing field of luminaries.

■ Dr. Bradley Nelson — "The Emotion Code"

This work is one of the foundational pieces of this methodology. Dr. Nelson is a renowned holistic chiropractor and lecturer who reveals how emotionally charged events from your past can become trapped emotions that literally inhabit your body. His book, "The Emotion Code" is easy to read, is comprehensive in the description of his methodology and includes helpful charts and illustrations.

How this work informed "The Alchemy of Becoming"

The entire alchemic process works within the field of energy. Early on I was introduced to the notion that everything is vibrating energy and that we each have a vibrational signature. Our vibrational signature is a unique composite of high and low frequencies. Raising one's level of consciousness is essentially manifested through raising your signature. The first step in raising that signature is to identify and release negative or low frequencies held in trapped emotions. These trapped emotions are indeed a form of disharmonic frequencies which cause dis-ease.

Dr. Nelson's Emotion Code is brilliant and has inspired the design of a code to be an interface vehicle between the Self and higher guidance. In the Alchemy of Becoming the coded words are slightly different and are not organized to coordinate healing with a specific organ. This is because the prime directive for the methodology in this book is to raise consciousness.

Healing is a by-product of raising consciousness. The premise here is that you cannot heal from the same vibrational frequency that caused the source of dis-ease. Lower frequency emotions are identified and released in order to elevate your vibrational signature and in so doing healing of body, mind and soul take place.

The code in this book is applied in a completely blind way, meaning the words are selected without reference to the chart. You simply determine which column and row the lower frequency word is in and ask if it is the first, second, third, fourth or fifth word. This has been helpful to avoid being influenced by a particular word as the thinking mind can take over. It has the added benefit of learning the feeling of achieving a neutral mind (you do not care if it is the first, second, third, etc. word). This neutral mind with no attachment to an outcome is key to a strong and accurate connection to higher guidance for this process and all subsequent applications in the alchemic methodology. The sway technique, as in using the body as a pendulum, is preferred unless there are physical limitations.

One of the *invariant laws* of this alchemic methodology is that something must be known before it can be released or un-manifested. Therefore, the process of releasing lower frequency emotions works best when the circumstances surrounding the event (age, whether inherited or from a past life, nature of trauma or suffering), can be identified.

This concept of a code is expanded to include a similar construct for clearing blocked emotions from the body's nine energy systems. Dr. Nelson refers to a "hidden heart wall" which in this methodology is understood (as channelled to me) to be coded wording for a blocked heart chakra. As it turns out, blockages can occur in all chakras and in all other energy systems. These energy systems act as currents of life force information running through and around the body and include the auric field.

This understanding in turn led to the code for *limiting personality traits* imbedded in the subconscious.

Likewise, a code is used to attract and balance the body's higher frequency emotions. This was channelled to me including the concepts of key words, and the analogy to dampening or strengthening emotions as a conductor would do in the context of an orchestra. Releasing lower frequency emotions starts the healing process, which is enhanced through the affirmation of, and replacement with finely tuned elevated emotions.

I remain grateful to Dr. Nelson's work and encourage exploring his book, "The Emotion Code", which has been revised in 2020. He has also expanded his work with "The Body Code" complete with an app for ease of reference.

■ Pam Grout — "E-Squared"; "E-Cubed"

These two books are written like lab experiments proving that reality is malleable, consciousness trumps matter and you can shape your life with your thoughts. All the experiments are fun, light-hearted, easy to do but contain serious messages and lots of wisdom. They are designed to prove the principles that there is an invisible energy force or field of infinite possibilities and that you impact this field according to your beliefs and expectations. Furthermore, the experiments are designed to demonstrate and confirm that you are connected to accurate and unlimited guidance and that the universe is limitless, abundant, and accommodating.

How these books informed "The Alchemy of Becoming"

I was led to this book early on in my personal journey with the emphasis that there are ways to bridge our third dimensional experience and physical senses with those of higher dimensions and the metaphysical realm. These experiments are powerful in helping to suspend disbelief, particularly for those at the outset of their journeys. There is nothing like proof of the existence of unseen energy forces at play and your connection to guidance.

■ David R. Hawkins, M. D., PhD — "Power vs. Force"

Dr. Hawkins brings a lifetime of clinical research to his discovery of a calibrated scale of human consciousness. He was able to analyze the full spectrum of the levels of human consciousness allowing a comprehensive analysis of the emotional and spiritual developments at the individual level and in the collective (societies, countries, etc.). This provides a universal guide indicating where we and everyone else is on the ladder of spiritual development. His scale of consciousness ranges from 0 to 1000 and forms a sort of database of consciousness with lower frequency emotions such as shame, guilt, grief, apathy registering below 200 with progressively higher emotional frequencies such as love, joy and peace registering at the high ends (500 +) of the scale. His premise is that there is a social distribution of the levels of consciousness and that these provide general determinants of behaviour whether individually or as a society. It is difficult to move from one level of consciousness to a higher level during one's lifetime. Very few individuals would ever be above 500 and only a handful worldwide would be above 700. Force is the expression of creation at lower held levels of consciousness where fear and control are commonly used to dominate and exert influence. Force always requires justification whereas power comes from within those held in higher consciousness and emanates from truth, requiring no justification.

How these books informed "The Alchemy of Becoming"

Long before I had heard of Dr. Hawkins, my charts and drawing all had this line running through them depicting a scale of consciousness. It went from 0 to 1000. I was told that everyone's vibrational signature fell somewhere on that scale and that you could tune in to a person's level of consciousness using the sway technique. This is a useful metric at the onset of one's journey as you can monitor the progression of consciousness throughout the methodology. It was only later that I was led to Hawkin's book on the subject. The sequence is important here as I came to understand that it is the scale of consciousness that is most relevant to the alchemic methodology. Unlike the time that Dr. Hawkins wrote this seminal work, we are now in the midst of a global rise in consciousness and that many will learn to transcend the consciousness level they were born into. The alchemic methodology is a bridge to do just that. Dr. Hawkins has given us a universal language and tool that helps understand and aspire to levels of higher consciousness.

■ **Bruce H. Lipton, PhD — "The Biology of Belief"; Inner Evolution Series (Gaia)**

Bruce Lipton is a renowned cell biologist and an internationally recognized leader in bridging science and consciousness and in formulating and giving voice to a new understanding of biology. Scientific discoveries about the biochemical effects of the brain's functioning show that the cells of the body are affected by your thoughts and that your fate is not controlled by our genetic make-up. This is the new science of epigenetics, meaning above genetics linking mind and matter and giving us a better understanding of phenomena like the placebo and nocebo effects. Once considered highly controversial, Lipton's work has gained international acclaim and is foundational to advances in functional medicine approaches.

How these books informed "The Alchemy of Becoming"

Science and spirituality are merging, converging through thought leaders like Bruce Lipton. This is key to empowering both fields. This book is about Lipton's own journey breaking free from conventional thinking to the convictions of his own beliefs. The science in this book defines how beliefs control behaviour and gene activity. He confirms the power and intelligence we have within each of our cells and as such, we need not be controlled by false and limiting beliefs about ourselves. I was led very specifically to his experiments with cells in Petri dishes. Lipton explains that the health of a cell is influenced by its environment and that the cell is reading, processing and communicating that environmental information throughout its lifespan. You put a healthy cell in an unhealthy Petri dish and it too will become unhealthy. Conversely, if you put an unhealthy cell in a healthy Petri dish, it will turn healthy. This led to the whole concept in the Fermentation and Distillation stages of the Alchemic Methodology that we are not separate from our lives and that we have the means to create a life in harmonic resonance with ourselves. In other words, the life we have is analogous to our Petri dish. When we change our perspective from being helpless victims and adopt an empowered approach of a life happening from within us, our Petri dish will manifest accordingly.

■ **Dr. Joe Dispenza — "Breaking the Habit of Being Yourself"; "Becoming Supernatural"; Rewired Series (Gaia)**

Dr. Joe Dispenza combines the fields of Quantum physics, neuroscience, brain chemistry, biology, and genetics to show you what is truly possible when you create your life from the inside-out. If you want to change your life, you have to change yourself, meaning breaking down the programming you don't even know you have. We are our programming, our beliefs which become patterns of how the mind thinks, how the body feels emotions, the behaviours we express and memorize and the experiences and relationships we attract that reinforce our very identity or persona. Dr. Dispenza contends that much of our programming is externally derived with limiting beliefs about ourselves. He puts forth the notion that you have to become greater than your environment, greater than your body and beyond the notion of time to make changes at the subconscious programming level. His considerable body of work focuses not only on the science that governs our brain but how we can rewire ourselves and why that rewiring is critical to evolving our health and spiritual well-being.

Dr. Dispenza also delves deeply into the science and benefits of meditation in his book "Becoming Supernatural" and how to access the Quantum field through a meditative practice.

How these books informed "The Alchemy of Becoming"

These works informed every part of the methodology. The theme of this first level of transformation is living your truth in a new-found inner sovereignty. Essentially this is about rewiring yourself from outside-in programming to inside-out, reordering yourself and your life from a place of inner awareness and power. It takes an understanding of how you operate and why you do so, before you can evolve yourself. You literally learn to reframe yourself through self-awareness and observation and learn to create life through choice rather than reaction. For those who love the science within spirituality or the spirituality within science, Dr. Dispenza explains the mechanics that connects them to each other. He successfully integrates his many scientific and metaphysical insights in the Gaia series entitled "Rewired". This series is compelling and well worth watching in the sequences as presented in the series.

■ Donna Eden — "Energy Medicine"

Donna Eden was born with the ability to *see* energies around and within the body. This book is the culmination of her understanding of the different energy systems that form a lattice field of unseen energy influencing the way you feel, think and live—your body, mind, and soul health. This is a comprehensive illustrative manual of how to access your body's systems and flows to create greater vitality, health, and joy. It is the basis of understanding that we have the ability within us to promote self-healing and well-being. It is complete with recommended daily energy routines which are also available on YouTube.

How these books informed "The Alchemy of Becoming"

Taking back power to promote your physical and mental health is fundamental in the journey to achieving higher consciousness. Many are drawn to their spiritual paths when bodies have broken down and minds are struggling with everyday life. Self-healing is a power that lies within us all and should be viewed as a vital complementary practice to conventional medicine. Even in optimal health, keeping ourselves mentally and physically fit requires upkeep and attention to our governing energy fields. This is a reference manual you will go back to again and again as you become increasingly aware of how to create energy habits and routines to complement your life. Donna Eden's teachings are consistent with long-held Eastern Chi beliefs, chakra energy systems, reiki and acupuncture practices; energy fields underpin them all.

■ Bill McKenna — "The Only Lesson"

This is an inspirational memoir of McKenna's life which is rich with profound messages about what is important in life. There are wonderful insights drawn from the ups and downs of his life on the power of forgiveness, surrendering, letting go of fear, and ultimately of love. This book is easy to read, authentic and filled with gems of insights. In addition to this book, there are interviews with Bill McKenna conducted by Regina Meredith on Gaia, well worth watching.

How these books informed "The Alchemy of Becoming"

This is one person's account of a spiritual journey from a place of deep reflection and authenticity. At the end of the day, we all have such an account within us: the events and people in our lives who proved to be the best teachers of ourselves and the best inspirations of who and what we could become. Becoming sovereign within oneself is taking responsibility for all that happens. There is no victimization or blaming in this journey. Every encounter with life is an opportunity to learn more deeply about ourselves.

■ Jude Currivan — "The Cosmic Hologram"; "The Eighth Chakra"

Jude Currivan is a cosmologist, planetary healer and futurist. Her works put forth evidence from a wide range of cutting-edge scientific discoveries showing our universe is an interconnected hologram of information. Her works explain how consciousness is a major component of the cosmic hologram of information. Demonstrating how information is physically real, Currivan explores how consciousness connects us to the many interconnected layers of universal *in-formation*, making us both manifestations and co-creators of the cosmic hologram of reality. Concurring too with ancient spiritual wisdom, Currivan contends that consciousness is not something we have but the fundamental nature of what we and the entire universe is. With this understanding, we can each transform our own lives and help co-create and inform the world around us.

How these books informed "The Alchemy of Becoming"

For those loving deep science and the connection to spirituality and consciousness in particular, you will be challenged by this work and find it fascinating. She explains how Quantum mechanics and Einstein's Theory of Relativity can at last be reconciled if we consider energy-matter and space-time as complementary expressions of information. In other words, the universe is made up of energy and energy is encoded information providing instructions on the underlying laws that govern the seemingly irreconcilable worlds of Newtonian and Quantum physics. The *Big Bang* was really a *Big Breath* containing all of the ingredients and instructions for a perfect universe to unfold with the incredible precision of both ingredients and instructions for our existence.

The invariant laws that govern the universe are the same that govern the Alchemic Methodology as presented. All the necessary ingredients and instructions for transformation and the evolution of higher consciousness are imbedded in the energy frequencies of the Alchemic transmission. As we evolve to higher consciousness so too do we evolve and create a higher consciousness universe. Jude Currivan's work is all about the responsibility and importance we collectively have in determining the outcome of the expanding universe through our own quest for higher consciousness.

■ Dr. Barbara De Angelis — "Soul Shifts"

Barbara De Angelis offers us a book for awakening. She takes us on a vibrational understanding of ourselves as *seekers* to an inner rebirth of spirituality. Soul shifts are radical, vibrational internal shifts that spontaneously and inevitably transform the way you relate to yourself, to others, and to the world. For transformation to be real and lasting, it must originate from the inside-out, so that instead of trying to constantly micromanage everything, you operate from true mastery at the deepest level of who you are—the soul level.

When you learn how to make these Soul Shifts on the inside, everything on the outside of your life shifts. Places where you've felt stuck or confused become illuminated with new clarity and understanding. Obstacles turn into possibilities, dead ends transform into doorways, all because you have made a soul shift.

How these books informed "The Alchemy of Becoming"

This book is one of the fundamental tenets of the Alchemy of Becoming. I was led to this book repeatedly to reinforce the notion that everything is energy, and that true and lasting transformations must be done at the energy frequency level or soul level. All other forms of transformation are not from inner power but of force and control. All change must first come from within. Furthermore, I was to understand that the very placement of words in a sequence can be more than just information but act as a transmission for transformation. You are not just informed but transformed through the reading and absorption of the words and learning.

■ **Jim Self and Roxanne Burnett — "A Course in Mastering Alchemy"**

A Course in Mastering Alchemy is a step-by-step set of instructions provided by the *Teachers of Light* to expand your understanding, your consciousness, and your ability to use the new energy tools and manifestation techniques. The *Teachers of Light* are ascended beings who have imbedded the instructions with frequencies of transmission as a means of transcending the limitations of the third dimension and to experience higher consciousness levels of the fifth dimension.

How these books informed "The Alchemy of Becoming"

Like the Alchemy of Becoming, Jim Self and Roxanne Burnett have put together a guide which empowers the reader to transform through the transmission of frequency. While the entire course is worthwhile and speaks to many on their spiritual journeys, I was led specifically to parts of this work dealing with the power of language. This compelling work puts forth the notion that all words, numbers and geometric symbols are encoded with energetic frequencies that, at their essence, are imbedded information and instructions. Use of precise language for setting intentions, manifesting and affirmations takes on new significance. While this theme runs through the entire course, it is most powerfully presented in the "Seven Living Words" as *a code of being or a code of values* to be embodied not only in ourselves but in all works, we create. The concept has been adopted in the "The Alchemy of Becoming" though some words have been modified without losing the essence of their intended meaning. For example, the word "senior" has been modified to "sovereign".

An understanding of how to work with and access the deeper encoded messages of words, is presented in the "Rays of Creation." This understanding has been loosely adopted in "The Alchemy of Becoming" as the notion that words contain dimensional fractals of themselves through other words that are either source of limitations or inspiration to embodying their power.

■ **Dr. Theresa Bullard—Mystery Teachings Series (Gaia)**

In an excellent series on Gaia, Dr. Theresa Bullard, bridges the scientific understanding of Quantum physics and the structure of our universe, with the metaphysical teachings maintained throughout the western Mystery School tradition. The series is a hopeful and inspiring look at the human experience. Theresa Bullard is a physicist with 20 years of study within the esoteric teachings of Alchemy, Kabbalah, and Hermetics. In this series, she weaves together a deep understanding of the scientific and metaphysical perspective to guide us toward an expanded view of what is possible for the evolution of human consciousness. Bullard puts forth the notion that perhaps this is our purpose; to grow and evolve, shining light on the human experience, and doing the work to continually refine ourselves toward a more loving expression of our spirit.

How these books informed "The Alchemy of Becoming"

The very framework of alchemy as the methodology for transformation came from an initial interview Regina Meredith did with Theresa Bullard on "Open Minds". The message was clear; the seven steps were to form the basis for a synthesis of scientific and spiritual teachings offered by so many brilliant minds. There had to be a way to connect them to each other by creating bridges in a specific sequence. There are many ways to do this and Theresa Bullard does this brilliantly through her deep knowledge and respect for the Hermetic and Kabbalah traditions. This series is captivating and as such, well worth watching.

■ **Anodea Judith — "Eastern Body, Western Mind"**

This is a classic text on the chakra energy system. Anodea Judith has created a practical system for healing energy imbalances and taking control of your physical and mental health. Each chapter focuses on a single chakra, starting with a description of its characteristics, identity issues and how to keep it in balance. The unique combination of Eastern and Western theories elucidates the spiritual nature of personality development and how it fits within the structural logic of the body.

How these books informed "The Alchemy of Becoming"

This is a comprehensive synthesis of the chakra system. It is foundational to understanding our inherent programming and to recognize the signs of a chakra system out of balance. There are few bodies of work that provide more than a superficial understanding of the chakra system. This book delves deeply into both the Eastern and Western understandings of the interplay of the chakras with both their strengths and demons illustrated. The book offers practical exercises to both identify and heal chakras out of balance.

■ Olympia LePoint — "Answers Unleashed"

Olympia LePoint is a mathematician and rocket scientist who worked for NASA launching rockets. Her book "Answers Unleashed" is a fascinating account of her life experiences in understanding how the brain functions and can be changed through mindfulness. Her theory of the brain's neuroplasticity is based on something she calls the "Triabrain Theory of Relativity" or three-sided brain. In addition to the left and right hemispheres of the brain, LePoint puts forth the theory that faith or spirituality is the third part of the brain allowing for intuition and mindfulness to shape our thinking and to heal our brain from traumas and chaos. She explains that traumas and chaos disconnect the three parts of the brain from functioning coherently. Her book is a practical guide to self-directed neuroplasticity, where the realization and power of choice (awareness) can overcome and change the brain's functioning by connecting the prefrontal cortex (executive power of the brain) with the striatum or habit centre of the brain, to break destructive habits and thinking. You remap your brain. The brain, according to LePoint is a divine and chaotic blueprint of your life's journey by design. Rather than chaos limiting your potential, you use chaos to jump-start a genius brain powered by faith.

How these books informed "The Alchemy of Becoming"

Chaos in life is inevitable. It is disruptive to a life we seek to control. And chaos often begets chaos. However, instead of being a victim of chaos in our lives, we have the choice to understand the forces of chaos and to respond to chaos in such a way that we are mindful of the opportunity for growth through a conscious remapping of our thinking. Chaos becomes our teaching moments. It is sometimes the crack that lets the light in.

We have loosely termed the concept put forward in her book as a *whole brain state*. One of the exercises adapted from her book, is the power of using your dominant and non-dominant hand to gain powerful insights into subconscious programming. There are many more practical exercises offered in her work worthy of exploring.

■ **Michael A. Singer — "The Untethered Soul"; "The Surrender Experiment"**

Michael Singer's book, "The Untethered Soul", is a beautifully told journey of consciousness—first tethered to the limitation of ego to the untethered state of liberation through surrendering to the universe. It delves into what you can do to free yourself from behaviours and habits that create limiting energy patterns and lowered levels of consciousness. It is a powerful book of freedom, of a quiet within, an authenticity of self that allows for the liberation of the soul.

In "The Surrender Experiment," Singer takes us on a captivating story of his surrender, of his increasing state of non-resistance to a life unfolding as it should and must. He discovers that his spiritual awakening need not be predicated on a solitary life in the woods but rather through life's experiences.

How these books informed "The Alchemy of Becoming"

Every day is an opportunity to be given precisely what your soul needs for its growth. A spiritual journey is not the journey of renunciation of the fullness of what life has to offer. It is not about sitting atop a mountain to remain pure and in a meditative state of awareness. Rather, it is to awaken through and by what life has to offer, come what may. Surrendering, letting go of underlying fear, the false sense of safety that comes with the need to be in control, is one of the most difficult concepts to fully embrace. Letting go of our persona, of the masks and identities we wear and surrendering ourselves to life's perfection is the central liberating theme to Singer's work and a foundational theme to anyone's spiritual journey.

■ Rev. Michael Bernard Beckwith — "Life Visioning"

Michael Beckwith is the founder and spiritual director of the Agape International Spiritual Centre. Agape is described as a trans-denominational centre with a global following. His book, "Life Visioning" is a spiritual growth process which applies to your life structures, including relationships, finances, livelihood and spiritual practice. He outlines four stages of consciousness: Victim, Manifestor, Channel, and Being and characterizes each stage and how we move through them. "When your thoughts and actions begin to align with the imperatives of your soul," explains Beckwith, "you enroll the full support of the universe. Unimagined possibilities begin to open up as you synchronize with the divine."

How these books informed "The Alchemy of Becoming"

As one of the great spiritual leaders of our time, Beckwith's book proved very validating to the methodology. I was only led to his book after coming up with a version of life structures, remarkably similar to his. The Petri dish influenced by Bruce Lipton's concept represents the relationship you have with your life, as your Petri dish. The Petri dish is segmented into characteristics of your life, but in more precise terms on how you spend your days—for example what you ingest, how you spend your leisure time, etc. The idea is that you are aligning your elevated vibrational signature in order to realize your evolving potential.

Beckwith's characterization of the stages of consciousness has been adopted with some modifications but is very much aligned to his concepts. I was told there are four levels of transformation. These are outlined in Part Five of this book. I have, for the most part used his characterization of the levels as they are simply brilliant and so relatable. There is much to be gained in reading Beckwith's book and in watching interviews or videos in which he is featured.

■ Vishen Lakhiani — "The Code of the Extraordinary Mind"

Vishen Lakhiani describes himself as an entrepreneur, author, and activist on a mission to raise human consciousness. He founded a spiritual internet platform called "Mindvalley" to bring together the world's top educators under one platform to "usher in a new era for humanity that is more empowered, connected, and collaborative than the status quo." His book, "The Code of the Extraordinary Mind," combines his life experiences with the insights gained through his own spiritual journey and through the creation of the Mindvalley Platform. Vishen has also created a six-phase meditation process available on his platform.

How these books informed "The Alchemy of Becoming"

Lakhiani's book reinforces the concepts of authenticity, the themes of Level 1 of "The Alchemy of Becoming". He describes how we are constrained from early on in our lives to the rules and identity society imposes on us, consciously and unconsciously. He coined the term, *Brules* for bullshit rules that in fact do not serve us well and are largely based on fear and the need to control. He is a bit of a spiritual rebel in this regard and effective in challenging our belief structures. He attributes and promotes Beckwith's idea of life structures and the stages of consciousness evolution. The book comes with several exercises to demonstrate spiritual concepts like bending reality or manifesting for outcomes.

Mindvalley features many master class interviews and courses with spiritual leaders.

■ Paul Selig — "I am the Word"; "The Book of Love and Creation"; "The Book of Knowing and Worth"; "The Book of Mastery"; "The Book of Truth"; "The Book of Freedom"; "Beyond the Known: Realization"; "Alchemy"

Paul Selig is a psychic, medium, and clairvoyant. His books are transcripts of words from the *Source Field*. They are not interpretations but transcripts. There are 8 such books to date and undoubtedly, more to come. Selig does not consider himself to be the author of these books but acts as a channel. Many of his questions during the channelled sessions are addressed by the Source Field providing clarification to concepts that are often difficult to grasp. Selig does not profess to understand all that is communicated through him but is faithful to the mission of passing on "The Word" to us all.

How these books informed "The Alchemy of Becoming"

I was led to these books later in my spiritual journey. There was a particular order I was to read Selig's books and even then, it was a sequence of chapters that went from one book to the other. No one book, cover to cover and curiously I was not led to the first book first. In reading what I was directed to, in the order I was directed to, I felt that it provided a personal map to my spiritual growth. It was as if one chapter in a given book was a key to opening another chapter in yet another book.

These are perhaps the most important spiritual works of our time. They are exciting and will most certainly underpin the subsequent levels of transformation as part of the series in "The Alchemy of Becoming." For some, they will not seem accessible, particularly to the just awakened or awakening. However, the growth they promise as your consciousness is elevated, is undeniable.

Long before I knew of Paul Selig's books, the alchemic methodology of this book was well entrenched as was the title, "The Alchemy of Becoming." As this first book is finished, Selig's latest book simply entitled "Alchemy" has just been released. Synchronicity.

■ **Culadasa (John Yates, PhD), Matthew Immergut, Jeremy Graves — "The Mind Illuminated"**

"The Mind Illuminated," is a comprehensive guide on meditation. It provides the reader with the best features of many meditation practices originating from Buddhist and Indian traditions along with the latest research in cognitive psychology and neuroscience. The authors have laid out this in-depth practice in 10 clearly defined stages from novice to the adept meditator. This book can be read from front to back or used as a reference guide, choosing chapters as needed based on a meditator's skill level. Not only does it articulate what is needed to progress but offers clarity and honesty about the challenges and hindrances so many experience in honing a meditation practice.

How these books informed "The Alchemy of Becoming"

Navigating our inner landscape is a skill and practice essential to connecting with our higher selves and higher guidance with the goal of achieving higher consciousness. While there are many books on meditation, I have found most lacking in the practical how-to department, able to take a beginner right through in stages and levels of learning and practice, to the seasoned, adept meditator. In this way, I found many parallels to the architecture of "The Alchemy of Becoming" which likewise advocates progression in stages and levels.

Furthermore, this book, unlike some others, views meditation not as an end in itself. The benefits of meditation, the authors argue, are not to remain *on the cushion*. The whole point of meditation is to transfer the practice to mindful living. Only through mindfulness can you truly achieve the conscious being that allows for your fullest expression of self in your lifetime. This is Awakening, the true purpose of the meditation practice.

Providing step-by-step guidance for every stage of the meditation path, this uniquely comprehensive guide for a Western audience combines the wisdom from the teachings of the Buddha with the latest research in cognitive psychology and neuroscience. Clear and friendly, this in-depth practice manual builds on the nine-stage model of meditation originally articulated by the ancient Indian sage Asanga, crystallizing the entire meditative journey into 10 clearly defined stages. The book also introduces a new and fascinating model of how the mind works and uses illustrations and charts to help the reader work through each stage. This manual is an essential read for the beginner to the veteran of meditation and can be read from front to back, or used as a reference guide, choosing chapters as needed based on the current state of the reader's practice.

■ Rob M Williams — "Psych K The Missing Piece/Peace of Your Life"

Through what Rob Williams describes as "intuitive flashes of insight," he developed a simple technique to change beliefs held within the subconscious mind. While simple, the concepts that underlie this technique are profound. The subconscious mind is where beliefs are held, and such beliefs create patterns of thought and behavioural habits. Breaking one's self of these patterns of thought and behaviour is difficult. He contends that most self-help books try to change our programming through facts, reason, willpower, positive thinking, and motivation. However much of this is in vain. Williams' research reveals that the subconscious mind is not capable of responding to the abstract structures of the language of the conscious mind. Rather, the subconscious mind responds to sensory-based language meaning visually, auditory, and kinesthetically (VAK) in nature.

His book also points out that reprogramming the subconscious mind takes *whole-brain integration* meaning the creation of crosstalk between the left and right hemispheres of the brain. Each side of the brain processes and houses different skills and attributes and that life experiences trigger dominance of one side over the other.

How these books informed "The Alchemy of Becoming"

Rob Williams concepts on deprogramming and reprogramming have been incorporated in the Separation Stage of the journey. The technique for isolating the subconsciously held habits and beliefs are identified in the code interface with higher guidance (limiting and positive personality charts). This interface technique does not rely on muscle testing, and as such can be done alone. We have used the technique of writing with both the left and right hands to create a whole-brain state and the required crosstalk between the two hemispheres of the brain. His book provides much of the research and reasons why this technique is effective and as such is a wonderful reference. Also, there are YouTube ideas where Williams demonstrates this technique which is also very helpful.

■ **Richard Gordon, Chris Duffield PhD, Vickie Wichhorst, PhD – Quantum-Touch 2.0 The New Human**

This book is one of several which provides techniques and exercises on the capabilities we all have to heal and to encompass new realms which involve working with life-force energy. It is designed to provide a new understanding of what and who a human being is and what we are capable of doing. It opens our minds to new potentials in science and technologies and provides new foundations for better and more compassionate lives and societies. Above all, this is a helpful, simple but powerful instruction manual on how to develop your powers to heal.

How these books informed "The Alchemy of Becoming"

There are many books on self-healing and more generally on healing. This book contains the essential ingredients that underpins all forms of energy healing and the instructions are presented in a practical and straight-forward way with an enthusiasm befitting of this great gift. We have chosen to highlight the instructions contained within this book to introduce all journeyers of *"The Alchemy of Becoming"* to their powers to self heal.

■ **Gaia Platform — The Series Worth Watching**

Regina Meredith—Open Minds
Gregg Braeden—Missing Links
Theresa Bullard—Mystery Teachings
Joe Dispenza—Rewired
Randy Vertenheimer—Quantum Effect
Caroline Myss—Sacred Power
Bruce Lipton—Inner Evolution
Sue Morter—Healing Matrix
Transcendence—Extended Interviews
Legacy—Barbara Marx Hubbard; Ervin Laszlo
Nassim Haramein – Quantum Revolution

■ Other Noteworthy Books/References

Lee Harris — "Energy Speaks"
Brené Brown — "The Gift of Imperfection"
Gabrielle Bernstein — "Super Attractor"
Elkhart Tolle — "The Power of Now"; "A New Earth"
Eben Alexander — "Proof of Heaven"; "Living in a Mindful Universe"
Oprah Winfrey — "The Path Made Clear"
Belinda Womack — "Lessons from The 12 Archangels"
Jon Kabat-Zinn — "Wherever You Go There You Are"
Neil Donald Walsch — "Conversations with God"
Madisyn Taylor—DailyOm

Diane Fulford

APPENDICES

Appendix 1: Metrics tracking

Metrics Tracking			
Metric	**Date**	**Measurement**	**Notes**
Map of Consciousness (Logarithmic 1-1000)			
Auric Field Size (Feet/Metres)			
Auric Field Strength (Logarithmic 1-10)			
Overall Physical Health (Logarithmic 1-10)			
Overall Mental Health (Logarithmic 1-10)			
Biologic Age (Age)			
Others			

Appendix 2: Lower frequency emotions log sheet

Lower Frequency Emotions Log Sheet						
Date Identified	Trapped Emotion	Age	Acquired	Inherited	Date Cleared	Notes

Appendix 3: Blocked energies log sheet

Blocked Energies Log Sheet							
Date Identified	Energy Blockage	Age	Acquired	Inherited	Energy System	Date Cleared	Notes

Appendix 4: Definitions of lower and elevated emotions

A	
Abandonment	Physical abandonment is being left alone; left behind or deserted (this is the type of abandonment that we most often see in childhood). Emotional abandonment is being given up on; withdrew from; emotionally deserted or separated from; a feeling of being left behind in a non-physical form.
Abundance	Abundance describes a state where there is more than enough of something. In a spiritual context it extends beyond the material world, embracing that which fills your soul with a never-diminishing supply of attributes such as love, trust, and compassion. Abundance can never be depleted as there is a never-ending cycle of replenishment.
Acceptance	Acceptance can signify a positive welcome, endorsement and/or a sense of belonging. Accepting the reality of a situation, good or bad, allows you to gracefully face what is before you without trying to alter, change or protest it.
Acknowledgement	Acknowledgement is a close ally of Acceptance, as the acceptance of a fact or situation is preceded by embracing it as truth. Acknowledgement can also be understood in the context of recognition of another for their contributions.
Anger	A strong displeasure and belligerence aroused by a real or supposed wrong; wrath. Anger is often used as a cover-up or form of denial for emotions of hurt or fear.
Anxiety	A generalized feeling of uneasiness and foreboding; a fear of the unknown; fear without a subject (e.g., she feels anxious and fearful all the time for no apparent reason).
Ashamed	Ashamed is a feeling of being embarrassed or guilty over one's actions or inaction.
B	
Balanced	Balance is a state of different elements co-existing in correct proportion and arrangement. The proper alignment of the elements results in harmony and peaceful existence. Balanced in the context of the journey implies an ability to perceive and evaluate situations with equanimity.
Benevolence	Benevolence is a quality of being kind and well meaning. This quality can also extend to a positive and compassionate perspective on others and the world around you.
Betrayal	Betrayed is to have your trust broken, to be deserted or hurt by a trusted one. Betrayal of another is to be unfaithful in guarding or fulfilling a trust; to be disloyal or violate a confidence, to desert someone who trusts you. Betrayal of the self is to break integrity; act against one's morals, to abuse the body or soul.

Bitter	A harsh, disagreeable, or cynical attitude. Being angry or resentful because of hurtful or unfair experiences.
C	
Calmness	Calmness is a state of being that is free from disturbance or agitation that is characterized by peace of mind, balance, and tranquility.
Capable	Capable refers to the ability to achieve tasks or goals with the appropriate knowledge and skills. This usually applies to all things that a person undertakes and thus can be thought of as a discernible quality.
Caring	Caring is an attribute that reflects kindness and compassion for others and can incorporate affection, sympathy, and helpfulness.
Certainty	Certainty is a state of being completely confident of one's views or beliefs, a firm conviction that is free of any doubt.
Compassion	Compassion literally means *to suffer together*—a sympathetic consciousness of others' suffering or misfortune, paired with a desire to alleviate that state in some way.
Confusion	A disoriented feeling; foggy thinking; chaos; lack of distinctness or clearness; perplexity; bewilderment; a disturbed mental state.
Contentment	Contentment is a state where one experiences quiet joyfulness and deep satisfaction with self and life. This is not a passive state, but one that allows you to fully express gratitude and live in a state of Grace.
Conviction	Conviction is a reflection of when one embraces a firmly held belief. Conviction comes from knowledge, understanding, and experiences that convince you of the truth of your beliefs.
Courage	Courage is the ability to act in a situation that is daunting, uncomfortable, painful, or that even frightens you. It can also mean that one is sovereign and brave enough to express one's beliefs even when they are not widely accepted.
Creativity	Creativity is the act of turning new and imaginative thoughts into reality.
D	
Defensive	A state of resisting attack or protecting oneself; being sensitive to the threat of criticism or injury to one's ego; being on guard against real or imagined threats to one's person, physical and/or emotional.
Depression	Depression is an illness characterized by, among other things, great sadness, feelings of hopelessness (depressed mood), loss of motivation and decision-making ability, diminished sense of pleasure, eating and sleeping disorders, morbid thoughts, and a sense of worthlessness as an individual.
Despair	A complete loss of hope; misery; difficult or unable to be helped or comforted.
Discouragement	Feeling a lack of courage, hope or confidence; disheartened, dispirited. Losing the nerve to try or attempt something.

Disgust	A feeling of loathing; when good taste or moral sense is offended; a strong aversion. (e.g., she felt disgusted when the killer was acquitted).
Dread	Fear of something that is about to happen; apprehension as to something in the future, usually real but sometimes unknown. (e.g., he dreaded going to the high school reunion and facing the bullies who had tormented him).
E	
Effort Unreceived	When one's work, achievement, attempts, or endeavours are not accepted or recognized; when one's best effort is not considered good enough; a feeling of being unappreciated. Not feeling approved of or validated.
Empathy	Empathy is the ability to feel other people's emotions and relate to them. This ability can cause a feeling of being overwhelmed and confused if one cannot distinguish where or who the emotion came from. It can also be a strength, especially for healers, if you are able to recognize the source and remain unattached to the feelings generated.
Empowered	Empowered means having the knowledge, sovereignty, confidence and means to be able to make decisions for yourself and/or to accomplish tasks.
F	
Failure	When one falls short of success or achievement in something expected, attempted, or desired; (e.g., The failure of a marriage or other relationship, being fired, bankruptcy, performing poorly in athletics, art, academics, etc.)
Fear	A strongly distressing emotion aroused by impending danger, evil or pain; the threat may be real or imagined.
Flexibility	Flexibility is the state of being malleable—the metaphysical state of being open and accommodating to new ideas and concepts. Physically it implies the ability to bend without breaking.
Forgiving	Forgiveness is the conscious and deliberate decision to release feelings of vengeance, resentment, and hurt towards another who has deliberately or inadvertently harmed you. Forgiveness does not imply condoning the behaviour, just releasing the emotions and density associated with the transgression.
Forlorn	Miserable; sad and lonely by reason of abandonment, desolation, or emptiness; hopeless; forsaken.
Freedom	Freedom is the absence of all constraints that allow you to freely move about and express your truth.
Frustration	Exasperation; being stuck or unable to progress; feeling blocked from causing a change or achieving an objective or goal.
Fulfilled	Personal fulfillment is the continual journey of self-discovery and contentment with your position in life. It's about achieving goals because they matter most to you instead of culture or society. The focus is entirely on your fulfillment in life and how you being yourself pushes humanity forward.

G	
Generosity	Generosity is the act of giving more than what might be expected of you. It can take the form of physical or monetary gifts or simply time and effort spent with someone in need, or on a project that benefits others.
Gratitude	Gratitude is the quality of being thankful. It can be felt or take the form of a physical acknowledgement of that thankfulness. It carries with it a high vibrational frequency that can uplift and deepen spiritual connection.
Grief	Intense emotional suffering caused by loss, disaster, misfortune, etc., an acute sorrow and deep sadness. A universal reaction to bereavement. Also, can be feeling harassed, vexed or exasperated (e.g., if someone gives you grief).
Guilty	The feeling of having done wrong or committed an offence. Feeling responsible for the harmful actions of another (e.g., abuse, parents' divorce, death, etc.) Often accompanied by feelings of depression, shame, and self-abuse.
H	
Happiness	Happiness is a pleasurable feeling that comes from external circumstances and stimuli.
Harmonious	Harmony is the combination of separate yet related parts that brings unity to self, relationships, well-being, art, music or architecture.
Hatred	To loathe; despise; great dislike or aversion. Often hatred is of a situation rather than a person (e.g., hatred of another's behaviour, unjust circumstances, etc.). Self-hatred creates destructive behaviours and illnesses.
Heartache	Anguish and pain of the heart; distress usually as a result of difficulty or sadness in a relationship. Felt as a crushing or burning physical sensation in the chest.
Helpless	Being unable to help oneself; being without the aid or protection of another. Having little strength or personal power. A common emotion for those suffering from a victim mentality. Feeling unable to change one's circumstances or state.
Honesty	Honesty is the act of bringing truth, honour, integrity and sincerity to any given situation.
Hopeful	Hopeful is a feeling of inspiring optimism. Hopeful can be an overall outlook/perspective, or it can apply to specific future events.
Hopeless	Devoid of hope; having no expectation of good; having no remedy or cure; no prospect of change or improvement.
Horror	A strong emotion of alarm, disgust, or outrage caused by something frightful or shocking (e.g., an event of extreme violence, cruelty, or macabre).
Humiliated	A painful loss of pride, dignity, or self-respect; to feel mortified; embarrassed.

I	
Inclusiveness	Inclusiveness is the quality of including many different types of people regardless of their differences and treating them all fairly and equally.
Indecisive	An inability to make a decision; wavering back and forth between one choice or another. Stems from distrust of the self or doubting the ability to make a good decision.
Insecurity	A lack of confidence; self-conscious; shy. Feeling unsafe from danger or ridicule.
Inspired	Inspired is to be driven by extraordinary quality, as if arising from some divine creative impulse.
Integrity	Integrity is the quality of being honest and having strong moral and ethical principles.
J	
Jealousy	Resentful and envious of someone's success, achievements, or advantages. Having suspicious fears; fears of rivalry or unfaithfulness. Results from a fear of not being loved and/or from insecurity.
K	
Kindness	Kindness is the quality of being friendly, generous, and considerate in a spirit of warmth and benevolence.
L	
Lack of Control	Lacking restraint or direction; unable to regulate or command; a feeling that someone or something else determines your course.
Letting Go	Letting go is a conscious choice to trust that life will unfold in a benevolent manner, fuelled by your positive thoughts and manifestations coming from within. Letting go is the act of freeing yourself from denser energies such as guilt, hatred, control, bitterness, and blame.
Lightness	Lightness is a state of being weightless and buoyant, not taking things more seriously than needed. Lightness can be associated with an optimistic and positive perspective that allows you to see the good and the divine in yourself and others.
Longing	To have a strong desire or craving; a yearning or pining; aching for; to miss someone or something; to want something you do not have (e.g., She longed for a different life).
Lost	Unable to see the correct or acceptable course, having no direction. Physically lost most often shows up from childhood— (e.g., being lost in the woods and can't find the way home, etc.) Emotionally lost refers to a feeling of being unable to see the right decision or direction, being unable to find emotional stability (e.g., He felt lost after his wife died; She hasn't done anything with her life, she seems really lost.)

Love	Love is a profoundly tender, passionate affection for yourself and/or another person or organism. Love can be felt both at a physical and vibrational level. At the physical level, it manifests as deep affection for others. At a vibrational level, it manifests as a frequency of benevolence and positive energy that comes from within and is expressed more widely.
Love Unreceived	A feeling that love expressed is or has been rejected. Feeling unwanted, not cared for; not accepted; a lack of love where it is desired.
Lust	Intense sexual desire or appetite; an overwhelming want or craving (e.g., lust for power); passion; to covet.
N	
Neglected	Neglected is a state of suffering due to not receiving adequate care, or of being disregarded.
Nervous	Unnaturally or acutely uneasy or apprehensive; fearful; timid; to feel jumpy or on edge.
Nurturing	Nurturing is the act of caring for and nurturing the growth and well-being of self and others.
O	
Oneness	Oneness is a state of being joined as one thing, and no longer separate. In spiritual terms it signifies the unity of body, mind, and soul.
Optimism	Optimism is a disposition or tendency to look on the more favourable side of events or conditions and to expect the most favourable outcome.
Overwhelm	To be overpowered in mind or emotion; extreme stress; feeling overpowered with superior force; feeling excessively burdened.
P	
Panic	A sudden, overwhelming fear that produces hysterical behaviour, unreasonably fearful thoughts or physical symptoms such as trembling and hyperventilation, a strong feeling of impending doom.
Patience	Patience is the capacity to gracefully accept that an outcome may take a considerable time to manifest. Not feeling angst or upset at delays or obstacles that impede progress is a characteristic of a patient person.
Peaceful	Peaceful is a state that is free from disturbances, allowing for calmness and tranquility.
Peeved	Irritated; annoyed; exasperated; irked; aggravated; ticked off.
Plentiful	Plentiful means than there is an adequate supply of something, or even more than enough. It can be thought of both physically, for example a food supply; or metaphysically in terms of an abundance of love, support, and belief.

R	
Radiant	Radiant is a state of being that exudes positive energy, usually thought of in terms of glowing light.
Regret	Regret is a feeling of sadness and disappointment over something that has happened or been done, or as the result of a missed opportunity.
Rejection	Feeling denied, refused, or rebuffed; discarded as useless or unimportant; cast out; unwanted; forsaken.
Renewed	Renewed is the state of being returned to original optimal conditions. Renewal in a spiritual sense can mean rediscovering one's authentic self and being able to start afresh.
Resentment	A feeling of displeasure or indignation at someone or something regarded as the cause of injury or insult; bitter for having been treated unfairly; unwilling to forgive. Often this emotion comes along with animosity (ill-will that displays itself in action, strong hostility or antagonism).
Respectful	Respectful is a perspective that accepts that something is important without trying to change it or cause offence. Even if you disagree, you allow others to voice opinions and accept them as possibilities without judgment.
S	
Sadness	Unhappy; sorrowful; mournful; affected by grief.
Safe	Safety is a circumstance of being protected from harm or other negative outcomes.
Secure	Secure means feeling confident, centred, and free from fear or anxiety.
Self-Esteem	Self-Esteem means confidence in one's self-worth and abilities. It is a foundation for self-respect, love, and authenticity.
Self-Sufficient	Self-sufficiency is a characteristic that embodies the concepts of being emotionally and intellectually independent, not reliant on others for physical and metaphysical well-being.
Self-Abuse	Abusing the self emotionally includes negative self-talk (e.g., "I'm such an idiot."), blaming the self, etc. Abusing the self physically includes mistreating the body by use of addictive substances; to not care for the body by lack of sleep, proper diet, or nutrition; to work beyond what one can or should endure; to punish or tax oneself excessively. This abuse may help atone for sins, real or imagined, and usually is driven by anger. Illnesses can be forms of self-abuse (e.g., "I don't deserve to be healed.")
Self-Assured	Self-assured is a characteristic that manifests in confidence in one's own abilities. A self-assured person feels no need to proselytize or draw attention to themselves, a quiet confidence.
Selflessness	Selflessness indicates concern more for the well-being of others over self.

Shame	A feeling of being wrong, defective, or disreputable. The painful feeling of having done or experienced something dishonourable, improper, or foolish; disgrace; humiliation; a cause for regret. The lowest vibration of all the emotions. Leads to guilt, depression and even suicide.
Shock	A sudden or violent disturbance of the emotions or sensibilities; extreme surprise; to feel traumatized or stunned.
Sorrow	A sad regret; distress caused by loss, disappointment or grief; to feel or express grief, unhappiness, or sadness.
Supported	Supported in a spiritual context means that one feels the encouragement, approval, and comfort of others.
Surrender	Surrender in a spiritual context does not mean giving up but giving into higher wisdom. Removing the tendency to try and stop or control a situation, allows higher guidance to offer the best choices that serve your highest good.
Sympathy	Sympathy is the capacity to internally share the feelings of others. It is less about feeling sorry for someone and more about understanding and sharing their feelings and emotions.
T	
Terror	Intense, sharp, overmastering fear; extreme fright; alarm.
Thankfulness	Thankfulness is a state of fully appreciating people, circumstances or situations and making a conscious decision to recognize that internally.
Thoughtfulness	Thoughtfulness is the quality of being kind and having consideration for the needs of others.
Tolerance	Tolerance is the capacity to respect the beliefs or practices that differ from, or conflict with one's own. Allowing for different perspectives creates an opening for deeper understanding, but tolerance has its limits—such as harming other living organisms.
Trust	Trust is a powerful feeling where one has a firm belief and knowing of the integrity and reliability of another person, organization, or institution.
Truthfulness	Truthfulness is the quality of being personally genuine and honest. There is a discernible lack of deceit in a truthful person and their authenticity is never in question.
U	
Understanding	Understanding is a quality that conveys comprehension and being sympathetically aware of the feelings of others which can support tolerance and forgiveness. It also conveys the quality of insight and good judgment.
Unnurtured	Unnurtured is a state of not being adequately cared for in terms of mental, or spiritual health.
Unworthy	Not good enough; beneath the dignity of; not commendable or credible; undeserving; not valuable or suitable; unbecoming.
V	

Valued	To be valued is to be considered to be important, beneficial and cherished.
Vibrant	Vibrant describes a person who is passionate, full of life and energy. Vibrant people tend to exude enthusiasm for life and seek to get the most out of it.
Vulnerability	Feeling susceptible to harm, either emotional or physical; unsafe; unstable.
W	
Worry	Dwelling on difficulty or troubles; unease or anxiety about a situation or a person; extreme concern over potential problems; concern about a loved one in possible distress.
Worthless	Of no importance or value; without excellence of character, quality or esteem; serving no purpose.
Worthiness	Worthiness is the state of being valued and appreciated, and being deserving of attention and respect.

ACKNOWLEDGEMENTS

We are so grateful to the people in our lives who freely offered an abundance of loving support and effort, contributing greatly to the realization of this work.

Julie Barrette, our skilled layout artist who endured so many changes and rewrites with never-ending patience—not to mention also providing several key insights that pushed our thinking forward.

Lise Gauley who inspired us with her visualizations of key concepts (especially the "vortex") and for clarifying our thoughts with diagrams and charts.

Valerie Fulford, a talented and generous artist who illustrated things visually far better than we could in words.

Our editors, Barb Sliter, Richard Fulford, and Diane Lanthier who picked up grammatical lapses, typos, and errors that we were too close to see.

Our original beta group of journeyers who encouraged us with their enthusiasm, challenged us with their questions, laughed with us through some awkward moments and allowed us to learn on our feet. You know who you are.

Our family and friends who stuck by us and kept an open mind, even when they thought we were losing our marbles as we journeyed, transformed, and worked on this book.

And finally, to our husbands Richard and Marc, without whom we would have starved during long days of planning, deliberating, writing, and rewriting. Their quiet and loving support allowed us the freedom to go where we were meant to be.

Printed in the United States
By Bookmasters